Carolina Currents
Studies in South Carolina Culture

Carolina Currents
Studies in South Carolina Culture
Volume 1. New Directions

"Understanding for the Common Good"

Carolina Currents is an annual peer-reviewed publication that connects academic research to the lived experiences and practical concerns of South Carolinians

Editor
Christopher D. Johnson, Francis Marion University

Published by the University of South Carolina Press in cooperation with Francis Marion University

Carolina Currents
Studies in South Carolina Culture

Volume 1. New Directions

Christopher D. Johnson

THE UNIVERSITY OF
SOUTH CAROLINA PRESS

Published by the University of South Carolina Press
Columbia, South Carolina 29208

uscpress.com

Printed in the United States of America

Library of Congress Cataloging-in-Publication Data can be found at
http://catalog.loc.gov/.

ISBN: 978-1-64336-463-6 (paperback)
ISBN: 978-1-64336-464-3 (ebook)
DOI: https://doi.org/10.61162/ARKU7824

The inclusion of this book in the Open Carolina collection is made possible by the
generous funding of the University of South Carolina Libraries and Francis Marion
University.

Contents

Volume 1, 2024

Reviews

List of Illustrations

Pee Dee Psalm
Jo Angela Edwins

This land sings its own poems,
winds dancing through pine and sycamore,
the gurgle of suburban creeks,
the lusty roar of rivers
teaching bank and bridge who's boss
at the stark slap of a giant storm.

Low of cattle, screech of mockingbird, rustle of cornstalks,
snap of a wayward turtle, whoosh of egret wings—
but listen too for the human noises,
midnight railroad whistles,
thump of boot heel on concrete or stone,
the holy chatter of clashing church bells
come a Sunday noon.

Where might sound take us?
How is it that, deep in sleep, or ears plugged, we feel
rhythms in muscle and bone?

How is it that, masked or muffled, we hum,
knowing something alive will catch the tune?

And we must join the chorus, each of us following
phoneme and syllable, fermata and crescendo.

We need no conductor. We need only lift our voices
to let the song carry us home.

Jo Angela Edwins is professor of English and Trustees' Research Scholar at
Francis Marion University. A widely published poet, she currently serves as
the Poet Laureate of the Pee Dee.

Acknowledgments

This volume is the product of many dedicated people, most notably the contributors, who have pushed onward despite the devastating pandemic. Special thanks must also go to Luther F. Carter, president of Francis Marion University; and Peter King, university provost, both of whom have provided vital resources. My department chair, Rebecca Flannagan, has offered endless encouragement and has turned a blind eye as I have wantonly abused my photocopying privileges. Melissa E. Dungan has been tremendously helpful in distributing the various calls for papers and helping maintain essential files and records. Tammy Sneed has helped me navigate the university's procurement policies.

Richard Brown, the former director of the University of South Carolina Press, provided vital direction early on. His colleague, MacKenzie Collier, worked quickly and efficiently to distribute review copies. The current director, Michael McGandy, has provided important support and guidance, particularly in moving the publication toward Open Access. Editor and 2022 Interim Director Aurora Bell has been wonderful during the volume's final stages. Ehren Foley, acquisition editor, and Lily Stephens, publishing assistant, have provided invaluable assistance, as have Kerri Tolan, production editor, and Pat Callahan, former EDP director.

My efforts have been aided by three outstanding student workers: Nikki Clark Costas, who has assisted in formatting the book reviews; Santana Christmas, who has worked on the bibliography; and Richard Frazier, who has also worked on the bibliography.

In addition to the members of the editorial board, there have been many generous scholars who have served as reviewers. I acknowledge my colleagues at Francis Marion University: Todd Couch, Erica Johnson Edwards, Jo Angela Edwins, Howard J. Frye, Adam Houle, Meredith A. Love, Kiley E. Molinari, Meredith L. Reynolds, Steven C. Sims, Rachel N. Spear, Russell E. Ward, Christopher Washington, and Lance Weldy. I also thank Scott Weiner of George Washington University and William Daniel of the University of Nottingham.

Final thanks must go to my wife, Christine, who has assisted with this volume and has now put up with me through five book-length projects.

Figure 1. *Testimonial Remnants*, 2022. Photograph © Julie S. Mixon. Mixon writes, "The Hewn Timber Cabins are on the campus of Francis Marion University. While the exteriors can be viewed anytime, the interiors, along with artifacts are only displayed periodically. The furniture and tools inside tell many stories and are as much a representative of the people who lived there as a photographic portrait."

Introduction

Creating Carolina Currents

Christopher D. Johnson

The plans for *Carolina Currents* began in early 2019. Conversations with Luther F. Carter, president of Francis Marion University, led us to imagine a scholarly publication dedicated to South Carolina. We envisioned an interdisciplinary, "public-facing" project that would maintain the high standards of a peer-reviewed journal but remain accessible to a variety of readers. We also wanted to publish scholarship with purpose, the sort of essays that would allow readers to understand the complicated interactions between the state's past and present. Equally important, we hoped to focus attention on those regions and populations that have received little scholarly attention. Such an approach would help our publication realize its motto: "Understanding for the Common Good."

Francis Marion University is an ideal institution for such an undertaking. In addition to fostering a dynamic scholarly community, the university celebrates the state's rich multiplicity of cultures and focuses on serving those who might otherwise be neglected. For more than fifty years, the faculty and staff have taken great pride in Francis Marion University's commitment to the Pee Dee and in the fact that our student body accurately represents the richly varied demographics of our region. We are also deeply committed to serving the community through extensive outreach efforts and our many successful centers of excellence.[1] A publication devoted to the entire population of the state and dedicated to improving civic understanding complements the most important facets of the university's mission.

Established in 1970, the university has always been integrated and inclusive. Still, the campus contains vestiges of the state's worst history. The university is located on land that was once a plantation, and reminders of that past survive. Our residential students walk by a cemetery where enslaved people are buried. The DNA that lies beneath the ground almost certainly matches that of some students whose family connections to the area predate emancipation. School children visit our hewn timber cabins, which once housed the families of enslaved workers. Seeing these features, one realizes that the land itself has undergone a remarkable transformation, progressing

from a site of oppression to a place of opportunity. In many ways, the cemetery and cabins remind us of the importance of our work. As educators, we
strive to build something better for those who will come after us. Relics of
past oppression insist that progress is possible, that our work has meaning
within and beyond the classroom and library. *Carolina Currents* extends
our efforts. Recovering and preserving stories from neglected communities, it promotes nuanced understandings of the state's cultures. It reveals
both what connects and what separates the many citizens of the state. Most
important, it reminds us of the abiding humanity and intrinsic dignity that
unites all people.

Among the many questions we faced at the beginning of the project were
those concerning publication. From the beginning, we knew we needed a
partner. The University of South Carolina Press was, of course, the ideal
choice. Established in 1944, the press has a proud history of publishing distinguished works focused specifically on South Carolina. Equally important, the press has long offered an impressive catalog of scholarly and creative
works that dovetail neatly with our focus on diverse peoples and cultures.
Well-known books, such as Jonathan Green's stunning *Gullah Images* and
Representative James E. Clyburn's thoughtful autobiography *Blessed Experiences: Genuinely Southern, Proudly Black* have set a standard for more recent
offerings, including Elizabeth J. West's *Finding Francis: One Family's Journey
from Slavery to Freedom* and June Manning Thomas's *Struggling to Learn: An
Intimate History of School Desegregation in South Carolina*.[2] These and similar
works define the press's commitment to accessible, meaningful scholarship
that captures the fullness of the state.

Once a formal agreement between the press and Francis Marion University was reached, the work of assembling an editorial board began. The
board would need representatives from a variety of disciplines. It would
also require scholars committed to connecting the academy to the public.
Among the first to sign on was Echol Lee Nix Jr., associate professor of
philosophy and religious studies at Claflin University. A graduate of More-
house College, the Vanderbilt Divinity School, and Boston University's
School of Theology, Dr. Nix saw genuine value in the purpose and scope of
Carolina Currents and looked forward to writing biographical essays about
several overlooked civil rights leaders. Our email correspondence and telephone conversations were both encouraging and directive, and I looked forward to working with Dr. Nix in the coming years. Tragically, Dr. Nix died
in an automobile accident in September 2020, before the first volume had
taken shape.

Christopher E. Hendricks, a distinguished scholar and public historian from Georgia Southern University, also agreed to serve on the editorial board. His generosity was followed by that of Eric Crawford, associate professor of music at Coastal Carolina University; William Bolt, associate professor of history at Francis Marion University; Samuel M. Hines, professor of political science, The Citadel; Laura L. Morris, assistant professor of English, Furman University; Shevaun E. Watson, associate professor of English, University of Wisconsin, Milwaukee; Mark M. Smith, Carolina Distinguished Professor of History, University of South Carolina; and Felice Knight, assistant professor of history, The Citadel. The members of the editorial board have helped sharpen the focus of *Carolina Currents* and have provided invaluable guidance in reviewing submissions. Their thorough, attentive work has helped move the project from concept to reality.

By fall of 2019, we were ready to begin assembling the first volume. We developed a list of potential contributors and sent a call for papers to department chairs across the state. Colleagues and friends distributed the call for papers at regional and national conferences, and soon we began receiving inquiries and a few essays. Then COVID-19 hit. As universities moved online, libraries restricted access, and archives closed, scholars—especially those with school-aged children—found it impossible to research and write. The work slowed but never stopped. Generous professors agreed to write book reviews, and referees continued to provide cogent assessments and thoughtful suggestions for the few articles that arrived. Enthusiasm for the project remained high, but the realities of pandemic life stalled many emerging essays. Eventually, of course, things got better. With masks, social distancing, vaccines, and effective antivirals, academic life slowly crept toward a new normal. Essays began arriving more regularly as scholars found the time and resources to finish works that had languished over many difficult, frightening months. And so this volume took shape.

Collectively, the essays fulfill the promise of our original proposal. Arranged in a loose chronological order and covering topics as diverse as dessert recipes, drama, civil rights, and foreign affairs, they provide detailed discussions of overlooked aspects of South Carolina life, demonstrating how the past has shaped the present and showing how the state has slowly inched closer to those cherished ideals of acceptance and understanding. In these still uncertain times, when loud voices foment fear and angry populists call for division and mistrust, the essays advocate for better possibilities. They also urge us to recognize the scholar's responsibility not only to face the public but also to provide context and perspective, to remind readers that although our current challenges may be unique, the struggle to create a more equitable, just, and humane society is not.

The collection begins with an autobiographical essay by Thomasina Yuille, a retired Navy chaplain and independent scholar. Tracing her efforts to verify that her great-great-grandfather was, in fact, Colonel Asbury Coward, the eighth superintendent of The Citadel, who enslaved her great-great-grandmother, Ellen Coward Hargrove, Yuille offers an intriguing narrative. Part detective story, part family history, Yuille's narrative explores the complicated legacies of South Carolina's past. Coward was a force of oppression, a man who sought to extend the state's right to deny others' humanity. But he was also a family member. Although we will never know its true dynamics, his relationship with Ellen Hargrove was certainly coercive, if not violent, yet he remains an inescapable part of Yuille's heritage, and his physical features appeared in the faces of those who loved and cared for her. Without erasing or simplifying this thorny history, Yuille finds peace through compassion and understanding.

Christopher Hendricks provides an engaging examination of early nineteenth-century cuisine. Structuring his paper around Mary Randolph's 1824 recipe for southern rice pie (recently confirmed to be delicious by the members of the Southeastern Society for Eighteenth-Century Studies), Hendricks explores how historical foodways both celebrated and obscured different kinds of knowledge. Randolph's cookbook, *The Virginia House-Wife*, recognizes the significance of domestic craft and provided its author with a respected position within the public sphere. At the same time, her work elides the skills of enslaved workers who were captured in West Africa specifically because they knew what plantation owners did not: how to grow rice. Hendricks's adept analysis reveals a complicated cultural web in which a seemingly simple recipe is both an instrument of empowerment and an inadvertent tool of oppression.

Playwright and scholar Jon Tuttle recovers a long-forgotten play, *Modern Honour*, by John Blake White, who is best known for his historical paintings. White's 1812 play provides a sentimental rebuke to South Carolina's dueling culture, arguing for a gentler society where disputes are settled peacefully and lawfully. Tuttle's analysis suggests that, then as now, the South Carolina stage served as an instrument of reform as well as entertainment.

Robert Alston Jones continues the discussion of representation and appropriation through his examination of Bernhard Heinrich Bequest, a nineteenth-century German immigrant to Charleston, who later played an unlikely role in Lost Cause propaganda. As a young man without many opportunities, Bequest worked briefly as a Confederate blockade runner. After the war, he rose to prominence as a local businessman and civic leader. Bequest eventually acclimated to the dominant culture in which he lived, but he was almost certainly never the daring swashbuckler willing to risk it all for a racist ideology, as Ellison Capers claims in the noxious *Confederate Military History*.

Moving into the twentieth century, Cherish Thomas and Meredith A. Love examine *Green Book* sites within Florence County. Connecting those businesses with traditions of Southern hospitality, Thomas and Love argue that the African-American community made real the best aspects of a culture that sought to oppress and silence them. Through convincing analysis of archival evidence and oral history, they show how *Green Book* businesses not only served travelers who were excluded from white-owned establishments but also became important gathering places for local residents.

Kerington B. Shaffer and Erica Johnson Edwards also focus on Pee Dee history in their study of student-led civil rights protests in Florence. Through extensive archival research and interviews with community members, Shaffer and Edwards capture a pivotal moment in Pee Dee history. The students, like those in the more famous lunch-counter protests, emerge as heroes, brave young people who took a principled stand and met hostility with dignity and restraint, even as voices within and outside their community urged them to accept segregation.

Shifting from historical analysis to creative nonfiction, Esther Liu Godfrey introduces McKrae Game, a former advocate for conversion therapy, whose ministry reached a level of prominence in the upstate. In time, Game accepted his own sexuality and denounced his earlier efforts to "fix" young gay people. His story calls attention to a particularly dangerous dynamic within South Carolina culture: the harmful confluence of rigid spirituality, restrictive sexual mores, and homophobia.

Faculty from Furman University provide a critical assessment of the Joseph Vaughn Plaza on the campus of Furman University. Named for the university's first African-American student, the plaza is a site of reconciliation, designed to honor Mr. Vaughn and make current students feel welcome and valued. In many ways, it fulfills these goals, but the authors also point toward potential complications, some of which relate to the physical architecture of the plaza, others to the perception that Furman may have appropriated Mr. Vaughn's story to promote itself. In this way, the essay provides important guidance for municipalities and universities seeking to build similar memorials.

In the collection's final essay, Lauren K. Perez and Jennifer L. Titanski-Hooper explore the various ways the current war in Ukraine impacts South Carolina. Using a feminist geopolitical lens, they show the real-world implications of Russian aggression and demonstrate how events thousands of miles away affect the lives of people living in the Palmetto State.

As a whole, the essays explore connections that might otherwise remain unnoticed. They help us understand that our present and future are tied to our past, that *place*—whether the state as a whole, a particular region, or even a college campus—has meaning that must be recovered and studied. In this way, the essays bring me back to the hewn-timber cabins on Francis Marion University's campus. My first-year students learn about the skills needed to build them and how those skills are unacknowledged in our histories. I show the students how the cabins were constructed with a variation of the same dovetail joint that has been used in furniture making for centuries. We think about the weight of the green timbers, and how the structures—square, plumb, and level—have survived for at least one hundred seventy years. We also learn a bit about the people who lived in the cabins, and we run our fingers along lines they carved to mark each row of timbers. Those workers, buried in unmarked graves on another part of campus, were almost certainly illiterate, but they had knowledge, much of which is now lost. They built competently with the materials they had, making precise joinery in oak beams twenty feet long and six inches thick. Work that would require cranes and power tools today, they did with their hands, with each other. My students and I search for ways to celebrate the accomplishment of those cabins without expunging the oppression and violence to which they are inseparably tied.

I think about those men and their families, about how different the land is now from when they knew it. Could they have imagined that a plantation of enslavement, segregation, and exploitation would become a place of education? If they had known their descendants would earn college degrees where they planted crops, would it have made their lives better—not easier, but better? Those carved lines haunt me, and I often study the individual timbers, wondering how they were rendered so straight, how the joints were cut so perfectly. I imagine the tools, some as familiar to carpenters today as they would have been to artisans during Shakespeare's age. Most often, though, I think of the builders and hope that their work, however arduous, however replete with injustice, brought some joy. When the axes, saws, and froes were put up for the evening, I hope that those craftsmen felt the significance of what they had done, understood that they had built a home for their families, that their hands had made something enduring and human. Their stories are worth recovering and cry out for preservation. They speak to the horrific, sometimes tragic, history of our state, and they remind us of the possibility of triumph. In that way, their histories share much with the essays contained in *Carolina Currents*, which also speak to possibilities, even as they gaze unflinchingly at the past and present. And so I am grateful for these stories, grateful for the scholars who have made this volume possible, grateful for all that they have discovered and shared.

Christopher D. Johnson is professor of English and Trustees' Research Scholar at Francis Marion University. His most recent book is *Samuel Richardson, Comedic Narrative, and the Culture of Domestic Violence: Abused Pamela* (Cambridge Scholars Publishing, 2023). His current project examines the rhetorical strategies of early-modern biographers.

NOTES

1. For many years, Francis Marion University has sponsored the Center of Excellence for Teaching Children of Poverty. More recently, the university added an additional Center of Excellence for College and Career Readiness and another Center of Excellence for Teacher Retention and Induction in the Pee Dee. In 2020, the National League for Nursing (NLN) named the university an NLN Center of Excellence for its achievements in training future and current nurses. For more information, see www.fmarion.edu.
2. Jonathan Green, *Gullah Images: The Art of Jonathan Green.* Foreword by Pat Conroy (Columbia: University of South Carolina Press, 1996); James E. Clyburn, *Blessed Experiences: Genuinely Southern, Proudly Black.* Foreword by Alfred Woodard (Columbia: University of South Carolina Press, 2014); Elizabeth J. West, *Finding Francis: One Family's Journey from Slavery to Freedom* (Columbia: University of South Carolina Press, 2022); June Manning Thomas's *Struggling to Learn: An Intimate History of School Desegregation in South Carolina* (Columbia: University of South Carolina Press, 2022).

Getting Under My Skin

Reckoning with My White Confederate Ancestor

Thomasina A. Yuille

Our nation continues to struggle with its various histories of enslavement and racial injustice. In the first decades of the twenty-first century, many voices have called for recognition and reconciliation as we see in the Universities Studying Slavery initiatives across the country. Other voices have sought to limit dialog. My essay seeks to move discussions of race, both past and present, away from partisan and ideological frameworks and toward the living dynamics of a particular family. Tracing my own efforts to discover and understand my ancestors' complicated past, I hope to show not only that history is never a simple narrative but also that it remains both vibrant and deeply personal.

My Flesh and Blood, 1960–62

My grandmother Mary Ann did not look like me, which gave me my first clue about him. She looked like a white woman. I knew that she wasn't white. She was my grandmother. She never pretended to be anything other than colored on the inside. Yet her appearance puzzled me. I recall a woman about the age I am now, the color of vintage lace, with gray eyes and long, straight, dark brunette hair that fell to the small of her back—a cultural mark of beauty. Her two chubby brown granddaughters, my twin sister Toni and I, used to playfully quiz her about her intriguing appearance. Secretly, we wanted to look more like her, but I didn't necessarily covet her skin tone.

Even though my brown skin placed me below the lighter skinned girls in the caste, I passed the "paper bag" test. My mother encouraged me to like the color of my skin. She wanted brown children. As a child, she had felt punished for being light-skinned and didn't want any of her children to experience the hardship and trauma she suffered. Heading to college, she decided that she would marry a dark-skinned man because she wanted brown children. She married my father, a man with melanin-rich skin. Coincidentally, my father wanted to marry a light-skinned woman because he also wanted brown children. At that time, Black equated to ugliness not only in the predominant white culture but also for those who had internalized white norms as a means of assimilation. Instead of Black, we referred to ourselves as colored or Negroes.

Subsequently, these two science majors genetically engineered me. I learned that it was best to be a brown colored girl, because my complexion wouldn't be a target for other colored people held hostage by the hierarchy of color where hue demarcated your level of privilege. The shade of my complexion made my status clear and acceptable to all.

But I did covet Grandma's hair. I wanted flowing straight hair, like Rapunzel, not the coils that required parting, yanking, pulling, and twisting to comply with the obligatory standards of beauty. Even so, hair plaiting offered welcomed intimacy. I savored the feeling of my grandmother and mother's fingers lacing around my hair and caressing the bergamot-scented emollient on my scalp.

When I was five years old, I asked Grandmother Mary Ann why she looked white. I wanted to know. She obliged me, and we had the talk. My grandmother shared that her mother Mary Ann, had blonde hair and blue eyes and was enslaved until she was five years old. Her father was a white man, but he wasn't her father: He was her master. Now my young mind started to turn a corner. Was he or was he not her father? She explained again that her mother was not his child; she was his slave. He did not act like a father but like a master. I found the whole concept perplexing and strange, like listening to a fairy tale gone wrong. She explained that some of the masters established schools to educate their house servants, and he was that kind of master.

Grandmother continued to share that we came from house slaves who did domestic chores and served as wet nurses. She chuckled and said with a hint of pride, "The mistress and the slaves nursed each other's babies, but my grandma [Ellen Coward Hargrove] affectionately known as *Madodo* nursed her own babies first." Common lore held that the bondswomen's milk contained more nutrients. She didn't unpack to my little ears the incest or the sex trafficking that happened in this laissez-faire environment of sex on demand by masters and their associates.

Grandmother said that her siblings' complexions ranged from a translucent pearl to varying shades of yellow to brown. Grandmother didn't talk about slavery for too long. She protected us from those memories. She said many shameful things happened to people and that colored people suffered a lot under chattel slavery while they fervently prayed for God's deliverance. Freedom took a while but happened in due season. She talked about

Figure 2. The author with her grandmother, Mary Ann McFall McNeil, and sister, Ernestine Yuille Weaver.

plantations as forced labor camps with colored people laboring for very long hours. These messages were instilled in me at a young age—that the color of your skin and the texture of your hair mattered. Like magic, they emanated power.

For many Americans, enslavement is recent history. I am one of those Americans. Consequently, the institution has a profound visceral impact on me. I knew people who knew people who were enslaved. My maternal great-grandfather was enslaved until he was in his teens. Reading about the inception and practices of our color caste system gets under my skin. America's historical and legal records are riddled with accounts of atrocities against Black and brown people to instill terror and thereby attempt to control their thoughts so that their bodies would yield to the enslavers' demands.

This dark history weighs heavily upon me. Sometimes I want to cease my research, because these ghastly narratives are repulsive and heartrending and harass my thoughts today. Like others, I want to see no evil and hear no evil, but that attitude lulls me into denial, a defense mechanism that dulls the pain at the expense of distorting my perception. My spirit is restored from the insightful words of Alexander Berkman: "Man's inhumanity to man does not have the last word. The truth lies deeper. It is economic slavery, the savage struggle for a crumb, that has converted mankind into wolves and sheep."[1] I must examine American history because these stories reveal the thought-world and prevailing culture of my ancestors. These ugly and disturbing passages disclose the origins of racialized enmities and inequities generated by the human chattel juggernaut. Had I lived earlier, the chains would have fastened me to people who looked like me. The origin of America's racialized caste system is a horror story, but horror frequently serves as a crucible for heroism—a kiln for our spiritual and societal transformation. For me, this is horror's redemptive purpose.

My grandmother's youngest sibling, Charlotte McFall Lacy, whom we called Aunt Lottie, acted as the family historian and griot. She kept the records of our family history through oral tradition. She didn't let the uncomfortable nature of the topic stop her. Aunt Lottie resembled my grandmother, but she didn't act like my grandmother. The first time I recall meeting my Aunt Lottie, she stepped out from behind the steering wheel sporting culottes, black and white saddle shoes, and bobby socks. Her wavy brown hair was fashionably short. On my first trip to Charleston, she ferried my sisters and me to the slave market. I recall tentatively tiptoeing through the chambers. The market held a strange solemnity. She told us about some of the brutalities that enslaved people suffered. Looking at the dark, rusty, chains, the cuffs, and the dingy walls, frightened me. Enslavement seemed far enough away and yet unsettlingly close.

I remember feeling jumpy throughout that short tour, especially when Aunt Lottie said that parents could be sold away from their children. For a six-year-old, it was worse than any spooky house that I could have ever imagined. Her words alarmed me. One false move and my whole life could change. I kept thinking I was glad that I hadn't been born back then. I worried that my mother would be sold away from us. She spoke her mind. She didn't like to be bullied. I wouldn't call her sassy, but opinionated. I recall Grandmother saying, "Laura, your mouth is going to get you into trouble!" I guess I followed close behind, because I used to hear that warning from my mother as well.

Looking back, I wonder if that was an age-appropriate field trip. The whole idea of being sold away in chains fastened to a coffle left an impression. Then again, this cultural practice happened to Black children, and it was undoubtedly cruel, violent, and traumatic. The harsh conditioning process of slave making began in childhood: If children resisted, they could be sold, maimed, or killed. As soon as enslaved children could take instruction, they worked. They ate in troughs designed for animals, eating with their hands or, if available, with seashells. Their eyes witnessed cruelties, and some experienced sadistic forms of torture. I can imagine the hollering, pleading, clinging, and whipping that happened in the slave market as the owners ruthlessly severed family connections.

It is an innate attribute of the human condition to want to hold onto the children we bear, but the child delivered by an enslaved woman did not belong to her. The spiritual song, "Sometimes I Feel Like a Motherless Child" was a common dirge.[2] Enslaved women and men realized that it would take a village to raise a child, but to remind enslaved people of their place in the caste system, the enslavers attempted to rob them of any semblance of a family. The racist laws reinforced the belief that enslaved people did not deserve love, emotional attachments, or any evidence of their shared humanity. However, despite this maleficent framework, like water, human love and connection fashioned its own groove.

Charleston was a "melting pot" because of the human chattel industry. While playing with my sisters on Palmetto Street, I saw the most striking combinations of Blackness—an earthen admixture of brown-skinned people with blue eyes, ebony-skinned people with straight hair, and blondes with tawny complexions. However, the closer these features were to white characteristics, the more they were valued. A pragmatist, my Grandmother Mary Ann used her light skin to leverage certain goods and services in the marketplace. She would chuckle about how she and her sisters would sometimes *pass* to enter stores that prohibited African Americans in the Jim Crow South. Grandma earned admission to study piano at Columbia College in

New York City, but World War I ended these aspirations. She didn't have the financial means and pivoted to other marketable skills. She remained in Charleston and sewed death shrouds and dresses for wealthy white Charlestonians.

My Aunt Lottie appreciated her light skin because of the opportunities her complexion afforded her. At a time when African Americans hesitated to travel for fear of racial animus and violence, she traveled extensively throughout the country and the world. In the 1920s, she earned her master's degree in mathematics from the University of Chicago. Eventually, she became a professor at West Virginia State University. Katherine Johnson, the human calculator in the movie *Hidden Figures*, studied under Aunt Lottie's tutelage and mentioned her in her memoir.[3] Aunt Lottie believed that her light skin accorded her a position of leadership in the African-American community, and she willingly accepted the mantle of service.

In the generation to follow, however, animus continued to grow toward light skin and the privileges it brought. Mother had a very different experience within the color caste system. During World War II, Grandma worked as a foreman in a sewing factory, a job that would have been prohibited for many discernibly Black women. However, she earned *good money*. My paternal grandfather graduated from Hampton Institute; taught carpentry at Central High School in Louisville, Kentucky; and purchased several homes on their street. My mother had enough, while those around her had negligible resources. She recalled a childhood of being bullied and threatened with physical violence by African-American children from impoverished homes. Malnourished, these children suffered from rickets and bowed legs, but my immaculately dressed mother had pretty legs. Her healthy appearance triggered their envy. "You think you're cute," or "You think you're better than us" became an unfortunate gibe in her childhood. Even though my mother didn't like being light-skinned, I felt proud of my light-skinned mother with brown, blowing hair. As a child growing up in a color caste system, I knew that her appearance garnered adoration and preference. The color caste system seeped into my consciousness. I was learning how to assimilate.

So the genetic trace of my white ancestry trickled throughout my maternal family, but I learned to keep the knowledge of it at, and below, a whisper. I was warned not to discuss any of these matters, especially in front of white people. Discussing cross-racial relationships was considered impolite and dangerous because, in many states, these bonds remained illegal. When Aunt Lottie even hinted at superiority because of her complexion, my mother retorted, "Aunt Lottie, the only thing that our light skin proves is that we were 'shitted on.'" In many ways, Mother's response was a brutal fact. When I unearth the stories of female house slaves, the archetype of Cinderella emerges but without the restitution of a happy ending through matrimony. Frequently, female house servants were second-class kin, the scapegoats doomed to respond to their masters' and mistresses' demands. By design, these women were made for the white man's purpose and pleasure.

Grandmother wanted to *let sleeping dogs lie*, but Aunt Lottie wanted to talk about the white side of our family lineage. She wanted to share the story of our heritage with all its complexity. When Aunt Lottie referred to the master, Grandmother and Mother smirked. They didn't want her to even get close to trying to brag on the connection. They felt deeply affronted by its abhorrent nature. But Aunt Lottie persisted. She thought that we needed to know our ancestry. She stubbornly refused to erase these connections. The Africans' footprints were swept away like ocean waves upon sand, but the white men had footprints in historical documents, and through her storytelling she prepared me to be ready at the right time.

Skin Deep, 1980–85

Prompted by my mother's suggestions, I went on a short vacation from my studies at Yale Divinity School and traveled to Charleston to visit Aunt Lottie. As she was getting on in years, I knew that I would need to listen to her stories more intently and document them. Accompanied by my cousin Frank, we took the road trip headed south on Interstate 95. I do not recall when I first heard his name, but I knew that knowing the master's name was a rarity. His name was Colonel Asbury Coward, the eighth superintendent of The Citadel. I thought it was a peculiar name, rather conspicuous and certainly ironic. One not easy to forget, that's for sure. One afternoon, Aunt Lottie drove us to The Citadel to view Colonel Coward's portrait. We walked across campus to where his oil painting hung in the refectory. She stood at attention beside it and said, "See, I have his nose." She appeared proud of her connection to him and proud of his ascent. I snapped my Polaroid and watched the photograph fade into view. Now, admiring his portrait, I felt like an Oreo cookie; secretly, I also wanted to admire his accomplishments and my connection to him. But he was an enslaver, and that reality created a sharp divide. After viewing the portrait, Aunt Lottie took us on a windshield tour along the Battery. She knew the old Charleston family names and pointed to the windows of the rooms where our female ancestors had lived as enslaved house servants in these grand plantation-like homes.

In the mid-1980s, I joined the military, another hierarchical system that made me ask myself whether I was a glutton for punishment. I gave my mother a great deal of influence over that decision. She persuaded me first on a spiritual level, and then on a political one, and ended on an economic reality. "What better job could God ask of you than to serve young people living and working in violence? Besides, you will learn how the white man thinks." She continued, "If the eagle isn't flying, nothing is." So, I donned the naval uniform and had my assumptions confirmed that many white men did not want to discuss matters that disturbed the status quo as it pertained to color. They denied their preferential treatment at every turn. Common statements such as "We are all blue," or "You're a Black woman, so you'll get promoted" were frequently declared, but they were woefully inaccurate statements. Many white male Navy chaplains avoided uncomfortable conversations that called to mind racialized inequities. As a result, they could unwittingly exploit their fundamental advantages in the system. However, occasionally, the Navy succumbed to outside pressure to address societal harms.

What's Love Got to Do with It? 1997

During a professional development training course, we candidly discussed our attitudes on race relations. Several white chaplains discounted the idea that color signified a barrier to equity. They endorsed the idea of meritocracy and accepted the political nature of assignments that leveraged promotions influenced by the *good ole boys'* network. They pretended that racism did not exist to protect their advantages. They did not see systemic inequities, only individual responsibility. The conversation started to get under my skin. As a way of jockeying for position in the hierarchy, one of these chaplains, an Episcopal priest, gloated about his alma mater, The Citadel. Finally, in the heat of discussion, I took the bait. I announced, "Here lies the problem when talking about race relations—Colonel Asbury Coward, a superintendent of The Citadel, is an ancestor of mine. He and my Great-Great Grandmother Ellen had five children, and I am not supposed to acknowledge it. Their relationship has been completely denied. Like it never even happened." Because of my color, I knew how quickly I could be dismissed. You could have heard a pin drop. I wondered to myself, "How do you like me now?" I felt like a schoolgirl chanting that my white ancestor is better than your white ancestor, and I'm Black, so there!

Then one of the white subject-matter experts, blurted out, "She was raped!" My plan for one-upmanship backfired. What was I thinking about, making this statement? Perhaps I wasn't thinking at all. I felt the sensation of falling off a cliff and yelling on the way down, "Why didn't I keep my big mouth shut?" I attempted to explain that they could have had a relationship. But it felt too preposterous for me to argue with his allegation of assault. At best, their relationship was a hostage situation. Again, he shouted, "She was raped! The customs and legalities of that period had no bearing. She was raped." No one said a thing. Nothing more to say.

To hear him say that word triggered shame in me, like shrinking inside my skin. His amplification felt jarring. To be raped was to be violated, discarded, shamed, and *even* blamed. Suddenly, I identified with the victim. I felt embarrassed and crushed by that four-letter word instead of furious at the perpetrator. Rape burst the idyllic, romanticized bubble that my Aunt Lottie's playfulness had unintentionally blown around their relationship. The word "rape" signified that Ellen was just a piece to Asbury and that she lived her life in pieces, like bed wench, wet nurse, chambermaid, ladies' maid, housekeeper, laundress, and seamstress. I had not grappled with the power differential between them. Laws defied acknowledging, dignifying, and preserving these relationships. Consensual sex was a misnomer within this system of power and disenfranchisement.

I imagined that Ellen had a privileged position among enslaved people because of her proximity to white privilege and her mulatto designation. I didn't want to imagine her suffering from coercive tactics like verbal and physical abuse, living with her children in the cellar, the attic, or under the stairs on pallets. In my childhood memories, Grandma told me, "Madodo was beautiful." I chirped, "What color was she?" "Your color." I felt a well of pride. Ellen was a "house slave"—a "higher" position than field slaves in the caste. The instructor disrupted my romanticism to even more discomfort. I, too, had become indoctrinated by our color caste system and ascribed value to one's proximity to whiteness. But more than that, I wanted to see her esteemed by him, instead of trafficked.

After the session, one of the senior chaplains discreetly approached me and suggested that I do some genealogical investigation. He hinted, "Colonel Coward has a large footprint. You can find some good information." The Black chaplains appeared gratified that I had attempted to deepen the conversation, yet even when I had blurted out the story, in the back of my mind I still wondered if the tale was true—a symptom of imposter syndrome. I could not provide any documentation. Great-Great-Grandmother Ellen did not have any legal papers substantiating their relationship. Through the passage of time, their connection was diminished to hearsay and *almost* became a work of fiction. *I mean, while it was happening, it "wasn't happening," so why would I think it happened now?* Verifying this relationship seemed futile, like looking for a black cat in a coal cellar. I knew the African-American descendants of Thomas Jefferson had met some dogged and oppositional resistance from his legitimate heirs. I didn't need to get into that ring without the right gloves.

I've Got You Under My Skin, 2012–14

With the election of President Barack Obama, the perceptions of those I brought into this conversation about race had shifted and expanded. A Black biracial man occupied the highest position in the political world. However, his election fueled tensions in our public discourse about race. During this seismic shift and inspired by the work of the Griot Institute for the Study of Black Lives and Cultures at Bucknell University, I began in earnest to verify my family's oral tradition.[4] Under the guidance of the late Professor Carmen Gillespie, the Griot Institute offered a seminar on the relationship between Thomas Jefferson and Sally Hemings. I attended those lectures, read books that explored this union, toured Monticello, and thought deeply about how notions of color have shaped our body politic.

Some of my ancestors would have been categorized as white Blacks—those who were phenotypically white but classified as Negroes. As if for the first time, I found myself shocked that some slaves looked white. The white elite had, indeed, learned how to enslave themselves. Journalists Brittany Luce and Eric Eddings, in a provocative segment on passing in the podcast *For Colored Nerds*, confirmed my observation.[5] They recalled how abolitionists garnered white support by instilling fear in white parents that their children could be mistaken for slaves and abducted into the trade.

Given how many white men had both white and colored offspring, unacknowledged, interracial relationships were prevalent. Intricate social practices and notions of propriety evolved around those relationships. These involved "acceptable" duplicities. In Charleston, the overwhelming number of slave manumissions were granted to mulattoes, their enslaved paramours, and the children of these unions. According to the *South Carolina Encyclopedia*, in 1860, mulattoes constituted five percent of the state's enslaved population but seventy-two percent of the freed people. Women were more frequently manumitted than men.[6]

My sister Toni interviewed a Black genealogist, the late Wilhelmina Kelly, who joined the Daughters of the American Revolution (DAR) through her white male ancestor.[7] One could claim membership through Black ancestors, because many Black men did, in fact, fight in the Revolutionary War, but their service is harder to corroborate. Within the limitations of the law, her white male ancestor discovered a way to legitimize his relationship, so she had a paper trail. The three of us put our heads together to devise a strategy to be admitted to the DAR through a white ancestor.

We wondered whether the Cowards fought in the Revolution and attempted to trace them in the documents available to us, but our lack of marital records and rudimentary paperwork impeded our discovery. Moreover, as Black women, we felt almost like traitors, searching for the confirmation that white soldiers would provide. My Black ancestors could have fought and died in that war, many receiving a booty of broken promises. We couldn't find the Cowards. Furthermore, we still needed to establish our kinship with them. The DAR did not accept DNA, and we didn't have any donors at that time, but that restriction planted another idea: Find the holy grail—DNA. Although genetic material would not satisfy the DAR, one minute sample from a legitimate descendant would answer the pivotal question.

Fitting together my pieces of information, I found a compilation of Colonel Coward's Civil War journal in *The South Carolinians*, edited by Natalie Jenkins Bond.[8] I purchased a copy. Sitting at my desk with the unopened book, I had the haunting notion that I shouldn't be "snooping around" in his private life. But curiosity got the better of me. I also heard my mother, my Aunt Lottie, and my grandmother encouraging me. I could hear my mother whispering in my ear, helping me to connect the dots. A perceptive woman, she enjoyed detective work and positing theories. When the book arrived with the "Stars and Bars" and palmetto ensign on its cover, I felt a moment of recoil and resistance. But when I opened the cover and saw his picture, I felt stunned! That's the man! He's my great-great-grandfather. My grandma bore a vivid resemblance to him. Gazing down at his photograph, I detected vulnerability. Something shifted inside me. I found I could not hate him, because he looked like people I deeply loved and sorely missed.

The next big hurdle was to read his war journal. I worried about the content and the language he would use to describe people that looked like me. Questions swirled. Would his words hurt? Would he refer to my people as "niggers"? Would he disparage them? He didn't use the term "niggers" in the narrative. Instead, he used "colored" and "Negroes." Sometimes he used the historically genteel but disparaging word "darkie," a term my mother declared equally repugnant.

I found myself taking a measured view of his morality, given his cultural conditioning. The racial caste system was the Southern—indeed, the American—way of life. That's a brutal fact. Asbury had his place within this color caste system. White supremacist ideology permeated his story; that's the narrative that he was taught and that sustained his social ranking in the racialized hierarchy. He learned to exploit the narrative of racial difference to leverage power and privilege for himself and those most like him. Initially, I felt shackled by the ill-begotten narrative of racial difference that fostered enmity instead of affinity between us. American culture drew bright lines of separation, and that division created wide disparities that exist to this day. Colonel Asbury Coward inherited a racialized caste system that gave his whiteness preference, privilege, and protection. Had I been in his position, I'm not quite sure how I would have managed this advantage. Fear of death, violence, terror, ostracism, family separations, and the threat of impoverishment forced and manipulated everyone's complicity in the caste system. Many of us still spend much of our time adapting to the structures we live in, figuring out ways to thrive or survive instead of working to dismantle and transform our social constructs from the ground up. When I approach that larger task, I identify with Sisyphus rolling a rock up a hill, only for it to slide down. Incremental change is a slow, at times imperceptible, process. I can feel frustrated by the apparent ineffectuality of the cause, and so I remind myself that doing good is good.

Consequently, I choose not to see Colonel Coward as a one-dimensional demon rampaging through the 1800s. It flattens him into a paper cutout and discounts the complexities of the human condition. The racialized caste system traumatized everyone in varying degrees, but power and privilege matter in the world of realpolitik. Therefore, in matters of human suffering, there was no equivalency between enslaved Black and free white people. By design, they lived in two distinct and remote worlds, one labeled Black and the other white. However, I also acknowledge the universality of the human spirit, which continues to inform my perspective. People are capable of both sacrificial love and horrendous evil. For better or worse, we are subject to each other's autonomy.

To understand him, I needed to gather as much historical background as I could to inform my perspective. Again, I wanted to enter this project with curiosity rather than hostility. I asked questions and followed leads. I read copious historical documents and literature depicting life during the antebellum period. To work through my resentment, I found photographs of Colonel Coward online and selected one as a screen saver—the one in which I thought I detected a twinkle in his eye. I referred to family notes and a family tree that my Uncle Frank, my mother's older brother, left stashed in the pages of the book *Initiatives, Paternalism, and Race Relations on the Charleston Avery Normal Institute.*[9] Prompted by Uncle Frank's encouragement, I discovered an extensive genealogy site that traced Coward's lineage back for generations and found tidbits of surprising information in obscure articles about him.

I used to look at my screen saver, at this elfin man and say, "Look, if you want to repair the breach, I need some paper that connects us." During a workshop at the Griot Institute, a prominent genealogist, Helen F. M. Leary, stated simply that any white man who had proximity to an enslaved woman had sexual access to her. I needed at least to establish the physical proximity between Colonel Coward and Great-Great-Grandmother Ellen. Without a piece of paper proving that she served as his bondswoman, my project could not advance. But I kept on, hoping the paper would turn up.

I wanted the man on my screen saver to help me with my project. From what I had deduced, he enjoyed being a prominent, influential figure, but he did have to scramble and strategize for the prestige that he eventually enjoyed. He wasn't born with a silver spoon, but his chubby little fingers held fast to a white card that alighted in the palm of his hand. At the moment of birth, his physical attributes gave him access to numerous cultural privileges.

Then, in early 2013, sitting in the lobby of the Hale Koa Hotel on Waikiki Beach, I received an email from my second cousin Lahnice McFall Hollister. She was doing genealogical research and came across a slip of paper naming our Great-Great Grandmother Ellen and her mother Charlotte as property intestate to Asbury upon the unexpected death of his father, Jesse. I had my piece of paper. Ironically, I felt thrilled. Although an odious proof of ownership should have hardened me toward him, that paper provided a piece of the puzzle.

In the following months, I drove to The Citadel to read through Colonel Coward's personal papers. I still felt like a trespasser. I didn't know my place—or I did know my place and didn't accept it. Essentially, all Black Americans have white ancestry. "Broadly, the genomic analysis found that, on average, the African-American genome was 73.2 percent African, 24 percent European and 0.8 percent Native American."[10] I am a BIPOC: Black Indigenous person of color. Yet, as I sorted through his material, I started to feel empowered and thought to myself, "Who's sitting in the catbird seat now? It took almost two hundred years, yet here I am rifling through all your stuff."

I got nosy. I spent several hours rummaging through his boxes and reading the microfiche ad nauseum. At times, I imagined an overseer in the corner waiting to swat me away for meddling. I felt naughty as I started to read his unpublished handwritten diary. The salutation read, "My dear children," a term of endearment that did not include me, yet here I am.

Colonel Coward's personal diary provided glimpses into his character. He wrote of his courtship with his apparently well-to-do wife, Elise, and referred to her as "the pink mantle"—one of many marks of affection and condescension—as he persuaded her to take his hand. Her father was a vendue master, an auctioneer. Although their marriage was, in part, an economic transaction, Elise was flesh and blood to him, whereas Ellen was a commodity to serve their various purposes, or perhaps just his. To justify this practice and validate their privilege, Coward and men like him referred to characters in the Old Testament such as Abraham, who had Sarah and Hagar. Coward had his wife, Elise, and his enslaved concubine, Ellen.

Initially, I assumed that Asbury Coward was of the planter class. Quite the opposite—the Cowards were yeoman farmers, the working poor, commonly referred to by the power elite as waste people, or poor white trash. This group found themselves wedged between a rock and a hard place: They could not compete with free labor. To escape grinding poverty, to gain financial stability and to elevate his position in the caste, his father, Jesse, made a Faustian bargain. He decided to work as an overseer on the Quimby and Hyde Plantations, where cruelty was a requirement for anyone working in the human chattel industry. Owners and overseers commonly used terror to compel compliance. Perhaps one of Jesse's motivations was to give his son, Asbury, the advantages of a good and costly education. For Jesse, the end justified the means.

Ellen and her mother's circumstances were ever more knotty, vulnerable, and precarious. They had no authority over their own lives, and their bodies were owned by a man who resorted to violence. For many overseers, corporal punishment—the cat-o'-nine-tails and the sugar house (a workhouse of torture)—were instruments to enforce compliance in a system that normalized and excused violence on Black skin no matter what the shade. I imagine enslaved women studied these men closely. Forced to sleep with the enemy, these women probably made themselves economically valuable to leverage some form of negotiation. They toiled to secure their utilitarian value to their owners and perhaps reap some of the privileges from their proximity to whiteness.

Colonel Coward had a harsh childhood reminiscent of a Dickensian novel. His mother's death when he was three months old left him shuttled between the bosoms of his maternal Aunt Sarah Jane and his Black mammy Elsy, who provided most of his care and nourishment. As a child, he experienced episodes of paroxysms. Several times in his handwritten diary, he laments that he could have injured and killed his kinfolk who got under his skin. With remorse, he wrote about different strategies like counting to ten, staring off in the distance, or boxing to manage his anger. Gaining some insights after reading Edgar Allen Poe's short story "Ligeia," Colonel Coward believed he conquered the demon of anger through an act of will.[11]

I wondered about the source of his violent tantrums. Perhaps his fits of rage were a result of childhood trauma. He may have witnessed his wet nurse, Elsy, being beaten. Perhaps, the enslaved people he became attached to disappeared. Perhaps he frequently witnessed corporal violence. Perhaps, as a child, he was trained to inflict violence on enslaved people as a weapon of control. Perhaps he got bullied. After all, in stature, he appeared to be a bit of a runt, but he could pack a mean punch.

One concern that nagged me was whether Asbury had affection for Ellen. They knew each other as children. I wanted her to have a better situation than what her circumstances appeared to have been. For me, love creates safety. I did not want to think of her being repeatedly raped and left emotionally ransacked. I wanted to see her loved and not simply worn out like a throw rug. Legally, Ellen would never have the status and the protections of his wife, but could she *at least* be an object of his affection?

Later in the year, I attended a conference with Coming To The Table, an organization that aims to link the descendants of the enslaved with those of enslavers.[12] I decided to contact Colonel Coward's legitimate heirs. Searching the web, I found one—his namesake. I discovered that we had one more thing in common: We both served in the Navy. I wrote to ask if he would be interested in exploring our common ancestry. My registered letter did not receive a response. Once again, I put the matter to rest and went back to work in the "real world." I moved to DC.

Skin in the Game, 2015–20

My employment as a resiliency facilitator for the US Department of Defense postponed my search, but as soon as my contract ended, I shifted my attention back to substantiating our oral tradition. Despite a full career as a Navy chaplain, I knew that *the pen was mightier than the sword*. I wanted to write this story before time erased it. One nagging question throughout this process of discovery was, "Why didn't I ask my ancestors more questions?" I had been busy living my life and asking other questions. After retiring from the Navy, I seized the opportunity to refocus my attention, synthesize the information, and begin writing the story. Although I had experience in homiletics, I needed to study the craft of writing and consequently enrolled in a writing program at Salve Regina University. My sermon writing was expository, interposed with some anecdotes, but a book requires another kind of prose. "Cut to the chase" was a common slogan in the military, but expediency doesn't always make for good storytelling, which invites the reader to slow down, imagine and reflect. Plus, my ancestors' story was going to be hard to tell, because the themes expressed in the narrative remain painful, emotionally charged, and controversial.

It is exceedingly hard to write because, for many, Asbury Coward epitomizes a villain—the perpetrator. The trouble is that villains are not villains to everyone, and all of us have played the part. Frequently, perpetrators are or have been victims. Besides, *Asbury was this and then he was that, and then he was this again and then he became that.* Human nature cannot be categorized as all good or all evil, nor does human growth mimic a straight trajectory. We are not stock characters but a string of moments, some good and some otherwise. We retrace and reintegrate.

I do not want to minimize his egregious behavior. He owned slaves. He fought for the Confederacy. He joined the Red Shirts, a ragtag, violent, and extremist wing of the Democratic Party. Writing about him challenges me, because he was the enemy, yet I want to make a connection. I would read something about Asbury Coward that I admired or some action that he took that reflected magnanimity and insight. Then I would read something that caused me to wince or to raise an eyebrow. Yet I pressed on amid the complexity, hoping that he wasn't a stock character.

The cultural climate played a critical role in facilitating my research through a groundswell of information. Over several years, a spate of books that reexamined American history emerged, telling hard, dark, under-told stories about enslavement, civil massacres, Jim Crow, lynching, convict leasing—the relentless drumbeat of strategic and perpetual confiscation of wealth. I saw how our sanitized historical narrative had reinforced the racialized caste system. Open conversations about racial disparities and the structures that perpetuated these harms became more acceptable, and even urgent.

The aftermath of George Floyd's murder and the toppling of numerous Confederate monuments motivated me to make the story public, regardless of where I landed in the authentication process. Racial reckoning had become a popular catchphrase. Feeling the urgency of the moment, I continued reading the works by thoughtful leaders like Ibram X. Kendi, Robin diAngelo, Isabel Wilkerson, Clint Smith, Daniel Hill, and Ta-Nehisi Coates. I also listened to the podcast of Nikole Hannah Jones's *The 1619 Project*.[13] These authors and the Black Lives Matter movement changed the conversation about race and color. They provided new ways to discuss the artificiality of race and the reality of structural racism. I heard legal scholar and civil rights advocate Kimberlé Crenshaw contend that race is fiction. Racism is a fact. I breathed a sigh of relief that we could discuss these social constructions instead of dismissing their reality and their potency in generating harms and sustaining disparities.

Despite the rising animus during the Trump years, the cultural climate seemed more receptive. Scholars made advancements in sharpening the terminology for discussing race relations. For example, the concept of erasure gave me tacit permission to explore my ancestry. I no longer felt gaslit by others' denial or skepticism. I felt validated and inspired to continue to search for the truth. Their scholarship also awakened me to what Kendi calls a "*dueling consciousness*" and revealed my personal complicities with assimilation.[14]

One evening, I watched a *PBS NewsHour* segment "Race Matters," which covered the Universities Studying Slavery programs. To familiarize myself with this undertaking, I located the website and noticed that The Citadel was listed. This university has a Truth, Racial Healing and Transformation Center Team (TRHT), which was codirected by Tessa Updike, an archivist, and Dr. Felice Knight, an African-American historian.[15] With these two individuals, I knew I had an opening to discuss my project, even though I still lacked credible DNA evidence.

To present my case, I met with the TRHT and was reminded that they needed DNA evidence. My second cousin, Lahnice McFall Hollister, had been extensively researching my grandmother's family, the McFalls of Charleston. In her article published in *The New England Historical and Genealogical Register*, "Three Generations of South Carolina Freedwomen," she recounted our family's oral tradition and identified Asbury Coward as the owner and possibly the father of Ellen's five children. Our great-grandmother, Mary Ann McFall, was the eldest daughter of this union.[16] She was the blonde-haired, blue-eyed girl who was enslaved until she was five years old. In my second meeting with the TRHT, I invited Lahnice to be my ally, because her work was extensive and documented. Although she had not set out to prove Coward's kinship, her findings did substantiate Coward's and Ellen's proximity.

Blood Is Thicker than Water, June–November 2021

Knowing that I must verify my oral tradition, I again googled Asbury Coward's name. I found an obituary with a photograph of Coward's heir, Captain Asbury "Sandy" Coward IV, a white-haired, blushed-complexion, round-faced man in his Navy choker white dress uniform. With some agitation, I read his obituary. As I perused the article, I found the name of his younger brother, Curtis Coward. I recognized this name from a previous search. Hearing the tick of the clock, I made a last-ditch effort. He might be the last living white male heir and the missing link. I sprang into action, located his email address, and contacted him. In my introductory email to Curtis Coward, I shared the story of my trip to The Citadel with my Aunt Lottie—Charlotte McFall Lacy—to see Colonel Asbury Coward's portrait. There she pointed out her resemblance to him. I explained my goal of verifying Asbury Coward as our common ancestor. He responded within twenty-four hours. I was thrilled. He seemed open, curious, and eager. Finally, after all these years, I was going to uncover a family mystery.

When we spoke, I offered my condolences and asked him, "Are you a descendant of Colonel Asbury Coward, a superintendent of The Citadel?" "Yes," he responded, "I'm wearing his signet ring as we speak." During our conversation, he reminded me in a crusty voice that I had reached out to his brother several years ago. He and his sister-in-law had discussed my letter, but the conversation dropped. He quizzed me, "Guess what my middle name is? McFall!" He did not challenge any of my claims, because the practice of taking enslaved women as concubines was customary. He reminded me that Thomas Jefferson had Black descendants. He also mentioned that he had two daughters whose work related to racial equity and that they were eager to meet me. We agreed to continue our conversation the following week.

Coincidentally, I had planned to meet Dr. Felice Knight at The Citadel that afternoon. When I met with her, she shared in the excitement of this phase of discovery, but she said that his agreement did not provide the evidence I needed. I had anticipated her response. The following week, I met virtually with Curt. This time, I asked if he would donate a DNA sample. I knew it was a big ask. Even though we might share an ancestor, we were total strangers. At the end of our conversation, though, he said he would do whatever he could to help me with my project.

On Thanksgiving Day, Curt informed me that his DNA information was now available. I uploaded my data on his site the following week. On December 3, 2021, I received confirmation: Colonel Asbury Coward was my ancestor. Curtis, his legitimate heir, and I shared the same great-great-grandfather. Through patience and persistence, I found him. My maternal ancestors had spoken the truth, and I had substantiated their story.

In My Blood, January 2022–Present

According to my female ancestors, all five of Ellen's children were fathered by Asbury Coward from 1857 to 1874. Dr. John Allen McFall, the eldest brother of my grandmother Mary Ann wrote in his journal that some of the former slave owners did provide a form of guardianship for their newly emancipated colored families. I imagine that this custom followed a patronage model, with favors discreetly bestowed by the patriarch to their colored relations. According to Dr. McFall, freed mulattoes fared better than freed Blacks because of the patriarch's oversight. In his writings, the name of Asbury Coward, his grandfather, was never cited. Consequently, it's hard to state with absolute certainty what Asbury *might* have done for his colored offspring. Erasure removed the trace of any intimate attachments. Through my research, I detected that Asbury might have offered some guidance and protection. Emancipation left Ellen marooned and pregnant, with their three children in tow. Countless newly freed females with children mentally collapsed. They didn't have a foothold in the prevailing winds of change. Emancipation found Black women with children in a no-win situation. Many perished.

In many foreseeable ways, freedom equated to severe deprivation for freed people. Jim Downs reports in *Sick From Freedom* that nearly one million enslaved people died from 1862 to 1870.[17] Black families suffered and died from a barrage of racialized hostilities, exposure, and communicable diseases such as smallpox. Their ailments went untreated. Many Blacks gradually withered away from starvation. So dire were their health problems that a white religious leader thought that Black Americans would vanish. "Like his brother the Indian of the forest, he must melt away and disappear forever from the midst of us."[18]

Asbury's actions could have helped to keep Ellen and her family alive. Although he had no legal obligation to his colored family, he had a moral and ethical one, which he could have attempted to fulfill. It appears that Asbury quickly devised a plan to restore his household and reinstate his school, Kings Mountain Military Academy. He went to the Freedmen's Bureau and disclosed his plan to distribute some of his freed people to the Lowcountry.[19] Others would stay in York County because of their family connections. Ellen and her mother, Charlotte, remained in York County for several years. Ellen continued as his concubine, which allowed her to remain under Asbury's protection during a volatile period. She worked as a laundress, a seamstress, and a domestic servant in exchange for food, shelter, protection, and education for her children. Charlotte also served as a laundress and domestic servant. This time, their arrangement seemed to be based on mutual need dictated by even more dire circumstances.

Although Asbury's disclosure to the Freedmen's Bureau appeared charitable, his decision could have been motivated by economic expediency and exploitation. When he returned home from the war to York County, Asbury rallied his spirit. He read a tattered sign that he adopted as a credo: "I had it. I lost it. I start all over again."[20] Like many men in his economic caste, he built on what he knew—the old order—and labor was on a fire sale. Consequently, Asbury relied on Ellen and Charlotte to support his aspirations. Before the war, their manual labor defrayed the cost for his attendance at The Citadel. He hired them out to meet his expenses and would use them again.

It is also possible that Asbury had genuine concern for Ellen and their children. There is some evidence that he was not entirely committed to the Confederate ideology. For example, he admired President Lincoln and considered the president's assassination a grave calamity. On hearing the news of Lincoln's murder, Asbury burst into a rant. A fellow Confederate colonel, Samuel Melton, did not share Asbury's sentiments. To quell the situation and calm Melton, Asbury stated, "Mr. Lincoln had much of the milk of human kindness in him. He would have been inclined to deal justly and reverently with the present condition of affairs. God help us all! New trials I see awaiting us ahead!"[21] By voicing this opinion, Asbury barely avoided fisticuffs with Melton. Asbury then shifted the topic, perhaps from fear of being perceived as a loose cannon or a victim of battle fatigue. Even so, his words suggest that he may have heard the still small voice of righteousness.

Asbury's statement about Lincoln accurately predicted the looming situation as an unmitigated disaster. Yorkville became an extremely fractious and hostile environment in which to live and work.

The Civil War ended, but the tensions between the Confederates and their sympathizers and Freedmen and their allies escalated. Even though the

Confederates lost the war, they refused to forfeit their power and privilege to the Freedmen who demonstrated their potency in every sphere. Former Confederates could not envision a biracial nation and conducted asymmetrical warfare on their formerly enslaved people.

Being married to Elise and with a growing family, Asbury's life became thornier and more complicated. During the Ku Klux Klan insurgency in York County, Asbury walked a tightrope, waffling between his competing connections. Many Klan members were his superiors, friends, and neighbors. He needed them. One of his close associates, a town's physician, Confederate General James Rufus Bratton, commanded the Klan and led in some of its most heinous and notorious exploits. Conversely, Asbury had intimate connections with Charles Bessear, his faithful manservant during the Civil War and later his cook at Kings Mountain Academy. Then there was Ellen, accompanied by his children. Though customary, Asbury and Ellen's relationship was illicit and grew more tentative with each passing year. Asbury's former privileges twisted into present liabilities. He got caught! He landed in a political and interpersonal quagmire with no easy answers. Ellen provided one. Elise probably breathed a sigh of relief.

In the mid-1870s, Ellen left York County for the Lowcountry, accompanied by her mother and five children. Her oldest, Henry, was about thirteen years of age, and her youngest was a toddler named Charlotte. Dr. McFall suspected that Ellen left York County because of the Klan, though she never confirmed his hunch. He reported that the Klan murdered over eight hundred Freedmen and destroyed hundreds of barns and homes.[22] Having surrendered their arms, Freedmen could no longer defend themselves, and race cleansing ensued. During this coup, the Klan drove the Freedmen out of the area, and some of those brave souls migrated as far as the West African coast. Others fought back or sought the protection of living in the woods instead of inhabiting their homes, where many of the Klan's night raids occurred. Despite the racial animus, Ellen's line flourished, and it's conceivable that Asbury Coward has more Black descendants than white heirs. A sturdy woman, his wife Elise had numerous pregnancies, but her children didn't have comparable longevity. She spent much of her childbearing years in and out of a black gown.

After Ellen's departure, Asbury's political alliances regained their former congruency. His school flourished. In 1876, he served as chief marshal of a Red Shirts parade in support of the political campaign of Wade Hampton III. Although Asbury wasn't a Klansman, he eventually backed the Red Shirts' white supremacist ideology and their use of violence to maintain control. In so many ways, he had already made numerous investments in this way of being.

As a political pragmatist, I think that Asbury assessed his situation and made choices that were based on his competing allegiances, alliances, and ambitions. His self-interests aligned with their supremacist ideology. His network consisted of a gang of elite, cantankerous, disaffected, traumatized, grief-stricken, and wounded former Confederate soldiers. He knew their ferocity as well as he knew his own. Resisting his band of brothers not only could have sealed his fate but also could have doomed his household. The Klan murdered both Blacks and their white sympathizers. Asbury may have feared the repercussions of resistance. Or maybe he kept his hands clean while letting others do the dirty work of reestablishing the South's repressive regime.

Despite Asbury's complexities and apparent contradictions, neither he nor I created our social and economic caste systems. We didn't hatch this plan. The planter elites did. By a consequence of birth, we landed on disparate rungs on the ladder, but we each bear responsibility for the harms we may have caused to others. Asbury did not construct the notion of *whiteness*, but the idea of whiteness became a moral hazard for him. Asbury's supremacist ideology perpetuated the narrative of racial difference and stirred the animosity that formed the bedrock for the socioeconomic injustices that barred Black people from equitable participation in the political structure that governed them. State legislators and institutions strategically stripped Freedmen of their hard-earned civil rights, which perpetually tormented and impoverished them. Whatever his feelings toward Ellen, Asbury chose not to share power or privileges with Freedmen. Instead, he dispensed benefits as he deemed equitable to those he favored.

Some white people found ways to use their whiteness as a lever for equity and the abolition of social injustice. They struggled to awaken a nation mesmerized by the love of capital, but they couldn't generate a critical mass to continue the process of reconciliation. There just weren't enough of them. Even though I desperately wish that Asbury and those like him had not resorted to or been complicit with violence and instead operated from a place of goodwill and equity, they didn't. Perhaps they couldn't. The white populaces could not overcome the centuries of negative conditioning and predatory behaviors toward Black people and resorted to the same vile tactics to victimize and disenfranchise newly freed people. Former Confederates recreated the Old South. That pernicious script provided them with a sense of order, comfort, and certainty but left them spiritually deformed and in so many ways morally bankrupt, for they had invested in a lie. In an episode on *Fresh Air* hosted by Terry Gross, historian Eric Foner shared that Lincoln had wanted to send Black people back to Africa because white people hated them so much.[23] These divisions didn't just happen.

As I researched Asbury's life, I realized that the human chattel system fastened everyone within its tight grip. The industry incarcerated Black people and insidiously reduced desperate and fearful white populations down to their lowest common denominators to maintain the racialized hierarchy, which calcified the divisions. In this scenario, I think everyone *could* be seen as a victim.

And so, I think I understand some of Asbury's choices. The caste system is a behemoth and greater than any individual. The colloquialism "hate the game but not the player" works for me. In the asymmetrical competition between Blacks and whites, Asbury had been dealt the white card. He was a player. He understood the machinations of hierarchy. Of course, he was going to play that card adeptly in alignment with his values, interests, and aspirations. The game was rigged. For him to do otherwise would have seemed irrational and foolhardy. He had family obligations. I can only imagine the political enticements and the incentives he received to remain loyal to his caste. In a sense, he was presented with keys to this kingdom. Eventually, he plotted and landed at the head of the fortress, The Citadel, formerly an arsenal established to violently quell any sentiment of liberation from the enslaved population.

Asbury had the safety net of his social status, but my great-great grandmother Ellen did not. Born of an enslaved mother, she started her life at the bottom rung of the social ladder. But she did have the presence of her mother, Charlotte, whom I acknowledge as one of the unsung heroes in our family narrative. Charlotte did everything she needed to do to keep her small family together. These women worked as a team. Under Charlotte's vigilance and tutelage, Ellen learned how to survive and, in many ways, overcome enslavement. Charlotte imparted to Ellen the tools she needed to keep her safe in a treacherous environment, the master's household. Charlotte held aspirations for her daughter, and I believe that she taught Ellen how to manage and overcome a life defined by adversity by leaning into her inner resources—intimacy with God. Ellen could find wisdom, solace, and dignity from within. These life skills contributed to Ellen's personal agency so that she could emancipate herself in due season and succeed. Their remarkable resiliency has been passed down from generation to generation and paved the way for the educated Black middle class.

As I attempted to walk in Asbury's leather brogans, I softened. He kind of got under my skin. I wondered whether the enslavement of others worked for him or whether it added multiple layers of complexities and conflicts. At times, I wondered if he quietly shared the same thought. I'm sure that there is more information to uncover about my great-great grandfather Asbury that would further disappoint, appall, and maybe surprise me, but I am certain that we all have clay feet. No one lives a perfectly moral, just, and virtuous life. We do the best we can with the hand we've been dealt.

Despite our damaged history, Asbury Coward is no longer my enemy, because I choose not to perceive him that way. When I label him, I make him into a caricature. If I reduce him to one motive, one trait, one flaw or one "ism," I negate his humanity and my ability to get under his skin. Clearly, he wanted to do good work, and he accomplished it. He led in the formation of a generation of leaders. I will not erase the good that he has done or depreciate his legacy for those who directly benefited from his actions. On his death certificate, his occupation was stated not as a soldier but as an educator. An ethic of service is an integral part of both vocations. I know this because I worked as an educator and served as a military chaplain. The University of South Carolina awarded him the honorary degree of Doctor of Laws for his work in education.

I think I recognize how difficult it was for ancestors like Asbury to surrender his power, his ambitions, his privilege, his influence, his connections, his family, his location, his comfort—his whiteness. It's a big ask. But for Ellen, it was an even bigger ask. She had to carry his debt. She carried the responsibility of raising his five white–Black children with fewer ways and paltry means to provide for them. She had to pay his debt, and I'm certain there were many other outstanding debts of his that she had to cover. I guess that's a part of the messy situation my late mother referred to when Aunt Lottie esteemed their light skin. Female house servants got the raw end of that deal.

Like many Black Americans, I inherited a complicated and fractured familial legacy. In many ways, I have benefited, and I stand on the shoulders of all of them. My mother used to comment when someone did something questionable or egregious, "There, but for the grace of God, go I." Surely, I can extend grace on this man, this very human soul. From the moment I saw Asbury's photograph on the inside cover of *The South Carolinians*, I knew he was my great-great-grandfather. He looked like family because we are family. Asbury Coward's paternity appeared on my DNA swab. Under our skin, we are kinfolk. When I shared my findings with my godmother, my late mother's longest friend, she quipped, "You look like him." I paused, surprised. Asbury Coward *is* a part of the people who look like me. He's under my skin. He's in my blood.

The Reverend Thomasina A. Yuille has provided spiritual leadership for diverse populations within the U.S. Navy, the Protestant Church, and within higher education. Currently, she is piecing together her family history to document her ancestor's oral tradition and to delve into their navigation of the complex American landscape of family, color, and race.

NOTES

1. Alexander Berkman, *Prison Memoirs of an Anarchist* (New York: Mother Earth Press, 1912), 225.
2. "Sometimes I Feel Like a Motherless Child" is a traditional Negro spiritual that dates from the time of enslavement. The song was popularized in the late nineteenth century by the Fisk Jubilee Singers. See www.allmusic.com.
3. The mathematician Katherine Johnson (1918–2020) was one of several African-American women employed in NASA's Flight Research Division. Her work identified the precise trajectories needed for the Apollo 11 moon landing. See "Katherine Johnson Dies at 101; Mathematician Broke Barriers at NASA," *New York Times*, February 25, 2020, A1. Her accomplishments were celebrated in Theodore Melfi's biographical drama, *Hidden Figures* (20th Century Fox, 2016).
4. The Griot Institute for the Study of Black Lives and Cultures was founded in 2010 and is currently directed by Dr. Cymore Fourshey. See https://www.bucknell.edu/academics/beyond-classroom/academic-centers-institutes/griot-institute-study-black-lives-cultures/about-griot-institute/our-history.
5. *Passing* is a 2021 film written, produced, and directed by Rebecca Hall and based on Nella Larsen's 1929 novel. Luce and Eddying's podcast is available at https://www.forcolorednerds.fm/.
6. Bernard E. Powers Jr., "Free Persons of Color," *South Carolina Encyclopedia* (Columbia: University of South Carolina Press, 2006), www.scencyclopedia.org.
7. Wilhelmina Rhodes Kelly (1946–2019) was an African-American genealogist and author of four books: *The Hines Bush Family: And Other Related People from the Barnwell District, South Carolina 1842-2004* (Tuscon, AZ: Hats Off Books, 2004); *Bedford Stuyvesant* (Charleston, SC: Arcadia Publishing, 2007); *Crown Heights and Weeksville* (Charleston, SC: Arcadia Publishing, 2009); and *The Long and Winding Road to Jamestowne, Virginian 1607* (Bloomington, IN: Xlibris, 2009).
8. Natalie Jenkins Bond, ed., *The South Carolinians, The Memoirs of Col. Asbury Coward* (Burlington, VT: Vantage Press, 1968).

9. Edmund L. Drago, *Initiative, Paternalism, and Race Relations: Charleston's Avery Normal Institute* (Athens: University of Georgia Press, 1990).

10. Arvind Suresh, "Sen. Elizabeth Warren Controversy: Almost every American has a sliver of Native American ancestry," Genetic Literacy Project, Oct. 16, 2018, www.geneticliteracyproject.org.

11. Poe's story was first published in September 1838 in the magazine *American Museum*. A revised version appeared in 1840 in *Tales of the Grotesque and Arabesque*. See John Ward Ostram, "Poe's Literary Labors and Rewards," in *Myths and Reality: The Mysterious Mr. Poe*, ed. Benjamin Franklin Fisher (Baltimore: The Edgar Allan Poe Society, 1987), 38.

12. Originally founded in 2006 on the campus of Eastern Mennonite University in Harrisonburg, Virginia, Coming to the Table is now associated with RJOY (Restorative Justice for Oakland Youth). See https://comingtothetable.org/.

13. *The 1619 Project: A New Origin Story* (New York: Random House, 2021) is edited by Nikole Hannah-Jones, Caitlin Roper, Ilena Silverman, and Jake Silverstein. It is an expansion of Hannah-Jones's earlier work, "The 1619 Project," which appeared in the *New York Times Magazine* in August 2019.

14. Ibram X. Kendi, *How To Be An Antiracist* (New York: One World, 2019), 29.

15. Universities Studying Slavery is a consortium created by the University of Virginia. There are currently seven South Carolina member institutions: The Citadel, Clemson University, College of Charleston, Francis Marion University, Furman University, the University of South Carolina, and Wofford College. For more information see https://slavery.virginia.edu/universities-studying-slavery/. Truth, Racial Healing and Transformation is a comprehensive organization, sponsored by the W. K. Kellogg Foundation, which works on both the local and national levels to "address the historic and contemporary effects of racism." See https://healourcommunities.org/.

16. Morna Lahnice Hollister, "Three Generations of South Carolina Freedwomen: Tradition and Records Reconstruct a Meaningful Heritage," *The New England Historical and Genealogical Register* 172 (2018): 41.

17. Jim Downs, *Sick from Freedom: African-American Illness and Suffering During the Civil War and Reconstruction* (Oxford and New York: Oxford University Press, 2015), 17.

18. Paul Harris, "How the End of Slavery Led to Starvation and Death for Millions of Black Americans," *The Guardian*, June 16, 2012, www.theguardian.com.

19. The Bureau of Refugees, and Abandoned Lands, commonly referred to as the Freedmen's Bureau, was established by the Department of War in 1865 for the purpose of managing "all matters relating to the refugees and freedmen and lands abandoned or seized during the Civil War." The National Archives provides a useful history of the bureau and its work. See "The Freedmen's Bureau," October 28, 2021, https://www.archives.gov/research/african-americans/freedmens-bureau.

20. Bond, *The South Carolinians, The Memoirs of Col. Asbury Coward*, 186.

21. Bond, 185.

22. McFall, *Autobiography*, 10.

23. "Lincoln's Evolving Thoughts on Slavery, And Freedom," *Fresh Air*, hosted by Terry Gross, October 11, 2010, https://www.npr.org/2010/10/11/130489804/.

WORKS CITED

Berkman, Alexander. *Prison Memoirs of an Anarchist*. New York: Mother Earth Press, 1912.

Bond, Natalie Jenkins, ed. *The South Carolinians, The Memoirs of Col. Asbury Coward*. Burlington, VT: Vantage Press, 1968.

Bressler, Martin and Linda Bressler. "A Study of Veteran-Owned Small Businesses and the Impact of Military Reserve Call-ups Since 9/11." *Academy of Entrepreneurship Journal* 19, no. 2 (2012): 1–22.

Downs, Jim. *Sick from Freedom: African-American Illness and Suffering During the Civil War and Reconstruction*. Oxford, England: Oxford University Press, 2015.

Drago, Edmund L. *Initiative, Paternalism, and Race Relations: Charleston's Avery Normal Institute*. Athens: University of Georgia Press, 1990.

Gross, Terry. "Lincoln's Evolving Thoughts On Slavery, And Freedom." *Fresh Air*, October 11, 2010, https://www.npr.org/2010/10/11/130489804/.

Hall, Rebecca, dir. *Passing*. Netflix. 99 min. 2021.

Hannah-Jones, Nikole, et al., eds. *The 1619 Project: A New Origin Story*. New York: Random House, 2021.

Hollister, Morna Lahnice. "Three Generations of South Carolina Freedwomen: Tradition and Records Reconstruct a Meaningful Heritage." *The New England Historical and Genealogical Register* 172 (2018): 33–42.

Kelly, Wilhelmina Rhodes. *Bedford Stuyvesant*. Charleston, SC: Arcadia Publishing 2007.

———. *Crown Heights and Weeksville*. Charleston, SC: Arcadia Publishing, 2009.

———. *The Hines Bush Family: And Other Related People from the Barnwell District, South Carolina 1842–2004*. Tucson, AZ: Hats Off Books, 2004.

———. *The Long and Winding Road to Jamestowne, Virginian 1607*. Bloomington, IN: Xlibris, 2009.

Kendi, Ibram X. *How To Be An Antiracist*. New York: One World, 2019.

Melfi, Theodore, dir. *Hidden Figures*. 2016. Hollywood, CA: 20th Century Fox.

Ostram, John Ward. "Poe's Literary Labors and Rewards," In *Myths and Reality: The Mysterious Mr. Poe*, edited by Benjamin Franklin Fisher, 37–47. Baltimore: The Edgar Allan Poe Society, 1987.

Powers, Bernard E. Jr. "Free Persons of Color." *South Carolina Encyclopedia*. Columbia: University of South Carolina Press, 2006. www.scencyclopedis.org.

Suresh, Arvind. "Sen. Elizabeth Warren Controversy: Almost Every American Has a Sliver of Native American Ancestry." *Genetic Literacy Project*, October 16, 2018, www.geneticliteracyproject.org/2018/10/16.

The Multicultural Nature of Eighteenth-Century Cooking in British America

The Southern Rice Pie

Christopher E. Hendricks

Among more than four hundred recipes included in Mary Randolph's 1824 cookbook *The Virginia House-Wife* appears one for a southern rice pie, an interesting (and delicious) variation on the more famous rice pudding:

> BOIL half a pound of rice in milk, until it is quite tender; beat it well with a wooden spoon to mash the grains; add three quarters of a pound of sugar, and the same of melted butter; half a nutmeg, six eggs, a gill of wine, and some grated lemon peel; put a paste in the dish, and bake it. For change, it may be boiled, and eaten with butter, sugar, and wine.[1]

Randolph's recipe, which adapts easily to today's kitchen (see recipe, "Southern Rice Pie"), captures the ingenuity and sophistication of early American cuisine. Her collection as a whole, America's first regional cookbook and the first published work on southern cooking, provides a record of both her considerable culinary skills and her impressive business acumen.[2] This recipe in particular and the book in which it is found bring to light a type of knowledge that often remains obscured in the history record: women's domestic craft. Hidden behind the recipe, moreover, is another form of knowledge that has too often been left in the shadows: the agricultural skills of enslaved Africans, who taught their enslavers to grow the rice that became a staple in many of Randolph's recipes and a crucial economic engine for early South Carolina. This essay explores the complicated cultural history of Randolph's cookbook, examining both what the text reveals and inadvertently hides. In doing so, the essay presents two related stories. The first concerns a resourceful and talented woman with a tenacious desire to support her struggling family. The second concerns generations of Africans whose accumulated wisdom made her success possible. At once intertwined and distinct, these stories show how America—and, particularly, South Carolina—depended on people who were forcibly oppressed by those most dependent on their knowledge.

Following in a long tradition of women copying their recipes into journals or binding them together into books, Mary Randolph assembled her collection of recipes she used regularly over the course of a lifetime. As a child, she learned the domestic skills necessary to run a plantation household, including the knowledge of culinary skills. She put that knowledge to use after she married her cousin David Meade Randolph in 1780. As a wedding present, David's father gave the newlyweds Presqu'île, a plantation along the James River. There, Molly, as she was known in the family, took charge of the domestic operations, overseeing the household, among which numbered forty enslaved servants—including those who did the day-to-day cooking—and handling the finances. She utilized her skills not only to provide for her family (four of the couple's eight children reached adulthood) but also to entertain guests in the manner expected of a member of one of Virginia's oldest and wealthiest families.[3]

In 1798, the Randolphs moved to Richmond, where David felt he could pursue a political career, and there built a large house a friend dubbed

Figure 3. Mary Randolph by Charles Balthazar Julien Fevrét de Saint-Mémin, 1807. Library of Congress, Prints and Photographs Division.

"Moldavia," combining Molly and David's names. The couple entertained Richmond society lavishly, and, thanks to Molly's legendary culinary skills and intelligent conversation, people flocked to her table. Chronicler of Richmond society Samuel Mordecai proclaimed her to be "one of the remarkable and distinguished persons of her day."[4]

Beyond its role in Richmond's social whirl, Moldavia became a center for political debate as the new republic was forming. Although the nation's founders hoped it would never happen, politicians started dividing into political parties. The divide affected families as well. With the assistance of his cousin, Secretary of State Thomas Jefferson, David got an appointment as a US Marshal and served through the Washington and Adams administrations. He naturally fell into the Federalist Party, putting him at odds with his cousin's politics. The strain on the family grew, even after Molly's youngest brother Thomas Mann Randolph married Jefferson's daughter Martha. But when Jefferson became president in 1801, though he must have known what the move would do to family relations, he fired David from his government job.[5]

David's dismissal could not have come at a worse time for his family; it coincided with a crash in the tobacco market and a recession. Molly and David's extravagant lifestyle became a thing of the past, and they had to watch their finances carefully. David was forced to sell lots and rental properties he owned in Richmond; his plantation; and finally, even Moldavia. Things got so bad that, in 1808, David moved to England to study the coalmining industry. An amateur inventor, he also pursued patents and sought sponsors to finance new business ventures. He remained in England for seven years.[6]

Left in dire financial straits, Molly refused to throw herself on the mercy of relatives and instead decided that she would flaunt social convention and start a business. Banking on her reputation as a consummate hostess and cook, in 1808, she opened a boarding house in rented accommodations on Cary Street. Although family members, including her sister-in-law Martha Jefferson Randolph, were convinced the venture would fail, Molly's business was a success. Her friends supported her, and she profited from the lack of good accommodations for fine ladies and gentlemen in Virginia's capital. Once again, Molly's home became the center for Richmond society, which dubbed her "The Queen." According to Samuel Mordecai, "The Queen soon attracted as many subjects as her dominions could accommodate, and a loyal set they generally were. There were few more festive boards than the Queen's. Wit, humour, and good-fellowship prevailed, but excess rarely.

Social evenings were also enjoyed, and discord never intruded."[7] Randolph ran her business from 1807 until she retired in 1819, operating it even after her husband returned home in 1815. Through her ingenuity, determination, and skill, she had become the family's breadwinner. Her reputation spread far and wide, attracting genteel customers, including South Carolinian Harriet Pinkney Horry, who herself kept a personal manuscript recipe collection, and stayed in Randolph's boarding house in 1815.[8]

After closing down the business, Molly and David left Richmond and retired to Washington, DC, where they lived with their son William Beverly Randolph. David continued to dabble in inventing, but Molly was occupied caring for their youngest son, Burrell Starke Randolph, a midshipman in the US Navy, who had fallen from a mast in 1817, breaking both legs, which never healed properly. Burrell described his mother as "a victim of maternal love and duty."[9] But Molly embarked on another vocation while she cared for her son. She began to write her cookbook, in one sense, the culmination of her lifetime of cooking. Indeed, commenting in the preface of the book, Molly observed, "The greater part of the following receipts have been written from memory, where they were impressed by long continued practice."[10]

Randolph's rice pie recipe is intriguing because of what it reveals about the multicultural nature of cooking in British America during the eighteenth century. This is even reflected in its title, "Rice Pudding," although the recipe is for what Americans would refer to as a pie. Randolph means pudding here in two senses. Although in British English, pudding or "pud" is rather a generic form for dessert, the *Oxford English Dictionary* dates the earliest reference to it as a sweet or savory dish in pastry as early as 1543. Before that, the word was used to refer to boiling various ingredients in an animal's stomach or entrails—1287.[11] But notice, at the end of Randolph's recipe, "For change, it may be boiled, and eaten with butter, sugar, and wine," implying the later North American meaning, which is more of a custard-like dessert without pastry.[12]

In colonial America, desserts generally were part of the realm of the elite, served in wealthy households as a symbol of status and refinement. This was especially true for recipes calling for large amounts of sugar, which would have been too costly for most households.[13] Instead, typically, eighteenth-century desserts were simple and light and included things such as fresh fruits and other items intended as palette cleansers. In wealthy homes, a silver or earthenware epergne set on the dining table served as a centerpiece, and people would have had their desserts in front of them for the entire meal. Even elaborate desserts like rich cakes, which were reserved for special occasions or important guests, tended to rely more on dairy products—milk, butter, and eggs—than refined sugar. Although sitting somewhat in that category, pies were exceptional. They were not only desserts. Colonial Americans also served pies as main courses. In colonial New England, for example, fruit pies—particularly apple—appeared on tables at breakfast, dinner (at noon), and supper, especially during the winter, when people were relying on dried fruits stored away during harvest.[14]

Colonial desserts included any variety of ingredients. The go-to American ingredient today—chocolate—was expensive and typically was used as a drink at breakfast. Although Mary Randolph included more than a dozen flavors of ice cream in *House-Wife*, that would have been expensive because of the ingredients (ice, sugar, etc.) and was also labor intensive.[15] Instead, colonial desserts tended to remain fruit based, although some included vegetables such as corn. Until the price of sugar began to drop around the time *House-Wife* came out in the next century, bakers tended to sweeten their desserts with molasses, or in New England, maple syrup. There are certainly regional variations in the ingredients people used in their desserts based on what items were readily available: New Englanders relied primarily on fruits and maple syrup; Germans in the Middle Colonies contributed doughnuts and the molasses-based shoofly pie, a variation on the treacle tart to American cooking; and in the South, cooks were using corn, sweet potato, and peanuts in desserts, as well as rice.[16]

African foodways account for the development of Randolph's rice pie recipe (along with explaining the use of sweet potatoes and peanuts in other southern pies). Rice consumption in England and France was limited before the modern era. In the Medieval Period, rice was largely used—again only in wealthy households, because it was imported from Africa—as a starch and thickening agent in dishes like blancmange. Perhaps it was the expensive nature of rice imports that led some of the first British colonists to try cultivating the crop in Virginia in 1609, just two years after founding Jamestown.[17]

But it was not until seventy-six years later, when, according to tradition in 1685, Charleston physician Henry Woodward obtained rice seed from Colonel John Thurber, who had arrived in Charleston from Madagascar, that successful rice cultivation began in British America. Rice planting spread quickly, and within ten years, the grain was so plentiful that it was being used as currency, much as tobacco was in Virginia. In 1691, Carolina's lords proprietors granted planter Peter Guerard a patent for a pendulum engine that removed rice hulls. By the turn of the eighteenth century, South

Figure 4. *Rice Culture on the Ogeechee, Near Savannah* by A. R. Waud. Library of Congress, Prints and Photographs Division.

Carolina was exporting four hundred thousand pounds of rice each year. In 1710, that number had risen to 1.5 million pounds, and by 1720, to 20 million. In 1714, the colony adopted a standard-size barrel to help in the regulation and sale of the crop; the "barrel," at one hundred sixty-two pounds, is still used in measuring rice yields today.[18] None of this would have been possible without African technology.

The ethnic cultures of the Senegambia region of Africa developed the rice farming techniques that were exported to colonial America. As rice production increased exponentially in colonial South Carolina and, later, in Georgia, slavers sailed to the west coast of Africa, seeking both labor and knowledge, intentionally capturing people from rice-producing communities to enslave and bring to America. Forty percent of all slave imports passed through Charleston, and 40 percent of those people came from the rice-growing regions.[19] One advertisement of a shipload of slaves specifically touted that it was made up of "a choice cargo of Windward and Gold Coast Negroes, who have been accustomed to the planting of rice," and such people brought a higher price, making an initial outlay for a rice plantation incredibly expensive.[20] An estimate at the end of the eighteenth century stated that a planter would require a minimum of two hundred acres of swamp, forty slaves, housing, storage, and milling facilities to turn a profit.[21]

Rice production is complex, because during certain times of the growing cycle, the fields have to be dry and at others, flooded. Thus, Africans developed a complicated system of dikes and trunks, allowing the fields to be flooded and drained at the appropriate times. Because the enslaved people were teaching the Europeans, a unique labor system developed in colonial rice culture. Africans designated the correct size of the fields, the locations of the dikes, etc. These rules became standardized from plantation to plantation, so much so that they even included how much labor would be performed during the day. Thus, the task system was born.

Whereas in tobacco-producing regions of British America, the gang system predominated, with bands of enslaved workers going out to the fields at sunrise and returning at sunset, under the task system, enslaved people in South Carolina and Georgia received their orders as a list of tasks at the beginning of each week. This enabled enslaved laborers flexibility in how they organized their time, making it possible to complete their work before the end of the day and to have remaining daylight hours for rest or personal work. Or they arranged their time so that they could complete their labor early, leaving a full day or so at the end of the week for themselves. That allowed these people to plant gardens; catch fish; raise poultry, pork, and cattle; and so forth. Not only did this improve their diets but individuals also carried the products they produced beyond their personal needs into the markets of Charleston, Savannah, and other colonial cities and earned cash or bartered for other goods in an elaborate system of exchange.[22]

Although the task system may have allowed enslaved workers to improve their lives somewhat, the geography of the rice-producing regions took its toll. Working conditions were horrific. In 1775, one writer observed, "the cultivation of it is dreadful: for if a work could be imagined peculiarly unwholesome, and even fatal to health, it must be that of standing, like the negross, ancle, and even mid-leg deep in water, which floats an ouzy mud; and exposed all the while to a burning sun, which makes the very air they breathe hotter than the human blood; these poor wretches are then in a furness of stinking putrid effluvia: a more horrible employment can hardly be imagined."[23] Planters often provided inadequate housing, food, and clothing. Mosquito-borne diseases—particularly malaria and yellow fever, whose causes were not yet understood—poisonous snakes, alligators, and brutal treatment took such a toll that up to one third of enslaved people in the Lowcountry died within a year of their arrival. However, because a single worker could produce rice worth six times more than his or her value in one year, planters

Figure 5. *The Old Plantation* (Slaves Dancing on a South Carolina Plantation) attributed to John Rose, ca. 1785–95. The Colonial Williamsburg Foundation.

felt that they could afford such losses.[24] The nature of diseases, though, had an unforeseen benefit for those people who survived. During the malarial season, planters and their families often retreated into the cities or traveled north, allowing for a level of autonomy, and meant both the greater retention of African folkways and the creation of unique cultural traditions, such as the Gullah language.[25]

Before 1750, planters in colonial South Carolina and Georgia typically avoided tidal areas when constructing their rice fields. That is because sea water would render fields useless. But, by 1758, Mckewn Johnstone, a planter near the Winyah Bay region close to Georgetown, developed a system of water gates. These allowed him to capture fresh water to flood his fields while keeping out seawater, opening thousands of new acres up to rice production, although these were vulnerable to hurricane damage caused by tidal surges. Tides became useful when Charlestonian Jonathan Lucas realized he could use them to run water-powered mills. One operation could mill more than one hundred barrels of rice a day, and mills sprang up across the Lowcountry.[26]

Two types of rice predominated in South Carolina. The first was the African *Oryza glaberrima*. Not surprisingly, its production in West Africa matches the area where the British captured people to bring them to the colonial South. Although this was the rice that arrived in Charleston in

1675, it was present in the Portuguese colony of Brazil by the mid-1550s. The second type, the famous Carolina Gold, was the more desirable because of its distinct color and nutty flavor. Scholars traditionally believed this strain originated in Southeast Asia but were stymied when trying to discover how it got to South Carolina. However, recent genetic research suggests that Carolina Gold may not be Asian at all but rather developed from a strain of rice from Ghana.[27]

By the middle of the eighteenth century, rice culture dominated South Carolina and Georgia to such an extent that it made its way into the decorative arts for both Black and white inhabitants. For example, during the milling process, enslaved women frequently used sweetgrass baskets for winnowing. Sweetgrass (*Muhlenbergia filipes*) is a native long-bladed grass that grows among secondary dune lines, on the edges of marshes, and in other wetlands in Coastal South Carolina and Georgia. Appearing in the historical record as early as 1730, this form of basketry, produced originally by male craftsmen, consisted of small bundles of sweetgrass (with sections of longleaf pine and black rush added occasionally for color) sewn together in coils with thin strips of palm.[28] The creators of these sweetgrass baskets helped them evolve from practical tools into an artform, often combining African and European shapes.

For those living on the opposite end of the economic scale, the famous Charleston cabinetmaker Thomas Elfe is credited with developing the rice bed, whose name comes from the decorative carvings of bundled rice on tall bedposts. The bed sits high off the ground and features a low (and sometimes detachable) headboard to allow for greater air circulation during hot weather but could be dressed with a canopy and bed skirt for heat retention during the winter months.[29]

Of all of rice's cultural gifts to eighteenth-century America, food reigns supreme and once again reflects and sometimes blends African and European cultures. Soon after Henry Woodward planted his field of rice, English colonists began trying to figure out ways they could incorporate rice into their diets. Planter John Stewart suggested substituting rice for barley to brew beer. Others proposed using it to feed poultry and livestock. And South Carolinians began to grind rice to produce flour and to substitute it for wheat and corn.[30]

Meanwhile, it was natural that people of West African descent used rice in their cooking; it was part of their cultural heritage. According to African-American culinary historian and winner of the 2018 James Beard Foundation Book Award Michael W. Twitty, in African households, "Rice for savoury purposes was nearly always paired with the Afri-Creole 'trinity' of toma-toes, onions, and bell or hot peppers, or was laid out as the bed for tradi-tional West African staples like okra, peanuts, black-eyed peas, greens or stews made from a combination of these or starring seafood or chicken."[31] And these people were not just creating these dishes for themselves. Just as in Virginia, enslaved cooks in South Carolina and Georgia were prepar-ing the meals for their master's households. This meant that "Mende, Temne, Fula, Limba, Loma, Bassari, Sherbro, Kru, Balanta and other West African peoples" were preparing foods from their unique culinary traditions and sharing them with members of the dominant English culture.[32] Such foods traveled north into regions that did not produce rice, so that in 1824, when Mary Randoph published *The Virginia House-Wife*, it should be no surprise that she included special instructions on "How to Cook Rice" to serve with dishes like Ochra Soup, as well as her recipes for johnny cakes, rice milk, rice bread, rice waffles, rice blanc mange, and, of course, rice pudding/southern rice pie.

Although historians are unsure whether she learned her recipe from an enslaved cook at Presqu'île or even what type of rice she used—*Oryza glaberrima* or Carolina Gold—Mary Randolph's recipe conceals a com-plex story. It is part of the tale of a determined woman who faced penury and worked to save her family from financial ruin in an age that normally would have frowned on a member of her class "lowering" herself into busi-ness. It also encompasses the story of an oppressed people forcibly taken into bondage for their knowledge who nonetheless survived in their new land and contributed significantly to its development and its culture. Exploring this recipe, drawing as it does on female agency and African technology and ingenuity, helps expose forgotten and often neglected parts of the history of South Carolina and the larger United States.

A modern version of the recipe for Mary Randolph's Rice Pudding:

Southern Rice Pie
(Serves 6)

2 cups whole milk
½ cup uncooked rice
¾ cup sugar
8 tablespoons butter

2 eggs

½ teaspoon nutmeg

2 ounces white wine

½ teaspoon grated lemon peel

1 pastry shell

Prepare the pastry shell.

Preheat the oven to 350 degrees.

Scald the milk in a saucepot over medium heat, but do not bring to a boil. Stir in the rice, reduce the heat to medium-low, and cook for 25–30 minutes, or until the rice is tender. Mash well with a potato masher or whip in blender or food processor.

In a bowl, stir together the sugar, butter, eggs, nutmeg, lemon peel, and wine and add this to the pot of rice.

Pour into the pastry shell and bake for 20–30 minutes, until top is brown.[33]

Christopher E. Hendricks is professor of history at the Armstrong Campus of Georgia Southern University in Savannah, where he specializes in early American history and material culture. He is currently completing a manuscript about the colonial towns of Piedmont, North Carolina.

NOTES

1. Mary Randolph, *The Virginia House-Wife. Method Is the Soul of Management* (Washington, DC: Davis and Force, 1824), 147.
2. Many culinary scholars credit Randolph with producing the first truly American cookbook. The only cookbook by an American author predating *The Virginia House-Wife* was Amelia Simmons's 1796 *American Cookery*. However, although she added some original recipes with American foods, Simmons mostly copied English cookbook author Susannah Carter's 1772 book, *The Frugal Housewife*. See Karen Hess, "Historical Notes and Commentaries on Mary Randolph's *The Virginia House-Wife*," in *The Virginia House-Wife by Mary Randolph: A Facsimile of the First Edition, 1824, Along with Additional Material from the Editions of 1825 and 1828, thus Presenting a Complete Text* (Columbia: University of South Carolina Press, 1984), xvi, xviii; John L. Hess and Karen Hess, *The Taste of America* (Columbia: University of South Carolina Press, 1989), 89; and Harry Haff, *The Founders of American Cuisine* (Jefferson, NC: McFarland & Company, 2011), 37, 41.
3. Haff, *Founders*, 38–39; Janice Bluestein Longone, "Introduction to the Dover Edition," in *The Virginia Housewife or, Methodical Cook: A Facsimile of an Authentic*

Early American Cookbook (New York: Dover Publications, Inc., 1993), 7; and Hess, "Historical Notes," xi, xl.

4. Samuel Mordecai, *Richmond in By-Gone Days* (Richmond, VA: George M. West, 1856), 97; and Haff, *Founders*, 39.

5. Jonathan Daniels, *The Randolphs of Virginia* (Garden City, NJ: Doubleday & Company, 1972), 199–200.

6. Haff, *Founders*, 39; Ann T. Keene, "Randolph, Mary," in *American National Biography*, ed. John A. Garraty and Mark C. Carnes, 24 vols. (New York: Oxford University Press, 1999), 18: 132; and Daniels, *Randolphs*, 202.

7. Mordecai, *Richmond*, 97–98; and Haff, *Founders*, 39–40.

8. Cynthia D. Bertelsen, "Introducing Sarah Rutledge, a Cookbook Author You're Going to Know Very Well!," *Gherkins and Tomatoes... Since 2008* [website], May 31, 2019, https://gherkinstomatoes.com/2019/05/31/. It is interesting that, although she lists rice recipes, including one called, "To Make a Casserole, or Rather a Rice Pye" (a base for a meat filling rather than a dessert) in the manuscript receipt book she began in 1770, Horry does not have a recipe for a rice pudding or pie. See Richard J. Hooker, ed., *A Colonial Plantation Cookbook: The Receipt Book of Harriet Pinckney Horry, 1770* (Columbia: University of South Carolina Press, 1984), 62. Other early South Carolina cookbooks, such as the anonymous *The Carolina Receipt Book* (1832) and Sarah Rutledge's *The Carolina Housewife* (1847), include recipes for rice custards/puddings (in fact, Rutledge includes six), but neither has one for a pie. See *The Carolina Receipt Book; or, Housekeeper's Assistant* (Charleston, SC: James S. Burges, 1832), 45; and Sarah Rutledge, *The Carolina Housewife; or House and Home* (Charleston, SC: W. R. Babcock & Co., 1847), 120, 126, 129–30.

9. As quoted in Daniels, *Randolphs*, 248; Haff, *Founders*, 40; and "Randolph Family," *William and Mary College Quarterly*, 1st ser., 9, no. 4 (April 1901): 250.

10. Randolph, *Virginia House-Wife*, x.

11. "Pudding, n." *OED Online*. www.oed.com.

12. Randolph, *Virginia House-Wife*, 147.

13. Lorena S. Walsh, "Consumer Behavior, Diet, and the Standard of Living in Late Colonial and Early Antebellum America, 1770–1840" (paper presented to the Institute of Early American History and Culture, Williamsburg, VA, September 25, 1990).

14. Maria Scinto, "About Colonial Desserts," https://oureverydaylife.com; and Jane Carson, *Colonial Virginia Cookery: Procedures, Equipment, and Ingredients in Colonial Cooking* (Williamsburg, VA: The Colonial Williamsburg Foundation, 1985), 5, 46, 82–83

15. Hess, "Historical Notes," xxxviii–xxxix. In the second edition of *House-Wife* (1825), Randolph included illustrations for a "refrigerator" or icebox that was extremely useful with her ice cream recipes. Harriet Pinckney Horry raved about the device when she saw it. Randolph's basic design was still in use until the development of electric refrigeration. See Mary Randolph, *The Virginia House-Wife: Method is the Soul of Management. Second Edition, with Amendments and Additions* (Washington, DC: Way and Gideon, 1825), 256, insert 3; Bertelsen, "Introducing Sarah Rutledge"; and Sue J. Hendricks and Christopher E. Hendricks, *Old*

Southern Cookery: Mary Randolph's Recipes from America's First Regional Cookbook (Guilford, CT: Globe Pequot, 2020), 123, 163.

16. Scinto, "About Colonial Desserts;" Walsh, "Consumer Behavior, Diet, and the Standard of Living"; and Kevin Mitchell and David S. Shields, *Taste the State: South Carolina's Signature Foods, Recipes & Their Stories* (Columbia: University of South Carolina Press, 2021), 48.

17. Daniel C. Littlefield, *Rice and Slaves: Ethnicity and the Slave Trade in Colonial South Carolina* (Urbana: University of Illinois Press, 1991), 99–100. A rice pie appears in European cooking traditions—the Italian rice ricotta Easter pie that developed in Naples—but often there is no pastry involved, and that particular dessert falls more in the category of a cake.

18. Steven Linscombe, "The History of U.S. Rice Production—Part 1," Baton Rouge: LSU AgCenter, 2006, https://www.lsuagcenter.com/portals/our_offices/research_stations/rice/features/publications/. For the sources of the Madagascar rice origins tradition; see James M. Clifton, "The Rice Industry in Colonial America," *Agricultural History* 55, no. 3 (July 1981): 266n1.

19. Hayden R. Smith, "Reserving Water: Environmental and Technological Relationships with Colonial South Carolina Inland Rice Plantations," in *Rice: Global Networks and New Histories*, ed. Francesa Bray et al. (New York: Cambridge University Press, 2015), 108–9; Judith A. Carney, *Black Rice: The African Origins of Rice Cultivation in the Americas* (Cambridge, MA: Harvard University Press, 2001), 80; and "African Passages, Lowcountry Adaptations," Lowcountry Digital History Initiative, https://ldhi.library.cofc.edu/exhibits/show/africanpassageslowcountryadapt/.

20. Judith A. Carney, "African Origins of Rice Cultivation in the Black Atlantic," *África: Revista Do Centro de Estudios Africanos* 27–28 (2006–2007): 108.

21. Joyce E. Chaplin, "Tidal Rice Cultivation and the Problem of Slavery in South Carolina and Georgia, 1760–1815," *William and Mary Quarterly*, 3rd ser., 49, no. 1 (July 1992): 46.

22. Philip D. Morgan, "Work and Culture: The Task System and the World of Lowcountry Blacks, 1700 to 1880," *William and Mary Quarterly*, 3rd ser., 39, no. 4 (October 1982): 563–99, passim, especially 564–66, 573–75, and 586–87.

23. *American Husbandry*, 2 vols. (London: J. Bew, 1775), 1: 393–94.

24. Gillian Richards-Greaves, "The Intersection of Politics and Food Security in a South Carolina Town," in *Black Food Matters: Racial Justice in the Wake of Food Justice*, ed. Hannah Garth and Ashanté M. Reese (Minneapolis, University of Minnesota Press, 2020), 55.

25. Julia Floyd Smith, *Slavery and Rice Culture in Low Country Georgia, 1750–1860* (Knoxville: University of Tennessee Press, 1985), 166–82.

26. Clifton, "Rice Industry," 275–76, 278; and "Linscombe, "History of U.S. Rice."

27. Judith A. Carney, *Black Rice: The African Origins of Rice Cultivation in the Americas* Cambridge, MA: Harvard University Press, 2001), 75, 144–54, 175, 176–77; Mitchell and Shields, *Taste the State*, 26; Karen Hess, *The Carolina Rice Kitchen: The African Connection* (Columbia: University of South Carolina Press, 1992), 17–21; and Michael W. Twitty, "How Rice Shaped the American South," *BBC*, https://www.bbc.com/travel/article/20210307. See also Erik Gilbert "Asian Rice

in Africa: Plant Genetics and Crop History," in *Rice: Global Networks and New Histories*, ed. Francesa Bray et al. (New York: Cambridge University Press, 2015), 212–28.

28. US Department of Agriculture—Forest Service, "Restoring Sweetgrass to the South Carolina Lowcountry," https://www.srs.fs.usda.gov/newsroom/newsrelease/2004/nr_2004-08-18-sweetgrass.htm. Native Americans also used a sweetgrass for basketry but utilized a different species, *Hierochloe odorata*.

29. Suzannah Smith Miles, "Rice Bed," *Charleston*, November 2014, https://charleston mag.com/features/rice_bed; and Bradford L. Rauschenberg and John Bivens Jr., *The Furniture of Charleston, 1680–1820*, 3 vols. (Winston-Salem, NC: Museum of Early Southern Decorative Arts, 2003), 1: 426, 427, 428, 429, and 2: 790. Elfe, Charleston's most famous cabinetmaker, ran a large production facility that included at least twenty "handicraft slaves" working as cabinetmakers and or carvers producing furniture for around three hundred customers between 1768 and 1775. See Rauschenberg and Bivens Jr., *Furniture of Charleston*, 3: 995–96.

30. Hayden Ros Smith, "Rich Swamps and Rice Grounds: The Specialization of Inland Rice Culture in the South Carolina Lowcountry, 1670–1861" (PhD diss., University of Georgia, 2012), 45; Judith A. Carney and Richard Nicholas Rosomoff, *In the Shadow of Slavery: Africa's Botanical Legacy in the Atlantic World* (Berkeley: University of California Press, 2009), 150–53; Carney, *Black Rice*, 84; and Smith, *Slavery and Rice Culture*, 84–85.

31. Twitty, "How Rice Shaped the American South."

32. *Ibid.*

33. Hendricks and Hendricks, *Old Southern Cookery*, 180.

WORKS CITED

Bertelsen, Cynthia D. "Introducing Sarah Rutledge, a Cookbook Author You're Going to Know Very Well!," Gherkins and Tomatoes . . . Since 2008. https://gherkinstomatoes.com/2019/05/31/.

The Carolina Receipt Book; or, Housekeeper's Assistant. Charleston, SC: James S. Burges, 1832.

Carney, Judith A. "African Origins of Rice Cultivation in the Black Atlantic." *África: Revista Do Centro de Estudios Africanos* 27–28 (2006–2007): 91–114. https://www.revistas.usp.br/africa/article/download/96064/95301/165661.

———. *Black Rice: The African Origins of Rice Cultivation in the Americas*. Cambridge, MA: Harvard University Press, 2001.

Carney, Judith A., and Richard Nicholas Rosomoff. *In the Shadow of Slavery: Africa's Botanical Legacy in the Atlantic World*. Berkeley: University of California Press, 2009.

Carson, Jane. *Colonial Virginia Cookery: Procedures, Equipment, and Ingredients in Colonial Cooking*. Williamsburg, VA: The Colonial Williamsburg Foundation, 1985.

Chaplin, Joyce E. "Tidal Rice Cultivation and the Problem of Slavery in South Carolina and Georgia, 1760–1815." *William and Mary Quarterly*, 3rd ser. 49, no. 1 (July 1992): 29–62.

Clifton, James M. "The Rice Industry in Colonial America." *Agricultural History* 55, no. 3 (July 1981): 266–83.

Daniels, Jonathan. *The Randolphs of Virginia*. Garden City, NJ: Doubleday & Company, 1972.

Gilbert, Erik. "Asian Rice in Africa: Plant Genetics and Crop History." In *Rice: Global Networks and New Histories*, edited by Francesca Bray, Peter A. Coclanis, Edda L. Fields-Black, and Dagmar Schafer, 212–28. New York: Cambridge University Press, 2015.

Keene, Ann T. "Randolph, Mary." In *American National Biography*, edited by John A. Garraty and Mark C. Carnes, 18: 132–33. 24 vols. New York: Oxford University Press, 1999.

Haff, Harry. *The Founders of American Cuisine*. Jefferson, NC: McFarland & Company, 2011.

Hendricks, Sue J., and Christopher E. Hendricks. *Old Southern Cookery: Mary Randolph's Recipes from America's First Regional Cookbook*. Guilford, CT: Globe Pequot, 2020.

Hess, John L., and Karen Hess. *The Taste of America*. Columbia: University of South Carolina Press, 1989.

Hess, Karen. *The Carolina Rice Kitchen: The African Connection*. Columbia: University of South Carolina Press, 1992.

———. "Historical Notes and Commentaries on Mary Randolph's *The Virginia House-Wife*." In *The Virginia House-Wife by Mary Randolph: A Facsimile of the First Edition, 1824, Along with Additional Material from the Editions of 1825 and 1828, thus Presenting a Complete Text*, ix–xlvi. Columbia: University of South Carolina Press, 1984.

Hooker, Richard J., ed. *A Colonial Plantation Cookbook: The Receipt Book of Harriet Pinckney Horry, 1770*. Columbia: University of South Carolina Press, 1984.

Linscombe, Steven. "The History of U.S. Rice Production—Part 1," Baton Rouge: LSU AgCenter, 2006. https://www.lsuagcenter.com/portals/our_offices/research_stations/rice/features/publications/.

Littlefield, Daniel C. *Rice and Slaves: Ethnicity and the Slave Trade in Colonial South Carolina*. Urbana: University of Illinois Press, 1991.

Longone, Janice Bluestein. "Introduction to the Dover Edition." In *The Virginia Housewife or, Methodical Cook: A Facsimile of an Authentic Early American Cookbook*, 1–14. New York: Dover Publications, 1993.

Miles, Suzannah Smith. "Rice Bed," *Charleston*, November 2014. https://charlestonmag.com/features/rice_bed.

Mitchell, Kevin, and David S. Shields. *Taste the State: South Carolina's Signature Foods, Recipes & Their Stories*. Columbia: University of South Carolina Press, 2021.

Morgan, Philip D. "Work and Culture: The Task System and the World of Lowcountry Blacks, 1700 to 1880." *William and Mary Quarterly*, 3rd ser. 39, no. 4 (October 1982): 564–99.

Mordecai, Samuel. *Richmond in By-Gone Days*. Richmond, VA: George M. West, 1856.

Randolph, Mary. *The Virginia House-Wife. Method is the Soul of Management*. Washington, DC: Davis and Force, 1824.

————. *The Virginia House-Wife. Method is the Soul of Management. Second Edition, with Amendments and Additions.* Washington, DC: Way and Gideon, 1825.

Rauschenberg, Bradford L., and John Bivens Jr. *The Furniture of Charleston, 1680–1820.* 3 vols. Winston-Salem, NC: Museum of Early Southern Decorative Arts, 2003.

Richards-Greaves, Gillian. "The Intersection of Politics and Food Security in a South Carolina Town." In *Black Food Matters: Racial Justice in the Wake of Food Justice,* edited by Hannah Garth and Ashanté M. Reese, 53–81. Minneapolis, University of Minnesota Press, 2020.

Rutledge, Sarah. *The Carolina Housewife; or House and Home.* Charleston, SC: W. R. Babcock & Co., 1847.

Scinto, Maria "About Colonial Desserts." https://oureverydaylife.com/about -colonial-desserts-12146117.html.

Smith, Hayden R. "Reserving Water: Environmental and Technological Relationships with Colonial South Carolina Inland Rice Plantations." In *Rice: Global Networks and New Histories,* edited by Francesca Bray et al., 189–211. New York: Cambridge University Press, 2015.

————. "Rich Swamps and Rice Grounds: The Specialization of Inland Rice Culture in the South Carolina Lowcountry, 1670–1861." PhD dissertation. Athens: University of Georgia, 2012. https://getd.libs.uga.edu/pdfs/smith_hayden_r _201212_phd.pdf.

Smith, Julia Floyd. *Slavery and Rice Culture in Low Country Georgia, 1750–1860.* Knoxville: University of Tennessee Press, 1985.

Twitty, Michael W. "How Rice Shaped the American South." *BBC.* Accessed June 9, 2022. https://www.bbc.com/travel/article/20210307-how-rice-shaped-the -american-south.

US Department of Agriculture Forest Service. "Restoring Sweetgrass to the South Carolina Lowcountry" [News release]. https://www.eurekalert.org/news -releases/521395.

Dueling Onstage in Charleston

John Blake White's Modern Honour

Jon Tuttle

In 1800, while in his early twenties, John Blake White left his Charleston home to study painting in London under Benjamin West, the American-born court painter to King George III and then-president of the Royal Academy of Arts. At one point, White toured Eton College, near Windsor Castle, with some friends, and reported in his journal that from his walk he derived "particular delight": "We felt ourselves treading on classic ground. Here the walls in every direction were scored with names and initials and dates, the simple record of thousands now reposing in the silent tomb, many of whom left no other traces behind them. . . . And so we sought in every direction for some idle traces of those who had since distinguished themselves in life's theatre."[1] On his return, in 1804, to the United States, White would go about distinguishing himself in his country's theatre, embarking on a career as a playwright and becoming, as Charles Watson described him in *The History of Southern Drama*, "the first dramatist in the South to write a substantial body of work."[2]

Indeed, White would likely be remembered as South Carolina's most prominent antebellum dramatist had he not also established himself as one of its foremost historical painters. Hanging still in the halls of the US Capitol are four of his paintings describing moments significant to South Carolina's role in the Revolutionary War. The most famous is *General Marion in his Swamp Encampment Inviting a British Officer to Dinner* (1836), which depicts General Francis Marion negotiating an exchange of prisoners during the 1781 occupation of Charleston.[3] The painting is generally considered a faithful rendering not only of "the Swamp Fox," but also of his slave-turned-soldier, Oscar Marion, who kneels beside the general, baking potatoes.[4]

Both Marion men were friends of White and his family. During the Revolutionary War, White's mother, Elizabeth Borquin, served as a spy for Marion's cause, and his father, Blake Leay White, fought at Fort Moultrie. White *pere* can, in fact, be seen manning a gun in White's *The Battle of Fort Moultrie* (1826), which also hangs in the Capitol, as do *Sergeants Jasper and Newton Rescuing American Prisoners from the British* (n.d.) and *Mrs. Motte*

Inviting General Marion and Colonel Lee to Burn Her Residence (n.d.). The former recounts the rescue, in 1779, by two of Marion's scouts of several American prisoners being conveyed to Savannah for trial and likely execution. The
moment described by the painting—the grateful wife of one of the prisoners
kneeling before his rescuers—was engraved on Confederate bank notes in
1861. The latter, based on an incident in 1781, depicts Rebecca Jacob Motte, a
wealthy widow, handing arrows to General Marion and Lieutenant Colonel
Henry Lee to be set aflame and fired at her roof to smoke out the British soldiers inside. Before that could happen, the soldiers vacated and surrendered,
and Mrs. Motte is said to have served dinner to officers of both armies.[5]

Until Sherman's troops burned it down in 1865, the senate chamber of the
Old Carolina State House displayed three of White's other paintings. *The
Unfurling of the United States Flag at Mexico* (n.d.) depicts Joel Poinsett, a
South Carolina native serving as American ambassador, attempting to quell
Mexican political discord with promises of American protectionism.[6] *The
Battle of Eutaw Springs* (1804) describes the last major engagement of the
Revolutionary War in the Carolinas, fought six days before White's birth at
Whitehall Plantation. *The Battle of New Orleans* (1816) celebrates Andrew
Jackson's dubious victory in the War of 1812 and would provide, three years
later, the subject matter for White's fourth play, *The Triumph of Liberty, or
Louisiana Preserved* (1819). That play was not produced, likely because Jack-
son was by then being vilified in the pages of the *Charleston Courier* for incit-
ing the first Seminole War and for executing two Britons, both mentioned
by name in the play.[7] White also painted portraits of such prominent South
Carolina statesmen as John C. Calhoun, Charles C. Pinckney, and Henry
Middleton. In 1821, he became director of the South Carolina Academy of
Fine Arts, and in 1845, he was made an honorary member of the National
Academy of Design.

One of the lessons West imparted as White's mentor was the moral and
historical authority residing in art. This was a lesson White would not immediately apply to his career as a playwright. His first two plays are derived
from continental romantic/revenge models and bear the standard attributes
of verse drama—exotic locales, elaborate sets, stock characters, and orotund
poesy. Both were produced by the Charleston Theatre, the first permanent
theatre in Charleston, built in 1794 at the corner of Broad and New Streets.[8]

The first, *Foscari, or The Venetian Exile*, premiered in January 1806 and
was reprised for one performance in January 1809. It told the story of a young
Italian nobleman who, falsely accused of murder and rejected by his beloved
Almeria, dies of a broken heart. The second, *The Mysteries of the Castle, or,*

The Victim of Revenge, included several gothic elements, including secret passages, hidden chambers, a ghost, and a spectacular explosion. It premiered in December 1806 and was remounted in February 1807.

In his later plays, White would turn his attention to matters more domestic and high-minded. His last, *The Forgers,* although unproduced, is considered the first American temperance drama.[9] It takes its title from the crime committed by its young, alcoholic protagonist, Mourdant, whose dissipations incite him to jealous rage and attempted murder. At play's end, he ingests poison, believing it to be liquor, and dies while suffering the first delirium tremens portrayed on the American stage. The play prefigures such later, more widely known plays as *Fifteen Years in a Drunkard's Life* (1841) by Douglass Jerrold, *The Drunkard* (1841) by W. H. Smith, and *Ten Nights in a Barroom* (1858), adapted by William Pratt from the novel by Timothy Shay Arthur.[10]

By the time the *Southern Literary Journal* published *The Forgers* in 1837, White was a prominent public figure who had served one term in the South Carolina general assembly, practiced law, run a paper mill, and worked at the Charleston Custom House. He had also become involved in the Reform Movement, likely inspired by his good friend Thomas S. Grimke, a Charleston lawyer and activist, after whom White named one of his sons. Grimke was involved in various causes and presided over a local chapter of the American Temperance Society, which had formed in 1826. It is likely that White was in attendance when Grimke delivered an address "On The Patriot Character [of] the Temperance Reformation" at the First Presbyterian Church, about two blocks from White's home.[11] White himself would later deliver an address to the Young Men's Temperance Society, arguing for the criminalization of intoxication. He also advocated against capital punishment and delivered, in 1834, an essay to that effect before the Literary and Philosophical Society of Charleston, of which he was a member.[12]

White's first dramatic foray into social reform came in 1812, with his third play, *Modern Honor,* an earnest rebuke of the culture of dueling. Dueling had migrated across the Atlantic to the American colonies and was widely practiced from as early as 1621, when the first recorded duel was fought, albeit with swords, in the Massachusetts Colony by Edward Doty and Edward Lester, both of whom arrived on the Mayflower as servants for the same family.[13] From 1800 to 1860, the US Navy lost more than half as many officers to dueling as it did in battle, including naval hero Commodore Stephen Decatur, who was killed by fellow naval officer James Barron for impugning the latter's courage.[14] In the decade before White produced *Modern Honor,*

Andrew Jackson had fought in at least two duels, suffering in one a bullet wound to the chest, and, of course, Aaron Burr had killed Alexander Hamilton. Whereas the New England states generally tended to dismiss dueling as barbaric, in the southern states, it gained in popularity. Ross Drake observed in *The Smithsonian* that, "to the touchiest among [Southern aristocrats], virtually any annoyance could be construed as grounds for a meeting at gunpoint, and though laws against dueling were passed in several Southern states, the statutes were ineffective. Arrests were infrequent; judges and juries were loath to convict."[15]

J. Grahame Long, in *Dueling in Charleston*, contends that "South Carolinians—Charlestonians especially—participated in more duels than any other group of people in the nation, possibly the entire North American continent."[16] Given that, it seems safe to assume that although White sets his play in "any part of the civilized world (5)," the milieu his play describes is markedly Charlestonian.[17] That White names one of his characters Caroline suggests to Watson "the women of Carolina whose husbands have died in duels."[18]

Modern Honor premiered at the Charleston Theatre and ran for the then-standard three nights, the last two to disappointing houses, which Watson attributes to the then-popular enthusiasm for dueling.[19] Indeed, during the post-colonial period, dueling had become so prevalent in the South that, according to Long, area newspapers "regularly announced the outcomes of concluding duels, not unlike modern-day sports pages," a claim he substantiates with a contemporary report:

> [August 1808] It is reported and we fear too much truth, that a duel was fought on Tuesday Last [August 9] on the Georgia side of the river between James Lesley, an attorney, and Dr. Bochell. . . . Mr. Lesley was shot through the body and died in a few hours. [August 2, 1853] Duel this morning about 5 o'clock [at] the back of the race course. Mr. J.D. Legare and Mr. Dunovant met to settle their disputes when the former was instantly killed. [May 25, 1839] Duel fought at the lower end of Broad Street between Fell and Herriot, the former shot in the foot to keep him from running and the latter in the mouth to keep him from jawing.[20]

Jack K. Williams observes that visitors from abroad recorded their amazement at the frequency of dueling, one reporting that he had met eleven men who "had killed a man each" and another, a German baron, writing that dueling was so common that a tourist "should be careful of what he says and what society he keeps."[21] Other indicators of dueling's prevalence include an item placed in the *Charleston Courier* on April 4, 1827, advertising "the Art of Self Defence [*sic*], Scientifically Taught" by one D. Mendoza, Jr.[22]

Modern Honor is, of course, sufficiently obscure that any discussion of it ought to be leavened with summation. It begins, as did most plays of that era, with a prologue written "by a friend" of the playwright and "Spoken by Mr. Green" (3)—specifically J. William Green, an actor familiar to audiences at the Charleston Theatre, having already distinguished himself on that stage as Macbeth, Richard III, Iago, and a raft of other roles.[23] In couplets, the prologue celebrates the origins of honor from "the first day of chivalry" when it "breathed its fascinations o'er the mind" and "softened, polished and improved mankind." Taking a darker turn ("But lo!"), it then warns of "false honor" as "the savage foe of life!/ Her god is Moloch, her Religion, strife" and concludes by praising the author's intent "to drive this monster from the light of day" (3–4).

Thus girded, we begin the play proper, discovering in the nursery of their apartment Charles and Caroline Devalmore, the play's deuteragonists, hovering tenderly over their sleeping babe while nearby their toddler plays with his toys. At once, then, in its very first breath, the play aligns itself with the postcolonial dramatic tradition of placing the American family at stake. In, for instance, Royal Tyler's *The Contrast* (1787), the very first American drama, the Van Rough family, sensible and honest, stood in for an America defending itself from corrosive continental influences represented by the dandified Billy Dimple.[24] In, for further instance, William Ioor's *Independence* (1805), the first South Carolinian drama, the Woodville family, sturdy and agronomical, stood in for southern small farmers losing their land to greedy cosmopolitan interests represented by lascivious Lord Fanfare.[25]

Modern Honor begins then with a recognizable trope: the American family in portrait, at home and rhapsodizing in blank verse about its own bliss and sanctity, with Devalmore asking at one point:

> What wealth, what grandeur, my dear Caroline,
> With that pure, heaven-born pleasure can compare,
> Which grows with the souls of those who love!
> Who, save a husband can appreciate
> Delight, with which the bosom overflows,
> When from the busy, bustling cares of life,
> He turns to home's enchanting scenes, beholds

A tender wife and smiling babes, anxious
To meet him: sees her smile, and hears them prattle[?] (7)

Because the play describes itself as a tragedy, we may correctly apprehend at this point that this family will over the course of the forthcoming five acts be torn asunder.

They are quickly joined by Devalmore's comely sister Maria, rosy-hued with "pellucid tinctures," who anxiously awaits the return from abroad of her beau, Henry Woodville, beloved by the family as "ever true," a "faithful constant friend" and possessing "what the world cannot corrupt,/An honest heart" (9, 10).[26] We may here apprehend, again correctly, that this couple's happiness is doomed.

When a letter arrives announcing that Woodville's return has been delayed, Maria is left alone and visited forthwith by "wild perplexing thoughts," wondering "Why writhes my soul with agonizing woe!/Why am I terrified by fears [?]" (12). Enter, of course and therefore, the play's antagonist, Colonel Forsythe.[27] Having apparently never recovered from his unrequited love for Maria, he observes in her current vulnerability an opportunity to declare that "by my soul/I vow that, you the only woman are,/Whom on this earth, with rapture I adore" (13). Maria deflects his overture graciously, then less so his suggestion that her Henry is purposefully loitering "in foreign climes, nor cares,/While in soft dalliance with the guilty fair,/Who nightly join his round of idle mirth" (13). When she chastises him for such slander, Forsythe threatens to impugn her honor:

Be guarded in your speech—remember well,
That you a woman are, whose boasted virtue
Hangs by most slender threads: the slightest breath
Might tarnish, e'en your fairest fame.
. . . .
The roses which in yonder garden blow,
Are safer than a woman's reputation. (14)

Through the rest of the play, and using such wiles, Forsythe pursues her doggedly until, at the end, a duel settles all the affairs, and badly.

The second act finds Forsythe at home with his man Flaurence, who apparently functions as Forsythe's arms dealer, as he enters with two new pistols he praises as "true as fate itself:/Destruction seems to perch upon their sights" (17). He is referring, no doubt, to pistols designed solely for the purpose of dueling, those typically being ornately decorated .52-caliber smoothbore flintlocks that came in their own custom cases, such as those made in Charleston by the J. M. Happoldt family, who, for three decades, were the leading gun manufacturers in the region.[28] Here, Flaurence seems to fetishize his pistol, sighing,

> For years, the pistol was my matin song,
> My noontide sport, my evening's recreation.
> Nor did I hold my life or honor safe,
> 'Till it was pastime, to bisect with ease,
> My ball, against a razor's edge. (17)

The two men settle quickly into extolling the efficacy of firearms as instruments of both protection and courtship. Flaurence proposes, oblivious to his own irony, that carrying a pistol is the only way for a "man of honor" to protect himself "in these rude days" when so many carry firearms (17). Forsythe concurs that, "The pistol has more civilized the world,/Than all the pratings of your grizzly sages" and dismisses as "boys and cowards" those who would resort to law (17). True gentlemen, he argues as he grips his pistol, would not waste "the tedious lapse of years" pursing legal redress that "in a moment, should be grasped at—thus" (18). Bachelors both, they conclude that the *summum bonum* of their code is the affection of women, who "legislate/On all nice points of Honor," for it is "Better to die than wear the badge of coward,/Fastened upon you by a woman's scorn" (19). Thus aroused, they conspire to penetrate Maria's chamber that very evening, when Forsythe claims to have an assignation arranged but, as part of his baroque plot to win her, offers to send Flaurence through her window in his stead.

Before their conversation, we have met Shadwell and Moore, essentially White's Rosencrantz and Guildenstern, whom Forsythe dispatches to assassinate his rival, Henry Woodville, but no sooner has Flaurence left than a bloodied Woodville staggers into Forsythe's chambers, having just fended off his assailants. Forsythe, having secretly just sought to kill him, now bids Woodville "thrice welcome" and tends to his wounds, but intimates, sensing that Woodville is in a froth, that his Maria has been "false as hell" (24, 26) and offers, that very night, to prove it.

Thus, in the third act, the play reenacts, in miniature, both *Othello* and *Romeo and Juliet*. Forsythe, as Iago, leads his hapless Moor, Woodville, to Maria's garden, where they spy her on her balcony, anxiously awaiting the return of her beloved, lamenting,

Ah would that thou wert come,
Dearest of my soul, to sooth the troubles
Of my aching heart!
. . . .
'Tis now eleven, and too late, I fear,
To hope for his arrival—whence that noise?
It was the owl, the watch-bird of the night,
Which flitted by seek yon distant grove.
No noise I hear, but all my soul is up,
In anxious expectation of his coming. (28)

The action that follows is dazzling: Flaurence, as arranged, arrives with a ladder and attempts to climb into her boudoir; Woodville, "in great agitation,"
subdues and chases him off (30). Devalmore, whose house this is, discovers
Woodville engorged with jealous rage. Honor is impugned, threats are made,
and fisticuffs ensue until finally a duel is arranged for the morrow between
two honorable men who have no quarrel with each other.

That duel occurs in the next act, but offstage; the spectacle of men shooting at one other must await the play's climax. Act Four instead traffics solely
in pathos. Early on, Devalmore bids a poignant adieu to his sleeping bride
and children and then, full of foreboding, steals out into the night to face
Woodville. He is reposited forthwith, shot dead, on a bier, followed quickly
by a now-horrified Woodville hoping to reanimate his old friend with
remorse. Failing that ("Moment of horror, too much for the damned!"
[44]), Woodville quickly calculates how he has been deceived and closes
the act by vowing revenge upon his deceiver:

Miserable wretch! What have I not done?
A tender husband killed, a father butchered,
Slaughtered a kind brother, murdered a friend—
But still the bloody scene shall not close here:
Fearful revenge shall first be satisfied:
So look to it Forsythe. Thou bloody monster!
Be this accursed act on thee, and thine—
Thy life or mine shall surely pay the forfeit—
Revenge is sweet, when duty points the way! (45)

Duty pointing the way, we move then to the final act, which presents,
in striking fashion, the act of dueling itself. The first to arrive at the secret

location—duels, being nominally illegally in Charleston, were conducted at undisclosed venues—are the two assassins, Moore and Shadwell. Before they hie to another part of the forest to lay again in ambush for Woodville, White allows one of them a show of remorse. Moore complains that

> . . . I do not like this work of murdering men.
> . . . .
> . . . from the first, I liked not this employment.
> In honest truth, I cannot reconcile it
> With my conscience. I passed a wretched night,
> Last night. (47)

It is for this very moment these two exist in the play. They will fail, as they did before, to murder Woodville, so their importance to the plot is negligible. But here, they feel for a moment the first pangs of conscience. Moore in fact resolves to "have no hand in it—/No scruples would I have to take his purse,/But, at the thought of shedding human blood,/I tremble every joint" (47). At the end of the play, he—but not Shadwell—will be arrested, the implication being that he has turned himself in.

Their conversation prefigures nicely the one that follows immediately between Woodville and his second, Hanmer. As a second—i.e., an assistant at a duel—Hanmer's responsibilities would have included enforcing established protocols and ending the affair in event of an injury. Those responsibilities had been codified across centuries and continents in, for instance, the Italian *Flos Deullatorum* (ca. 1410), the Irish *Code Duello* (1777), *The British Code of Duel* (1824), and Joseph Hamilton's *The Royal Code* (1829). In 1838, roughly a quarter-century after the play, but certainly while dueling was still in fashion, former South Carolina Governor John Lyde Wilson drew from such primers in publishing his own how-to manual, *The Code of Honor, or, Rules for the Government of Principals and Seconds in Dueling*, which included eight chapters—for instance, the "Person Insulted," "The Party Receiving a Note Before Challenge," and the "Principals and Seconds on the Ground"—instructing all parties as to the proper procedures for inciting, conducting, and concluding a duel.[29]

Primarily, a second's responsibility was to mediate or suggest alternatives to combat. In his *Code*, Wilson instructs seconds to "use every effort to soothe and tranquilize your principal; do not see things in the same aggravated light in which he views them. Extenuate the conduct of his adversary whenever you see clearly an opportunity to do so, without doing violence to your friend's irritated mind. Endeavor to persuade him there must have been some misunderstanding in the matter."[30] Much of Act Five is a Platonic dialogue. It, in fact, reimagines much of *The Crito*.[31] Hanmer attempts to soothe and tranquilize Woodville, entreating him to "Ponder yet upon this fatal measure./Permit the anger of your mind to cool" (48), and presenting appeals to religion, reason, friendship and obligation to family, none of which countervails Woodville's insistence on defending his honor:

> **HANMER.** How can this act, one step advance your cause?
> In what your honor profit anything?
> Should you this monster slay, the task is still
> T'expose his horrid crimes: what should prevent
> Th' exposure while he lives? But should you fall,
> You leave your loved Maria, honor, fame,
> All in the power of that very man,
> Whom neither love nor fear could influence.
> O vile, O mad infatuation this,
> It cannot stand the test of sober truth!
> **WOODVILLE.** Should I from this guilty field retire,
> Who'll vindicate my honor with the world?
> **HANMER.** What is the world to you, in competition
> With your soul? (50)

Hanmer, besides being the most interesting character in the play, here serves also as White's raisonneur; he was played by J. William Green, the same actor who delivered the play's prologue, and so embodied in this character the gravitas of its message as well as the reputation of the actor.[32] To, however, no avail: Woodville quickly rebuts him, his response echoing, at first glance, Shakespeare's Brutus, who "love[s] the name of honor, more than I fear death," and Hector, who "Holds honor far more precious-dear than life."[33]

> **WOODVILLE.** Ah nothing! Yet—yet everything!
> How shall I meet the friends whom once I knew?
> How brook the killing smiles of pity? How
> Bear up against th' unfeeling laugh of scorn?
> How stand that sharp reproaches of Maria?
> How 'scape from orphan's cries and widow's curses?
> How pass through life, with coward on my brow?

Ah me! No door, no hiding place is left,
Saving the silent mansions of the grave!
You argue, Hanmer, to the heedless winds:
Trust me, I've made my fixed determination.
Prepare the pistols. (50–51)

However sympathetic Woodville's motives may appear, they are hardly noble. In the pointless shootout about to unfold, White asks us to distinguish between the clashes of legendary forces determining the course of history and the grievances of pettifoggers hoping to avoid embarrassment. This is the distinction White, through Hanmer, draws between honor and modern honor, just before the duel itself,

Honor, mystic name! To lengths how boundless
Wilt thou conduct thy votaries! 'Tis strange,
That, through the fear of temporary ill,
Which merely a day, an hour can endure,
They should the hazard run of endless ruin! (51)

This "hazard" was one with which White was and would remain personally acquainted. In 1796, his friend Alexander Placide, manager of the Charleston Theater and one of the town's leading theatre figures, challenged one Louis Douvillier, a ballet dancer, to a sword fight in St. Michael's Alley over the affections of a woman.[34] Neither was harmed, but the woman chose Douvillier.[35] Six months after the premiere of *Modern Honor*, White attended the funeral of one William Bay in Charleston who had died in a duel over political differences. Obviously moved, White wrote in his journal, "There was an immense concourse of people at the funeral, there were many eyes overflowing with tears. His venerable parents followed his remains to the grave, witnessed [their son] consigned to the bosom of the earth, heard the earth closing forever upon him, and the feelings of the father burst forth in loud, articulate sobs."[36]

In 1817, five years after the play, White's friend Dennis O'Driscoll would also perish in a duel. His assailant, John Edwards, was arrested and tried in what would amount to a test case for antidueling laws in South Carolina. But charges against Edwards were dismissed when witnesses refused to testify, partly not to self-incriminate but also in deference to the gentlemanly code of honor.[37] That code, according to Clement Eaton, had its roots in the south's chivalric military heritage and in southerners' hyper-sensitivity about their honor: "To accuse a gentleman of an untruth, insult him, or attack his honor was to provoke a duel. . . . Many a high-minded man recognized the evil of dueling and yet accepted a challenge of a duel in order to escape the odium of being regarded a coward and thus lose his influence in society."[38] The premium placed on honor was common among not only the aristocracy, but social climbers as well. Honor, as Watson writes, "became more inexorable than any civil or moral law. Any man wanting to be regarded as a gentleman conformed, or he suffered contempt from the high and low."[39] Public figures—Henry Clay, Alexander Stephens, John Randolph, Sam Houston—all admitted to or bragged about having dueled, and all benefited socially or politically for it, a fact not lost on planters, members of the military, or even two students at South Carolina College who, in 1833, joined in the practice over a dining hall dispute. One was killed and the other, maimed.[40]

It was an affront to honor that apparently spelled the doom of Dennis O'Driscoll, who, several days before he died, wrote the following in his will:

> I do pray God of his infinite mercy and goodness to pardon all my sins: and forgive me for the Conduct I am about to pursue, to which I have been forced and every possible endeavor on my part to avoid it; and please Almighty God that I shd [sic] fall a victim to defense of my character & my Honor; I will devise all my estate or property of which I am now possessed, or may be entitled to, to my most dear and affectionate Wife Harriett C. O'Driscoll, & I pray God to grant her firmness to withstand her misfortune.[41]

O'Driscoll's death appears to have been a heavy blow to White. Among the deaths he recorded in his family Bible, indeed immediately after an item about the passing of his own wife, Eliza, appears the following:

> Died at Savannah, Geo. On the 17th August, 1817 my valued friend Dennis O'Driscoll, Esq. Attorney-at-Law, only son of Doct. Mathew O'Driscoll, of Charleston, aged 23 years, & 6 months. He fell in a duel with Mr. John D. Edwards, of Charleston, on Sunday morning, the 16 August, at Sunrise. Both fell at the first fire, Edwards severely wounded in the loins, and O'Driscoll mortally, in the abdomen (the ball at entered just below the naval [sic] and passed through his body). He possessed his reason to the last moment, was perfectly aware of his approaching dissolution, and dictated a letter to his father. . . . He expired the next morning, about 3 o'clock. . . . He was a man of extensive reading and varied information,

and so commanded the respect of all who were acquainted with him, and the love and admiration of a great number of friends.[42]

Two years later, in 1819, White would marry O'Driscoll's sister, Ann Rachel, and with her have eight children.

But to return to the duel: Hanmer fails to discourage Woodville from this folly, and the two are met in the forest by Forsythe and Flaurence. The protocol is reviewed—the combatants are separated by ten paces, then, one at a time, beginning with the aggrieved, aim and fire—and the duel begins. Woodville, at Hanmer's command, fires first—and misses, as was typical. Forsythe then levels his pistol at Woodville and, at Flaurence's command, fires—whereupon a "piercing shriek is heard from without. Woodville drops his pistol and staggers" (55). He collapses into Hanmer's arms, entreats him to make right all his wrongs by proving "a friend unto my loved Maria,/And a father to Devalmore's children" (56), and so expires.

The shriek, of course, has come from Maria, who arrives too late and "throws herself on the corpse" (57). An officer arrives and sends his men off in pursuit of Forsythe and Flaurence, though no justice is administered during the action of the play. Indeed, the only characters who escape neither aggrieved nor arrested, nor deceased are those who act the most dishonorably. Fittingly, then, the officer, the play's ostensible minister of law, asks its central questions:

When will this modern Moloch be appeased—
When glutted with the blood of human victims?
When will the light of reason dawn on man,
And shew this custom its deformity? (57)

Such questions went unanswered during White's lifetime. He died on August 24, 1859, and reposes now in his own silent tomb in his family's plot at St. Philips Church in Charleston, near Ann Rachel and his first wife, Elizabeth Alston, who died in 1817. There is no record of later productions of his plays, though a bronze bust, the gift of his son, Dr. O. A. White, still stands in Charleston's City Hall. White was inducted into the South Carolina Academy of Authors in 2018.

Dueling was finally outlawed in South Carolina in 1880, owing primarily to an infamous duel near Bishopville. There, on July 5, after two years of open bickering and in front of hundreds of spectators, Colonels Ellerbe B. C. Cash and William M. Shannon took aim at one another, the former killing the latter, a father of fourteen whose neighbors were so appalled that they threatened Cash with lynching. Thereafter, the editor of Charleston's *News and Courier*, Francis W. Dawson, himself a veteran duelist, began so fervent an editorial campaign against the practice that it was taken up in newspapers across the state. Under public pressure, the state's general assembly outlawed dueling and added an amendment to the general statues stipulating that anyone convicted of mortally wounding another in a duel would be subject to the death penalty.[43]

Jon Tuttle is professor of English, director of University Honors, and the Nellie Cooke Sparrow Writer-in-Residence at Francis Marion University and is a recipient of the South Carolina Governor's Award in the Humanities. His most recent book, *South Carolina Onstage*, published by Academica Press, is now available.

NOTES

1. John Blake White, "The Journal of John Blake White," ed. Paul R. Weidner, *The South Carolina Historical and Genealogical Magazine* 43, no. 1 (Jan. 1942): 36–37.
2. Charles S. Watson, *The History of Southern Drama* (Lexington: University Press of Kentucky, 1997), 37.
3. Exact dates for these paintings are sometimes uncertain. The dates cited here are recorded by the US Senate Catalog of Fine Art. See US Senate, "Arts and Artifacts." https://www.senate.gov/art-artifacts/art-artifacts.htm.
4. See "Gen. Marion in His Swamp Encampment Inviting a British Officer to Dinner," The American Revolution Institute of the Society of the Cincinnati, https://societyofthecincinnati.contentdm.oclc.org.
5. *Ibid.* See "Mrs. Motte Directing Generals Marion and Lee to Burn Her Mansion to Dislodge the British," https://www.govinfo.gov/content/pkg/GPO-CDOC-107sdoc11/pdf/GPO-CDOC-107sdoc11-2-92.pdf.
6. The dates here and below are identified in "John Blake White," *Virtual American Biographies*, http://www.famousamericans.net.
7. Hugh Davis, "John Blake White," *South Carolina Encyclopedia* (Columbia: University of South Carolina Press, 2006), https://www.scencyclopedia.org.
8. The Dock Street Theatre, the most famous of Charleston theatres, opened in 1736 as a temporary space for touring companies. It burned down several times and at one point became the Planter's Hotel but was finally reestablished as a permanent performance space in 1937. The Charleston Theatre, also called the Broad Street Theatre, opened in 1794 and, save for a hiatus during the War of 1812, continued operations through 1833. It was the site of the notorious Charleston Theatre riot of 1817, which arose from a dispute between manager Joseph George Holman and an actor, James Caldwell. That dispute began as an exchange of letters in the *Southern Patriot*, each principal leveling slander against the other, and climaxed when the

audience interrupted a performance to engage in what was essentially a class war, turning on one another and the property, including the chandelier, until the Civic Guard arrived to disperse the crowd. Ironically, the dispute is said to have ended in a duel fought on Sullivan's Island, which claimed neither man but ended Holman's career. See Charles Dorman, "Possible Contributing Causes and the Riot Itself," Theatre Symposium: Theatre in the Antebellum South 2 (1994): 36–39.

9. Charles S. Watson, *Antebellum Charleston Dramatists* (Tuscaloosa: University of Alabama Press, 1976), 99.

10. For a fuller discussion, see Watson, *Antebellum*, 99–103.

11. The first Presbyterian Church is at 53 Meeting Street. White's will placed him at 21 Legare Street at the time of his death in 1859. See Watson, *Antebellum*, 94.

12. Watson, *Antebellum*, 98, 100.

13. "The Duel: The History of Dueling in America," *American Experience*, PBS, November 11, 2012, https://scetv.pbslearningmedia.org.

14. *Ibid.*

15. Ross Drake, "Duel! Defenders of Honor or Shoot-on-Sight Vigilantes? Even in 19th-Century America, It Was Hard to Tell," *Smithsonian Magazine*, March 2004, www.smithsonianmag.com.

16. J. Grahame Long, Dueling in Charleston: Violence Refined in the Holy City (Charleston, SC: The History Press, 2012), 10.

17. *Modern Honor, a Tragedy in Five Acts* (Charleston: J. Hoff, 1812), 5. Subsequent references are to this text, a facsimile of which was provided courtesy of the College of Charleston's Special Collections & Pamphlets library.

18. Watson, *Antebellum*, 97.

19. Watson, *History*, 39.

20. Mabel Trott Fitzsimmons, "Hot Words and Hair Triggers." Charleston, SC: (F266 F112 394.8 Fi) Charleston Museum Archives, 1934. Quoted in Long, 11.

21. Jack K. Williams, *Dueling in the Old South* (College Station: Texas A&M University Press, 1980), 10.

22. Long, 74, 67.

23. Cast lists for each of the Charleston Theatre's productions through 1812 occur in Richard Phillip Sodders, "The Theatre Management of Alexandre Placide in Charleston, 1794–1812," (PhD dissertation, Louisiana State University, 1983), 779, https://digitalcommons.lsu.edu/cgi/.

24. That is, the first play to be written by an American citizen and produced professionally in America. For a more complete discussion, see Arthur H. Nethercot, "The Dramatic Background of Royall Tyler's The Contrast," *American Literature* 12, no. 4 (Jan. 1941): 435.

25. That is, the first play written and produced by a native of South Carolina. It too premiered at the Charleston Theatre on March 30, 1805. See Watson, Antebellum, 56.

26. This Woodville is no relation, of course, to William Ioor's Woodville family in Independence (Charleston, SC: G. M. Bounetheau, 1805). That both playwrights chose the same name is interesting, though, in that it evokes both English nobility (descending from the Wydeville line) and postcolonial American DIY ruggedness, a quality that typically distinguished American character types from

the more effeminate European. See "The Woodville Family," English Monarchs, www.englishmonarchs.co.uk.

27. In the first performance of "Modern Honor," Forsythe was depicted as a Colonel. Watson reports that, according to the *Charleston Times* of March 12, 1812, some members of the audience were affronted by the depiction of a military man as dishonorable. White, therefore, not wanting "to wound the feelings of a single honest man," made Forsythe a civilian for the rest of the run. See Watson, Antebellum, 97.

28. "South Carolina Percussion Dueling Pistol by JM Happoldt of Charleston," College Hill Arsenal, https://collegehillarsenal.com.

29. John Lyde Wilson, *The Code of Honor or, Rules for the Government of Principals and Seconds in Dueling* (Charleston, SC: James Phinney, 1838), 11, 18, 24. Quoted in Williams, *Dueling in the Old South*, 92.

30. Wilson, *Code of Honor*, Quoted in Williams, *Dueling in the Old South*, 92.

31. *Crito* is a dialog written by the Greek philosopher Plato. It records Socrates's defense of his own upcoming execution and contains an early expression of what would later be called the social contract theory of government. See Richard Kraut, *Socrates and the State* (Princeton, NJ: Princeton University Press, 1994).

32. See Sodders, 779.

33. William Shakespeare, "Julius Caesar," ed. Barbara Mowat and Paul Werstine, *The Folger Shakespeare*, 1.2.95-96https://shakespeare.folger.edu.

34. Lillian Moore, "Douvillier, Suzanne Theodore Vaillande," in *Notable American Women, 1607–1950: A Biographical Dictionary*, Vol. 2, ed. Edward T. James, Janet Wilson James, and Paul S. Boyer (Cambridge, MA: Belknap Press, 1971), 513.

35. "Suzanne Théodore Vaillande Douvillier," *Encyclopedia Brittanica*, www.britannica.com.

36. Quoted in Fitzsimmons, n. p.

37. Williams, Dueling, 68.

38. Clement Eaton, *A History of the Old South: The Emergence of a Reluctant Nation*, 3rd ed. (New York: McMillan Co., 1975), 396–97.

39. Watson, Antebellum, 95.

40. Williams, Dueling, 28.

41. Quoted in Long, 33.

42. "Records for the Blake and White Bibles," annotated Mabel L. Webber, *The South Carolina Genealogical and Historical Magazine* 36, no. 2 (April 1935): 46.

43. Walter Edgar, *South Carolina: A History* (Columbia: University of South Carolina Press, 1998), 417.

WORKS CITED

"Arts and Artifacts." US Senate. Accessed July 19, 2022. https://www.senate.gov/art-artifacts/art-artifacts.htm.

Davis, Hugh. "John Blake White." *South Carolina Encyclopedia*. Columbia: University of South Carolina Press, 2006. www.scencyclopedia.org.

Dorman, Charles. "Possible Contributing Causes and the Riot Itself." *Theatre Symposium: Theatre in the Antebellum South* 2 (1994): 36–39.

Drake, Ross. "Duel! Defenders of Honor or Shoot-on-Sight Vigilantes? Even in 19th-Century America, It Was Hard to Tell," *Smithsonian Magazine*, March 2004. www.smithsonianmag.com.

"The Duel: The History of Dueling in America." *American Experience*. PBS. Nov 11, 2012. https://scetv.pbslearningmedia.org.

Eaton, Clement. *A History of the Old South: The Emergence of a Reluctant Nation*, 3rd ed. New York: McMillan Co., 1975.

Edgar, Walter. *South Carolina: A History*. Columbia: University of South Carolina Press, 1998.

Fitzsimmons, Mabel Trott. "Hot Words and Hair Triggers." 1934. Charleston Museum Archives, Charleston, SC. F266 F112 394.8 Fi.

Ioor, William. *Independence*. Charleston, SC: G. M. Bounetheau, 1805.

"John Blake White." *Virtual American Biographies*. www.famousamericans.net.

Kraut, Richard. *Socrates and the State*. Princeton, NJ: Princeton University Press, 1994.

Long, J. Grahame. *Dueling in Charleston: Violence Refined in the Holy City*. Charleston: The History Press, 2012.

Moore, Lillian. "Douvillier, Suzanne Theodore Vaillande." In *Notable American Women, 1607–1950: A Biographical Dictionary*, Vol. 2. Edited by Edward T. James, Janet Wilson James, and Paul S. Boyer. Cambridge, MA: Belknap Press, 1971.

Nethercot, Arthur H. "The Dramatic Background of Royall Tyler's *The Contrast*." *American Literature* 12, no. 4 (Jan. 1941): 435–46.

"Records for the Blake and White Bibles." Annotated Mabel L. Webber. *The South Carolina Genealogical and Historical Magazine* 36, no. 2 (April 1935): 42–55.

Shakespeare, William. *Julius Caesar*. Edited by Barbara Mowat and Paul Werstine. *The Folger Shakespeare*. https://shakespeare.folger.edu/shakespeares-works/julius-caesar.

Sodders, Richard Phillip. "The Theatre Management of Alexandre Placide in Charleston, 1794–1812." PhD dissertation. Baton Rouge: Louisiana State University, 1983.

"South Carolina Percussion Dueling Pistol by JM Happoldt of Charleston." Nashville, TN: College Hill Arsenal. https://collegehillarsenal.com/South-Carolina-Percussion-Dueling-Pistol-by-JM-Happoldt-of-Charleston.

"Suzanne Théodore Vaillande Douvillier." *Encyclopedia Britannica*. www.britannica.com.

Watson, Charles S. *Antebellum Charleston Dramatists*. Tuscaloosa: University of Alabama Press, 1976.

———. *The History of Southern Drama*. Lexington: University Press of Kentucky, 1997.

White, John Blake. *The Journal of John Blake White*, edited by Paul R. Weidner. *The South Carolina Historical and Genealogical Magazine* 43, no. 1 (Jan. 1942): 36–37.

———. *Modern Honor, a Tragedy in Five Acts*. Charleston: J. Hoff, 1812.

Williams, Jack K. *Dueling in the Old South*. College Station: Texas A&M University Press, 1980.

"The Woodville Family." *English Monarchs*. https://www.englishmonarchs.co.uk/plantagenet_56.html.

Charleston's Nineteenth-Century Germans

Co-opted Confederates?

Robert Alston Jones

Charleston's almost forgotten community of nineteenth-century German immigrants of predominantly North German origin underwent a process of acculturation and assimilation that naturally required its members to accommodate local customs and mores. The German immigrants to Charleston came to the United States in search of freedom and prosperity, but after 1861, they found themselves in a rebellious Confederacy defensive of its character and institutions. The following account of the life of a German immigrant to Charleston, one Bernhard Heinrich Bequest, reveals how the "redemption" of the postwar Confederacy affected the immigrant, gradually transforming him into a conservative Southerner inclined to align himself with the native-born disciples of the "Lost Cause," the latter actively promoting and celebrating the Confederate past. Bequest's story demonstrates how this particular immigrant's life in Charleston was representative of the process of acculturation experienced by many in the nineteenth-century German ethnic community: Their becoming Charlestonians ran in parallel with the course that the Confederate South took in transitioning from its defeat to its reinvention, secured in the halo of its romanticized Lost Cause past.

The unprecedented rates of immigration of Europeans to America during the nineteenth century had begun to decline by the late 1850s, and the Civil War in the United States stifled the number of immigrants choosing America as a destination and decreased the percentage emigrating from German lands. Those trends notwithstanding, one North German teenager risked a late departure from Bremerhaven to arrive in Charleston just as the firing on Fort Sumter signaled the beginning of the war. Seeking his fortune but not quite ready to settle in Charleston, this young German emigrant was quick to take advantage of the Confederacy's war effort to earn his keep as a blockade runner.

According to an account in a volume on Confederate military history authored by a former brigadier general, young Bernhard Bequest "took to the sea" as a teenager. When he arrived in Charleston "two weeks after the capture of Fort Sumter," that is, toward the end of April 1861, he was not yet seventeen years old.[1] The *Gauss*, one of the ships captained by the legendary Heinrich Wieting, had departed Bremerhaven in mid-March carrying only eleven passengers. Given his age, it is likely that Bernhard Bequest got to Charleston as a member of the ship's crew.

The author of the biographical sketch was South Carolina–born Ellison Capers, as noted, a former brigadier general in the Confederate Army. According to Capers, "the Confederate flag was flying," and it was only a few months later in 1861 that Bequest

> hid himself on the little blockade-running steamer, Ruby, and on revealing his presence after the boat was at sea, was put to work as coal-passer during the trip to Nassau. At that port he shipped on the blockade-runner Stonewall Jackson, Captain Black commanding, which on the first trip out was sighted and chased by the United States cruiser Tioga, and compelled to throw overboard part of her cargo and put back to Nassau. This unfortunate vessel at her next attempt to reach Charleston was fired upon and struck as she was crossing the bar, and run ashore, where she was burned with the cargo, young Bequest making his way thence to the city with the mail pouch. His next voyage was from Wilmington, and reaching Nassau he shipped on the Fanny, Captain Moore, with which he made four successful trips. Later he was on the Cyrene, but being taken sick at Nassau, he returned to his home in Germany in June, 1864, and remained until September, when he sailed to Nassau by way of New York, and made a trip into Wilmington on the Rosso Castle. Sailing again on the Watson, they reached the Wilmington bar in time to witness the terrific bombardment of Fort Fisher, upon the fall of which fort blockade-running came practically to an end. Returning to Nassau, he opened a small store and remained there until October, 1865.[2]

Capers called his account of the young immigrant a "romantic story," seemingly impressed that the German native had begun his seafaring life at the age of fourteen. The escapades of Bequest as related by Capers are, indeed, impressive, if only cursorily outlined. Each of the ships he is said to have worked on can be accounted for: The rescue of the mail pouch by young Bequest after the destruction of the *Stonewall Jackson* was noted in a report of the vessel's capture in the Richmond, Virginia, *Daily Dispatch*, with a "Charleston, April 12" (1863) dateline. Capers's *Rosso Castle* is more accurately the ship, *Rothersay Castle*; his *Cyrene* is the long-serving *Syren*. The *Watson* was still at work in early 1865 when Wilmington's Fort Fisher fell in

January. Maritime records show that the *Watson* sailed for Nassau in mid-February 1865, possibly taking Bequest back to Nassau where, according to Capers, he stayed until October of that year.[3]

The language of Capers's account of Bequest's blockade-running days is one of admiration of the latter's youth and daring. In the course of his work on numerous blockade-runners, Bequest had apparently become an acknowledged actor in the Confederacy's efforts to carry out its defiance of the Union blockade. At some point—likely postwar—the blockade-running immigrant's story came to the attention of the brigadier general, who then registered his admiration by including his biographical sketch in the volume on South Carolina that was part of the formidable twelve-volume *Confederate Military History: A Library of Confederate States History,* edited and published in 1899 by fellow Confederate Brigadier General Clement A. Evans under the imprint of the Confederate Publishing Company.[4]

The reality of Bequest's blockade running was likely not all that romantic, and it was doubtless not the case that he simply "took to the sea" looking for adventure. He came from a family of seafarers in the Hanoverian village of Geestendorf who, for generations, had lived and worked the North German coast as sailors of one kind or another. His great-grandfather, a Frenchman, was known as a "navigateur." His grandfather had at one time been employed as a ferryman and sailor. His father worked as a ship's carpenter, a boatman, a skipper, and a ship pilot.[5] For certain, the sea was in his blood, but when he began his seafaring life at age fourteen, it was likely because his father had died in 1859, age thirty-nine. As the eldest of six children, the teenager would have been expected to assume his position as head of the family. But these were not the times—in North Germany and elsewhere—for the younger generation to accept traditional expectations. After his father's death, opportunity for advancement in his native Geestendorf—which, by this time, had been incorporated into the city of Bremerhaven as the latter became the main port of embarkation for emigrants from German lands—would have been overshadowed by the pull of opportunity in the United States. That he should set out across the sea to arrive in Charleston in early 1861 undoubtedly had to do with the fact that he could make the crossing with Captain Heinrich Wieting, a fellow Geestendorfer, plus the fact that the teenager had relatives in Charleston and knew of other emigrant families from the Geestendorf community now settled there.

Bequest continued to work as a blockade runner until it became increasingly difficult for the Confederacy to evade the Union's blockade of the South's Atlantic ports. He had done quite well for himself on the

Charleston-Nassau run and, according to the Capers account, had garnered sufficient financial means to start a business in Nassau. Undoubtedly, the blockade runner knew what he was doing beyond the challenges of the operation. Despite Capers's enthusiastic report suggesting that Bequest jumped at the chance to serve the Confederacy, there is good reason to doubt that the young German came ashore in Charleston with a sense of loyalty to the rebellious states or that he developed one while working to supply it. For the mature teenager, the thrill of adventure and opportunity for financial gain likely outweighed any ideological drive to further the South's rebellion. It is, in fact, hard to imagine why a young German would have felt compelled to defend the recently seceded South Carolina and its warmongers because of some romanticized patriotism for a country not yet his own. Bequest was working for himself and whatever ship's Captain he managed to sign on with. It was not incumbent on this adventuresome German sailor to become a committed Confederate during the war to later become a German-American Charlestonian.

Capers confirms that he did, indeed, become a Charlestonian. After opening a small store, Bequest remained in Nassau until October of 1865, when he "came to Charleston and engaged in business and planting at the town of Mount Pleasant, on the bay." Capers's account continues: "Since 1885 he has conducted a successful business at Charleston, is a member of the German Artillery, and has twice served as king of the German Rifle Club. By his marriage in 1866 he has a daughter living, Teresa L., wife of John Gishen, and by a later marriage he has one son, John F."[6] Capers saw in Bernhard Bequest a daring young German who made his mark on behalf of the defeated Confederacy and then successfully established himself after the war as an upstanding Charleston business- and family man. Capers's outline is accurate enough, but it elides the complexity of Bequest's journey. More important, Capers shaped his story to give credibility to a toxic creed of oppression that Bequest may have embraced later in life, but for pragmatic rather than ideological reasons.

It is worth investigating what it was about the immigrant German that drew the attention of the influential former Confederate military officer and to consider why Capers chose to eulogize the foreign-born Charleston merchant along with other military leaders of the Confederacy. By including the brief Bequest biography in one of the volumes in the "library" of Confederate military history, the ex-brigadier general presented him as a noteworthy Confederate fellow traveler. In this way, his brief biography lends ideological support for the Lost Cause, and his daring adventures give rhetorical punch to the multivolume history. The actual tale of this member of Charleston's nineteenth-century German community, however, is considerably more complex and provides insight into the relationship between the ethnic community and the cultural framework of postbellum Charleston and South Carolina.

After living and operating a small business of an undisclosed nature in Nassau, Bequest returned to Charleston to start over. The twenty-one-year-old's decision to go back to the city where he had worked previously was doubtlessly influenced by the commercial stagnation in Nassau caused by the Atlantic blockade. Bequest would opt for opportunity in Charleston rather than muddle through the anticipated decline of Bahamian commercial conditions. Convinced that Charleston would provide a more stable business environment now that the war was over, Bequest nonetheless must have recognized the challenges he would face coming back to a city and community all but destroyed by the war. It was almost certainly a combination of his youth and a kind of immigrant courage that allowed him to believe that Charleston, despite its wracked state, was a place where he could be successful. The move to Charleston signaled his intention to become a citizen of the United States—which, at that point, had not formally been reunited and which had barely begun the process of healing—and, by capitalizing on the city's new beginnings, make a future for himself. Like his earlier work as a blockade runner, his actions were driven by practical, material concerns, not Confederate ideals.

Bequest was back in Charleston by October 1865. In February of 1866, he married another North German immigrant from a small town not far from Geestendorf at the Lutheran church (St. Matthew's) founded in 1842 by North German immigrants who preceded him. There is little question that the young couple's married life was challenging. Immediately after the war, Charleston would have been an inhospitable host community. General William Tecumseh Sherman visited in May and wrote, "Anyone who is not satisfied with war should go and see Charleston, and he will pray louder and deeper than ever that the country may in the long future be spared any more war."[7] In September, a reporter from the North toured Charleston and described it as "a city of ruins, of desolation, of vacant homes, of widowed women . . . of deserted warehouses, of weed-wild gardens, of miles of grass-grown streets."[8] Nonetheless, conditions slowly improved. Within three years of his return, Bequest became a naturalized US citizen at age twenty-three. In 1868, he purchased property, as reported by Capers, in the rural village of Mount Pleasant across the Cooper River from the Charleston peninsula, and by 1870, the federal census recorded him with the anglicized name of "Benjamin," age twenty-five, a merchant, with his wife "Sarah," age twenty-two, "keeping house." Both are officially noted as of German birth with parents of foreign birth. It was unsurprising that Bequest initially established himself as a merchant: doing so had been the antebellum pattern for many of the North German immigrants to Charleston. He would become an early commuter, crossing to Charleston by boat (likely his own sloop) from his residence across the bay to run a store in the city proper, as well as one in the village of Mount Pleasant.

A sense of the cultural sensibilities that Bequest encountered when he came to Charleston in 1865 can be culled from a letter written by Henry Slade Tew to his daughter in February 1865. Tew was a fellow storekeeper and, at the time, the mayor of Mount Pleasant.[9] The letter was written approximately eight months before Bequest returned to Charleston and gives an account of the occupation of Mount Pleasant by Union troops. Tew describes the frightening circumstances in Mount Pleasant and acknowledges that the situation in Charleston was worse: "The burning buildings public and private, the repeated explosions, the gun boats and other vessels burning in the harbor all presented such a scene as but few ever witness in a lifetime, and surely one which none would ever desire to see repeated. Oh God! What a night of horror that memorable 17th of February was." The residents in the village were fearful of "violence and insult" by the arriving Union troops, the "women and children . . . greatly apprehensive at the presence of the coloured troops. . . . Many of the negroes from the Plantations came down in the Army train, and together with those of the village made quite a multitude of shouting wild creatures whom the thought of freedom had changed from quiet to transports of uproarious joy." When the troops moved to Charleston proper, the village was left with "only six men as a guard and our negroes noisy, stealing all they could lay hands on and moving into the houses that were vacant. It was a sleepless night to us." On "Sunday 19th," Tew and his family attended the Episcopal church, and, to their general dismay, saw "a mulatto girl with a white soldier" sitting in the pew in front of them. That very Sunday,

> the Episcopal Church was taken possession of by negro troops. Their regiment is commanded by Col. Beecher the brother of H. Ward Beecher and Mrs. H. B. Stowe and we hear that his wife who is with him declines all acquaintance with the whites, but has called upon the colored ladies and invited them to her quarters—from this time forth until matters are settled I suppose that the Church is to be abandoned by the whites, as no

one will care to subject themselves to the annoyance of having a colored gentleman or lady perhaps both walking into your pew and overpowering you with their odor or filling you with vermin.[10]

The letter serves as a testament to the idiosyncrasies of life in Mount Pleasant in 1865 and resonates with the biases, antipathies, and prejudices endemic in the South when defeat left a vanquished people feeling their way out of chaos and unable to adjust to new rules of order. Immigrants like Bequest would have found themselves in a new context with new rules. In time, Bequest would accede to the demands of the local culture, as well as those imposed on the host society itself.

Bequest and his wife were married only six years when she died in 1872, shortly after giving birth to the daughter mentioned in the Capers account.[11] Less than a year later, Bequest married the daughter (eleven years his junior) of a family that had immigrated to Charleston from the vicinity of Geestendorf before the war. Census records list Bequest as a "planter," a farmer, likely raising produce to be sold in his store. In 1882, the couple moved from rural Mount Pleasant into the city proper, close to where Bequest had operated his in-town store. The one surviving child of the German-born couple was—like his half-sister—an American born in Charleston.

Bernhard Bequest's story as briefly outlined here leaves plenty of room for details—the daily pursuit of "health and happiness" as an immigrant to Charleston. Although those immigrants who had come to Charleston during the years before the Civil War accommodated themselves to the unique character of the antebellum city, the first years of both Bequest couples' existence in the defeated South coincided with the complete revision of everyday life under the aegis of Reconstruction. When Bernhard Bequest relocated to the city in late 1865, he was attempting to establish himself as a grocer in Charleston and a farmer in Mount Pleasant at the same time the state— affronted by being under US military command—was being reprogrammed under Andrew Johnson's Presidential Reconstruction so that it could be admitted back into the Union.

It was a less-than-propitious time to undertake a new beginning. We can assume, nonetheless, that the German immigrant, new in town, had little choice but to adapt to the context in which he found himself. A month before Bequest returned to Charleston, a convention, held in Columbia, drew up the state's new constitution, adopted its version of the Black Codes, and moved the state's governmental offices from Charleston to Columbia.[12] Only shortly thereafter, South Carolina ratified the Thirteenth Amendment, which canceled slavery and released from bondage a perceptibly large population of Black freedmen. A year later, the state rejected the Fourteenth Amendment, effectively declaring that it was not interested in the matter of citizenship and equal protection for the formerly enslaved.[13] When, in late 1866, the state passed legislation to name a commissioner who would encourage the immigration of European whites as a means to diminish the Black majority, Bequest might have questioned the white host community's intent to further disempower its Black community, although his concerns were possibly put to rest when the city's own German "influencer," John Andreas Wagener, was appointed to the post in 1867.[14] The unusualness of the 1867 "event" whereby former slaves were "allowed" to participate in the election of state and local officials would not have escaped him. After a few years living and working in Charleston, the immigrant Bequest would likely have appreciated the implications of the fact that the state's 1868 constitution was drawn up by a convention whose elected Black representatives were a majority in a legislative body in which they had never previously participated. When Bernhard Bequest was naturalized in 1868, South Carolina's population consisted of approximately 290,000 whites and 416,000 Blacks.[15] By late 1870—likely to the dismay of the native-born whites in Charleston—a number of "firsts" were recorded for the state's majority population: Jonathan Wright was elected to the State Supreme Court, Alonzo Ransier was elected as the state's lieutenant governor, and Joseph Rainey was sworn to the US Congress—each an African American. The University of South Carolina would admit its first Black student in 1873.[16]

More likely than not, the newly arrived foreigner could feel overwhelmed by the "new" reality taking shape during the early postwar years. Not surprisingly, the German native would find comfort in his own, less politicized, heritage. Bequest sought out his fellow Germans by joining the Deutsche Schützengesellschaft in 1868. Recognized as the oldest rifle club in the United States, the Charleston club had been founded in 1855 and was a close-knit German society unto itself within the larger Charleston society. Belonging to the Schützen allowed the immigrant and his family to maintain something of their heritage in what, at times, must have seemed like an alien world. The Schützengesellschaft would become a cornerstone of life for many in the ethnic community, a center and nexus of social relationships that would sustain them whatever their personal circumstances might be.

Because of the war, the rifle club's annual, much-enjoyed festival, the Schützenfest, had not been held for eight years. In May of 1868, a month after Bequest was voted in as an active member, the club, with permission from the federal government in Washington, again put on its festival. The German sharpshooters paraded in full complement down the streets of Charleston amid the acclamation of the crowds and the lively strains of music. Participating in the activities of the German Rifle Club would become the focal point of Bequest's social life and define his identity within the German community. As was the case for many of his fellow immigrants, membership in the rifle club facilitated the members' goal of establishing themselves within the Charleston community: Participation in the club's activities and the favor that the club found in the community would facilitate the transformation of the German immigrant into a Charlestonian of German heritage.

Before the war, the annual Spring Schützenfest of the German Rifle Club had become a major event for Charleston's inhabitants. Its revival in 1868 signaled that it had not lost any of its popularity in the local community. Effusive praise was the topic of the two-column article on the front page of the *Charleston Daily News* of May 8, 1869:

> The fact that yesterday would be the concluding day of the Schuetzenfest, drew together the largest crowd that has ever been seen at the Platz. The trains, omnibuses, private and public vehicles were tasked to the utmost to convey the immense number of visitors. These were not confined to the Teutonic element. All nationalities and all classes flocked to the gay scene to enjoy the occasion, and witness or participate in its joys and amusements. The city was deserted; many stores were closed, and avenues of trade were as still and quiet as on Sunday. The very best spirit prevailed, and all seemed to enjoy themselves. It would be unwise even to guess at the amount of lager consumed. Kegs and barrels were emptied and replaced, and these again ran dry. Yet, to the honor of the Schuetzen be it said, there was not one riotous person on the ground. So much for lager, with our good Germans to drink it. No unpleasant incident jarred the harmonies of the day. The participants were all too good humored to get vexed with anybody. In the matter of courtesy, the German hosts were masters of the situation, and dispensed their heartfelt hospitality in a free and whole-souled manner.

At almost every annual Schützenfest, Bequest took a prize in the shooting contests. His talent with the rifle earned him first prize at the 1871 Schützenfest, when he became its King for the following year.

German men were regaled as heroes at the annual Schützenfests, and the members of the German Ladies' Society played an equally important social role in the Charleston community. The report in the *Charleston Daily News* of November 1, 1870, on "The German Fair" put on by the Ladies' Society speaks volumes about how Charlestonians regarded the Germans at the time:

> THE GERMAN FAIR / A TRIUMPH OF TASTE AND SKILL. . . . The sterling worth and unselfish feeling of the German citizens of Charleston are always displayed to best advantage when charity or religion appeals to the hearts which beat so warmly for God and Fatherland. They are thorough in their amusements. There is no lackadaisical enjoyment in the gala doings of the German. But when the religion of their fathers calls upon them for help and aid, their serious souls are stirred to the depths, and they labor with a zeal and devotion which no people can surpass. . . . The Germans are always staunch and true, and never have their finest qualities been shown to better advantage than in the Fair of the German Ladies' Society, whose triumphant opening we chronicle today. The object of the Fair, we need hardly add, is to obtain the means of completing the new German Lutheran Church in King Street, whose tower already rears its head above the neighboring buildings.

The newspaper reporter concluded that "the opening night of the Fair of the German Ladies' Society was successful beyond expectations. . . . The Germans of Charleston are never backward in giving their help to any measure which is for the good of the community."

Despite the hyperbole inherent in newspaper reporting during this period, it is difficult to overlook the fact that, during these years, there was more than a modicum of judgment being passed by the host society on the German ethnic community. Charleston and its ruling class have not infrequently been accused of being paternalistic, and there is no lack of that in the aforementioned passages: *They* are a separate entity from *Us*, viewed and judged from a distance, as if the viewer in the center is looking at something on the periphery, ready and able to comment on *them*, "the Germans," "*their* serious souls," "the sunny splendor of *their* smile," "*their* finest qualities," "*our* most valuable citizens." Although "the Germans" had, for some time, been making a very good impression on the natives, and even though they were well behaved and valuable members of the Charleston community, "old Charleston" would subconsciously keep the immigrants somewhat marginalized for yet a number of years. Nonetheless, and in spite of the host society's perceived separation between themselves and the industrious immigrants, it is clear that the German community had become an important sector of Charleston's populace.

During the politically tumultuous first decade of Bequest's tenure in Charleston, the milestones of his personal life would take shape against the background of social expectations and attitudes of the Reconstruction years. As if to demonstrate a strong commitment to the native community that he wished to become a part of, three years after the war had ended and while Reconstruction was underway, the now-naturalized Bequest ran for the office of warden in the Mount Pleasant election in November of 1868, when Henry Tew was again elected as the town's mayor. In the *Charleston Daily News* report of the election results, Bequest was one of eleven candidates for Warden: six were reported as Democrats, four were reported as Republicans and "colored," and Bequest was reported as "white" and Republican. He received one vote—likely his own. The following day, the newspaper ran a retraction: "We are requested to say that the statement in the report of the Mount Pleasant election, published in our last issue, that Mr. Bequest is a Republican, is wholly incorrect."[17] The six Democrats had run away with the votes, the Black Republicans—likely "radical" Reconstructionists— were defeated, and the white immigrant with a mistaken political affiliation learned a lesson about playing in Reconstruction politics. In the next election in 1870, Bequest did much better, tying for the second highest number of votes (127) of the six wardens elected. The *Charleston Daily News* of September 13 reported that "the election passed off quietly. The parties chosen were all Reformers except the last." Running as a Reformer was obviously preferable to running as a Republican. By age twenty-six, the German immigrant had assumed a more local identity. As would have been expected, in the course of five years, the host community had left its imprint, although it would not yet have transformed him into the fellow traveler to which ex-Brigadier General Ellison Capers would later lay claim.

Operating as a local merchant and public servant attuned to the politics of the community, Bequest would subsequently be elected mayor of Mount Pleasant. Not incidentally, his election in 1876 took place when the local and statewide politics led to the turbulent South Carolina gubernatorial battle between the "carpetbagger" incumbent, Daniel Chamberlain, and South Carolina's Democratic scion, Wade Hampton. The deal with President Rutherford Hayes to withdraw federal troops from the State House in Columbia and put the Democrat Hampton in charge as governor effectively signaled the "redemption" of the state and its release from the intolerable demands of "Yankee" Reconstruction.[18] An account of Mount Pleasant's historic landscape notes that the 1876 election, which effectively overturned Black Republicanism and restored white Democrats to power in the district, state, and region, caused the town's Black Republicans to seize the streets for an entire night while resident white Democrats, together with their few Black political allies, barricaded themselves in their homes.[19] Absent evidence to the contrary, it is not unreasonable to suggest that Bequest played a small role in "overturning" Black Republicanism and "restoring" white Democrats to power, although it is doubtful that he stood for election *intending* to play such a role. It is safe to say that eleven years after his immigration, he was elected mayor because his constituents considered him a fellow Democrat, a respected villager who had demonstrated the German immigrants' admirable qualities and who, it could be assumed, was one of their own. Given that the former German blockade runner had previously worked "on behalf" of the now-defeated Confederacy, it would have been typical of Mount Pleasant voters to assume that he had forsaken his heritage and become a Southerner devoted to the Confederacy's peculiar history, its heroes, and its battlefields. While *intending* to be counted as a good citizen in the host community, Bequest would later find himself admired by fellow Southerners, such as ex-Brigadier General Ellison Capers, an "esteemed" ex-Confederate who considered the upstanding German immigrant worthy enough to be included among the Confederate brethren in the volume on South Carolina's military history he was editing.

There is no dispute that the Southern states of the former Confederacy did not take Presidential—or any subsequent—Reconstruction efforts lying down. The indignities that Southerners had to suffer only strengthened their resolve to resist every modification that was to be made to their sacred past. Their defeat in the war made Southern elites increasingly more defensive about their right to exercise white supremacy and radicalized their response to being told how they should accept their loss and accommodate the new order. South Carolinians were recognized as the most profoundly resistant to the changes installed under Reconstruction, although it should be stated that Charleston's nonnative population was, by and large, not to be counted among the indignant or radical.

Bernhard Bequest would not have been the only German immigrant to be challenged by, and likely accede to—indeed, benefit from—the character and mood of the Reconstruction and post-Reconstruction years. Looking both backward and forward, the Bequest story demonstrates that although it took fortitude, determination, and a good measure of entrepreneurial spirit to become a successful businessman, it would also be necessary to tolerate and accommodate the values of the native-born community if one wanted to be accepted as a productive citizen. The immigrant had to accept the challenges of a society struggling to become part of a "new" South at the same time it was reluctant to forget its past and accept its future. Within the unsettledness of the radicalized political, social, and economic reconstruction that marked the last quarter of the century, Bequest—the immigrant German husband, father, and businessman—had little choice but to rise to the occasion.

In his analysis of how German immigrants became "white Southerners," Jeffery Strickland claims that they were "a middleman minority community, occupying a middle tier on the racial and ethnic hierarchy below white southerners and above African Americans," who after the Civil War "increasingly exhibited their desire to become white southerners."[20] As a postwar resident landowner in Mount Pleasant since his immigration, Bequest could be considered a case in point: from his naturalization in 1868 to his service on the town council, to his election to Mount Pleasant's mayoralty during the years when Democrat Wade Hampton and his conservative allies represented and monopolized the South Carolina political scene, Bequest's desire to become a "white Southerner" was manifest in everything he did, as he and his fellow German immigrants accommodated the expectations of the host society.

As the Germans had gone through stages of asserting their cultural heritage on the local scene—for example, establishing the Schützengesellschaft and other paramilitary "social" organizations—they had, indeed, occupied a middle ground by inviting the enslaved and free Black population to attend and participate in the rifle club's public functions. At the same time, however, they conscientiously displayed their martial uniforms and guns in exhibitionistic parades—the latter affirming the sense of white superiority assumed by the mostly native white crowds in attendance. By virtue of their increasing social and financial ascendancy, the Germans would become increasingly attuned to the platform of the Democratic Party. By 1871, they were sufficiently politically organized and recognized that one of their own—the much recognized, prominent, ethnic leader and former Confederate general John A. Wagener—could run for mayor of Charleston. In that election, a large-enough number of white Southerners endorsed Wagener's candidacy that he would win a two-year term. By the middle of Reconstruction, however, Charleston's Germans would be accused of having modified their initial openness to Charleston's Black population by moving from the center to the right. African-American Republican politicians lashed out at the Germans for their efforts on behalf of the Democratic Party. The state's

Republican African-American lieutenant governor, Alonzo Ransier, proclaimed it "the basest ingratitude in General Wagener and the Germans to support a ticket in opposition to the rights of the colored people." Ransier argued that the Germans had betrayed the African-American community: "So far as the negro is concerned—let the Germans remember when they came here in their blue shirts—you patronized them, traded with them, and through your patronage they are enabled to-day to raise their heads and now desire to govern us."[21]

As an immigrant German grocer-become-white Southerner, Bequest could enjoy certain perquisites. For example, he could take advantage of the lien laws that existed at the time.[22] There is record of him—a kind of sharecropper himself, farming a leased plot of one and a half acres—in his capacity as store owner providing supplies on credit to Frank Wallace, a less fortunate sharecropping citizen of the new, postbellum South. As furnishing merchant, Bequest functioned both as supplier and creditor in his community, practicing as the lien laws intended. He had become a man of his time in South Carolina, a merchant playing the role the state had created for his—and certain others'—benefit.

As was the case with most of his fellow immigrant businessmen, Bequest was on the lookout for additional opportunities that would improve his financial base and solidify his position in the community. By the time Reconstruction was on the wane, he had established a wood and lumberyard business in the city, prescient enough to predict that wood products would be in demand by a city physically constructing and reconstructing itself. The increasingly acculturated immigrant's business acumen—or perhaps the readiness to take risks—is attested by the financial maneuvers he undertook to transition from Mount Pleasant storekeeper to the owner of a lumber business in the city itself. The sale of properties he had earlier acquired was, likewise, testimony to the immigrant inclination to own property, a privilege and right beyond the expectations of most European emigrants.[23]

In 1886, the new Palmetto Company of the Fraternal Order of Knights of Pythias's Uniform Rank was formed in Charleston. In January of 1887, the Company held an organizational meeting where the main order of business was taking measurements for the members' uniforms—black frock coats and pants, white helmets and plumes, gilded belts, and swords and side arms. Bequest served as "Sir Knight Treasurer." His role in organizing this new fraternal entity and his serving as its treasurer suggest that he was expanding his circle of contacts and involving himself in what might have been considered a more "American" fraternal association than his German-oriented rifle club. The similarities between the Schützen and the Pythians are, nevertheless, striking. The Schützenfest in 1885 was reported to have begun with "becoming military and Terpsichorean honors"—no doubt featuring splendidly impressive (to both spectators and "performers") uniforms; the Pythians founding the Palmetto Company in 1886 were comparably thrilled with their handsome and imposing uniforms as well as with the prospect of marching in a parade to display their finery, swords, and side arms.[24] During the years after 1886, Bequest's name is more often in the record in connection with the Pythians than with the Schützen, suggesting that he was possibly more comfortable in the company of the one fraternal group, dedicated as it was to "friendship, charity and benevolence," as he transitioned into a citizen of Charleston at the end of the century. It could be argued that the former German sharpshooter was subtly modifying his identity through membership in a brotherhood that was more American, one that was "dedicated to the cause of universal peace and . . . pledged to the promotion of understanding among men of good will as the surest means of attaining it."[25]

In 1892 the members of the German Artillery—the venerable old and the sentimental young—celebrated the organization's "semi-centennial" in October with an impressive parade, an event that received a lot of coverage in the local press.[26] If the columns in the *News and Courier* are accurate, most of Charleston's citizens turned out to admire the marchers in their very impressive finery, and the adults, at least, to reflect on what the German Artillery stood for. The celebration once again certified that the Germans were held in high regard by the local citizenry. In a stirring speech before the parade got underway, Theodore Melchers, a member of one of the city's prominent German families, presented a custom-made badge to the group's leader, Capt. Frederick Wagener:

> It is your untiring exertion which has made this company what it now is. It is through your influence and your work that to-day it owns this magnificent armory, second to none in the Southern States, and it is your untiring zeal which has made this day such a success. This beautiful jewel has been chosen with special care to commemorate your various services. You here behold the shield or battle flag of the 'Lost Cause,' surrounded by rays of glory, surmounted by the emblem of the Artillery, crossed cannons and the eagle—above which you see our national colors and those of Germany, united and held together by the coat-of-arms of our beloved State, South Carolina. These emblems are to denote that you fought as a true and brave defender of the 'Lost Cause': that you are a true son of the Fatherland,

a loyal citizen of the United States, and a prince (a merchant prince) of South Carolina. Wear it near your heart as a perpetual memento of the love and esteem which your comrades bear you.[27]

On this occasion, Bernhard Bequest rode with three of the German organization's leaders in one of the eight carriages in the torchlight-parade spectacle celebrating the accomplishments of Frederick Wagener, a Confederate war hero who had fought bravely for the "Lost Cause" and then become one of Charleston's leading businessmen.[28]

Bequest's honorary participation in this 1892 celebration of a fellow German as a "true and brave defender of the Lost Cause" affirms that, by the 1880s, he and likely many of his fellow compatriots had absorbed the "traditional conservative values of elite rule and local government" promoted and defended by South Carolina's Confederate hero, Wade Hampton—whose 1876 election to the state's governorship had framed Bequest's own election to political office at the local level.[29] Later, when Hampton and his conservative followers were endorsing Black suffrage (which they expected to manage and "guide"), Bequest would have been receptive to the idea of extending the hand to the Black population as the Germans had done previously, notwithstanding the fact that Charleston's Reconstruction Blacks felt betrayed by the Democrat-leaning Germans during the 1870s. The German-American businessman could much more comfortably side with the pro-Hampton elitists than affiliate with the antiaristocratic, less privileged whites who, in the 1880s, aligned themselves with the anti-Hampton demagogue, "Pitchfork Ben Tillman." During this period, we cannot know whether Bequest continued to read the ethnic community's German newspaper, the *Deutsche Zeitung*, to apprise himself of the political climate in Charleston. More likely, he satisfied his inherent (and learned) conservatism by regularly absorbing the "ardently pro-Hampton"[30] conservatism of Charleston's *News and Courier* and its frequent promotion of Lost Cause issues.[31]

In June 1898, the *Evening Post* carried a condensed biography of the wood dealer:

> In mentioning our citizens who have made a success by energy and business ability the name of B. H. Bequest stands among the leaders of Charleston's prosperous men.
>
> Mr. Bequest is a native of Germany, where he was reared and educated. In 1861 he entered Charleston harbor in the bark Goss under Capt. Vieting, that well known seaman (now deceased). The morning he entered the

harbor the confederate flag was flying over Fort Sumter, and a short time after, Mr. Bequest, true to the cause he believed right, entered the Confederate service and experienced some thrilling adventures in the blockade service under Capt. Moore, steamer Fannie. He was on the Stonewall Jackson/Sirene with Capt. Black, and others.

Mr. Bequest is an old and tried seaman, having serviced in England, Scotland, Russia, Mexico, West Indies, etc.

After the war Mr. Bequest started in the grocery business on a very small scale at Mount Pleasant, remaining there for sixteen years. He was one of the leading citizens and enjoyed the confidence of the people. He was honored by the people, serving in the city council and four years as mayor.

In 1885 he came to Charleston and established his present business, which at that time was on a very small scale. But when, as before, hustling, coupled with untiring energy, and strict honest business principles won, and Mr. Bequest was enabled gradually to build up his now large and lucrative business. His plant is large and commodious, covering an acre of ground. He is a wholesale and retail dealer in oak and pine wood, oak and pine blocks, gravel and white sand, wood sawed and delivered to any part of the city. Vessels supplied at low rates. Mr. Bequest has all the modern conveniences for the successful prosecution of his work, the capacity of the plant being fifteen cords per diem.

Eight wagons are run and ten men given employment. To say that he has made a success is but to read the above.

Mr. Bequest stands high both commercially and socially in the city. He is a member of the German Artillery, a K. of P. Uniform rank, having been treasurer for many years. He is also a member of the German Rifle Club, having been king twice.

Mr. Bequest is also a member of several other organizations of the city, and a public spirited, progressive gentleman who believes in pushing Charleston and the Palmetto State to the front.[32]

If this laudatory biographical summary of Charleston's "Mr. Bequest" rings familiar, it is because the newspaper reporter has blatantly plagiarized the biographical account of the "successful" Bequest by Ellison Capers that initially brought the immigrant blockade runner to our attention.[33] In addition to following Capers's biographical outline, the reporter also unambiguously mentions the "cause" to which Mr. Bequest was "true" and "believed right." In 1898, there was no other "cause" other than the lost one.[34]

As suggested earlier, the former Confederate brigadier general's turn-of-the-century enthusiastic endorsement of the immigrant Bequest's life in Charleston—from the latter's youth as a blockade runner to his maturity as a successful businessperson—was tantamount to Capers's appropriating Bequest for his purposes in presenting and memorializing the foremost men in South Carolina's military history. Both Ellison Capers, the ex-Confederate brigadier general and editor of the account of South Carolina's valorous military past, and Clement Evans, Capers's fellow ex-Confederate brigadier general and series editor/publisher, were unhesitatingly happy to claim the immigrant as one of their own.

Engaged as he was in reliving and re-presenting the past, it was easy for Capers to relate to Bequest's youthful "military" accomplishments as a blockade runner and, in particular, note that the mature, successful merchant was a member of the German Artillery. There were, in fact, other markers of militarism peculiar to the city's German immigrants that would resonate with the guardians of the Confederate cause. It was a fact that Charleston's Germans had long been associated with the city's military presence. When the newspapers were calling the 1874 Schützenfest "The People's Festival," it was advertised as "a Grand Military Pageant." In the annual parade, the Germans were more than noticeable among the host of paramilitary organizations marching by.[35] This blatant military pageant/display marching through the streets of Charleston was, at the time, a white show of force during some of the darkest days of Reconstruction.

By the late 1880s, when the Lost Cause "religion" was reaching its zenith,[36] a number of Charleston's German "militia-like" groups (e.g., the German Fusiliers) were still active participants in the city's protective services involved in keeping the peace.[37] It was not by accident that Charleston's German volunteer militias, like other ethnic militias in "the martially charged culture of the South," would early on assume a protectionist role.[38] Similar to the Schützen, these paramilitary organizations persisted for decades in "protecting" Charleston. The city's perceived need of protection, combined with the Germans' readiness to function as protectors was a case of mutual dependency: Charleston's native white population had, since the early 1820s, been intent on defending itself against the threat of those under its control. That context, together with a resident ethnic population ready to offer its "military sense" in protecting the larger community against its enemies, was a mutually beneficial arrangement.

Undoubtedly, when Capers was editing his volume on South Carolina's Confederate military history in the 1890s, he was aware of Bequest's political orientation as mayor of Mount Pleasant; more specifically, that he was elected in 1876, the year when Wade Hampton played such a pivotal role in the state's history. It was then that Hampton had effectively "redeemed" South Carolina, and Bequest, innocently or purposefully, had played his part in "overturning" Black Republicanism to restore white Democrats to power. It may have actually been the case that Bequest came to mayoral "power" on the coattails of, or at least the general enthusiasm for, Hampton. Charles J. Holden has argued that "South Carolina's conservatives, like their antebellum forefathers, persistently fought to stem the national tide toward mass democracy. Their effort to reconfigure a regime of elite rule over the former slaves and poor whites succeeded in part through their constant promotion of Hampton and his war exploits and his role in the 1876 election."[39] By virtue of their enthrallment with Wade Hampton, conservatives' belief in elite rule dovetailed neatly with the general precept of the Lost Cause that held Confederate leaders to be the better men.

Bequest's participation in the German Artillery's 1892 ceremony honoring Frederick Wagener as a true and brave defender of the Lost Cause would have been reason enough for Capers to claim him as a fellow Confederate. Perhaps Capers himself was a participant in the ceremony, inclined to take it for granted that the entire membership of the German Artillery—all conservative Charleston Germans-become-Southerners—could be counted as devotees of the South's Lost Cause. However he knew of Bernhard Bequest, Capers could see in the Artillery's German immigrant a specimen worth co-opting as one of the notable "better men" of South Carolina's past and present.

What happened with Bernhard Bequest would have been similar to what happened to many members of the nineteenth-century German ethnic community as they underwent the process of becoming citizens of the host community. The native-born who fought the war and remembered it long afterward found the German immigrants to their liking when their criteria for "adopting" them were met so admirably. It was inevitable during these times that the values and ideals the immigrants had come with would be overtaken by what developed as a postwar "religion" that ever so fervently focused on the Confederacy of the past.[40] Bequest was an exemplary case of the Charleston immigrant whose original intentions—to become a naturalized, successful, free, and independent American businessman—were diverted by the postwar host society's attitudes, ideals, and beliefs. Consumed for decades by remembering its communal past and hesitantly facing a less sectional future, by the turn of the century, the host community's manifest Lost Cause ideology had successfully captured the immigrant guest in its midst and brought the foreigner into the fold of the Confederacy's defenders.

In the early morning hours of October 28, 1899, Bequest died unexpectedly in his home at the age of fifty-five. The funeral was held the next day—Sunday—at St. Matthew's German Lutheran Church at three o'clock in the afternoon. The funeral notice in the Sunday morning *News and Courier* included the call to the Pythian Palmetto Company to attend "in citizens' dress," as well as to the Pythian Stonewall Lodge, whose members were to assemble at Pythian Castle Hall to pay tribute "to your late brother Member B. H. Bequest." On Monday, October 30, the *News and Courier* took notice in its "All around Town" column: "The funeral services of the late Mr. Bernhard H. Bequest were held at St. Matthew's German Lutheran Church yesterday afternoon, and the remains interred at Bethany Cemetery with Pythian ceremonies. Mr. Bequest was an estimable citizen of Charleston, and had been for many years in business here." That he died "an estimable citizen of Charleston" was validation of a thirty-four-year-long struggle through the hard times of Reconstruction and the fading of Charleston into the backwash of the New South during the final decades of the century. A life that had begun with daring adventure and a vision of opportunity had progressed through service to the public and dedicated efforts as a landowner, merchant, and entrepreneur, ultimately to be acknowledged and admired by leading proponents of the Confederate Lost Cause as one of their better men.

Robert Alston Jones is a Charleston native and emeritus professor of German at the University of Wisconsin–Milwaukee. He holds degrees in German Literature and Language from Duke University and the University of Texas–Austin. He has recently published *Charleston's Germans: An Enduring Legacy*, an examination of Charleston's nineteenth-century community of German immigrants and the role it played in the evolution of ante- and postbellum Charleston.

NOTES

1. Ellison Capers, "South Carolina," Vol. 5 of *Confederate Military History: A Library of Confederate States History*, ed. Clement A. Evans, 12 vols. (Atlanta: Confederate Publishing Co., 1899), 455.
2. *Ibid.*, 455.
3. P. C. Coker, III, *Charleston's Maritime Heritage 1670–1865: An Illustrated History* (Charleston, SC: CokerCraft Press, 1987), 304.

4. The biographies of the two editors (Capers and Evans) are remarkably similar: Both enlisted early in the war and served until the surrender at Appomattox; both were wounded multiple times in the course of the war; both were raised to the rank of brigadier general (Capers in March, 1865; Evans in May, 1864); both became church ministers after the war (Capers: Episcopal priest, then bishop of South Carolina; Evans: Methodist minister from 1866 to 1896); both were conscientiously involved in the affairs of the United Confederate Veterans organization, Capers as chaplain general, and Evans as commander-in-chief at the time of his death in 1911; and both carried memories of the Confederacy's valor in the Civil War with them until they died. When Evans published his Confederate military history series in 1899, he would have considered both himself and Capers as "distinguished men of the South," each devoted to retelling the valorous history of the Confederacy. The title page in each of the volumes carries the subtitle, "A library of Confederate states history, in twelve volumes, written by distinguished men of the South, and edited by Gen. Clement A. Evans of Georgia." In his preface to Volume 1, Evans further confirms that "the authors of the State histories, like those of the volumes of general topics, are men of unchallenged devotion to the Confederate cause and of recognized fitness to perform the task assigned them. It is just to say that this work has been done in hours taken from busy professional life, and it should be further commemorated that devotion to the South and its heroic memories has been their chief incentive," iv.

5. See Erika Friedrichs and Klaus Friedrichs, eds., *Das Familienbuch des Kirchspiels Geestendorf (heute Bremerhaven-Geestemünde), 1689 bis 1874*, Bd. 1 (Bremerhaven, Germany, 2003), 47.

6. Capers, "South Carolina," 454–55.

7. Walter J. Fraser Jr., *Charleston! Charleston! The History of a Southern City* (Columbia: University of South Carolina Press, 1991), 273.

8. *Ibid.*, 275.

9. Tew served a second term from 1868 to 1870.

10. The text of Tew's letter is quoted in "An Eye Witness Account of the Occupation of Mt. Pleasant: February 1865," *The South Carolina Historical Magazine* 66, no. 1 (January 1965): 8–14. Colonel Beecher is James Chaplin Beecher (1828), half-brother to Harriet Beecher Stowe, the author of *Uncle Tom's Cabin: Or, Life Among the Lowly* (1852). See https://www.harrietbeecherstowecenter.org/harriet-beecher-stowe/family/.

11. The daughter, Theresa Louise Bequest, would later marry immigrant John Henry Gieschen—not "John Gischen" as reported by the English-speaking brigadier general.

12. "The Black Codes, passed by the former Confederate states during Presidential Reconstruction, were part of a complex web of postwar economic, legal, and extralegal restraints designed by white conservatives to maintain broad control over the freedpeople." *Encyclopedia of the Reconstruction Era*, Vol. 1: A–L, ed. Richard Zuczek (Westport, CT: Greenwood Press, 2006), 72.

13. The Fourteenth Amendment was ratified in 1868, as it was a requirement for readmission into the United States.

14. An inveterate organizer, Wagener had been in Charleston since 1833. He founded a German Fire Engine company, led the effort to found a German Lutheran Church (St. Matthew's), helped start three German ethnic organizations, established a weekly German newspaper, and was instrumental in creating the "German Colonization Society of Charleston" that would ultimately establish the town of Walhalla in upstate South Carolina. With Wagener as commissioner, the additional "whites" would likely be additional Germans, who would strengthen the ethnic community rather than suppress the Black community.
15. 1870 US Census.
16. George C. Rogers Jr., and C. James Taylor, *A South Carolina Chronology 1497–1992*. 2nd ed. (Columbia: University of South Carolina Press, 1994), 105.
17. "Local Matters," *Charleston Daily News*, November 14, 1868.
18. See Eric Foner's chapter, "Redemption and After," in his *A Short History of Reconstruction: 1863–1877* (New York: Harper & Row, 1990), 238–53.
19. See Amy McCandless, ed., *The Historic Landscape of Mount Pleasant: Proceedings of the First Forum on the History of Mount Pleasant* (Mt. Pleasant, SC, 1993), https://www.tompsc.com/DocumentCenter/View/569/MTP_First_Historic_Forum_1993?bidId=.
20. Jeffery G. Strickland, "How the Germans Became White Southerners: German Immigrants and African Americans in Charleston, South Carolina, 1860–1880," *Journal of American Ethnic History* 28, no. 1 (2008): 52.
21. *Ibid.*, 62.
22. The crop lien system of credit that "allowed the farmer to place a mortgage on his future crop with the person or persons who advanced him supplies for his operations. Normally those who made advances only accepted liens on an easily salable crop which was inedible and difficult to steal.... No other crop planted in the lower South so completely satisfied these requirements as did cotton." See Thomas D. Clark, "The Furnishing and Supply System in Southern Agriculture since 1865," *Journal of Southern History* 12, no. 1 (February 1946): 44.
23. Five years after the war and during the first half of the Reconstruction decade, under the duress of labor inadequacy and the evolution of lien laws, property was readily available and relatively inexpensive for all but the emancipated. For the German immigrant, ownership of land would have been a driving force and a means of achieving a status only imagined in the homeland. There and in Charleston the "propertied" were the people who mattered. As his financial situation improved, Bequest took advantage of the local conditions and conscientiously acquired property. During the years between 1867 and 1879, records of the Charleston Register of Mesne Conveyance show him involved in a number of real estate transactions.
24. The "military department" of the Order was referred to as the "Uniform Rank." The current website notes that the Uniform Rank (UR) "came into being in 1878. A great many Pythians were Civil War Veterans and some lodges formed their own military drill teams. This would in time evolve into the Uniformed Ranks. The Pythian UR was sometimes known as the Army of the Lily." See "About Us," Knights of Pythias, http://kophistory.com/History/index.htm.

25. "About Us," Knights of Pythias.

26. Capers calls attention to Bequest's membership in the German Artillery. See "South Carolina," 454.

27. *News and Courier*, October 19, 1892. Frederick Wagener was a younger brother of John Andreas, the leader of the ethnic community's early *triumvirate* (J. A. Wagener, Heinrich Wieting, and Franz Melchers), which worked to integrate fellow German immigrants into the native community.

28. "Frederick W. Wagener's contribution to Charleston's economic development was profound and indisputable. Wagener arrived at the height of German immigration to Charleston. He began his business career as a retail grocer like so many other Germans. On returning to Charleston in 1865 after his service in the Confederate Army, he partnered with other Germans to form a wholesale grocery establishment that grew into a significant business in the community." See Jeffery Strickland, "Frederick Wagener, 1832–1921," *Immigrant Entrepreneurship: German-American Biographies 1720 to the Present*, 2015, http://www.immigrantentrepreneurship.org/entry.php?rec=24.

29. Charles J. Holden, "'Is Our Love for Wade Hampton Foolishness?': South Carolina and the Lost Cause," in *The Myth of the Lost Cause and Civil War History*, ed. Gary W. Gallagher and Alan T. Nolan (Indianapolis: Indiana University Press, 2000), 61.

30. *Ibid.*, 69.

31. Although publicly immersed in the increasingly widespread development of the Lost Cause, Bequest may have been privately "connected" to those issues through his daughter, Theresa Louise, who, in 1894, was employed as a housekeeper for Edward McCrady, the prominent Charleston County representative in the state legislature noted for having developed the "Eight Box Law" in 1882. A former Confederate lieutenant colonel, McCrady was a man "well-connected by family, church, politics, and the military with South Carolina's 'master class,'" who devoted more and more time to justifying 'the Lost Cause' in speeches and writings, condemning the selfishness and aggressiveness of the North on the eve of the Civil War and justifying the South's secession." See Fraser Jr., *Charleston! Charleston*, 314. We can only speculate as to what kind of employer McCrady was and wonder whether he shared his ideas with the young Miss Bequest, his domestic employee.

32. *Evening Post*, June 11, 1898.

33. Although published with an 1899 imprint, the content of Capers's Volume 5 of Clement Evans's *Confederate Military History* was already in circulation and could readily be referenced and relied on as authoritative.

34. The reporter embellishes the Capers account with a few adventures that are unverified in the Bequest record and misstates the date Bequest "came to Charleston" to start his wood yard business. As an English speaker, the reporter can be forgiven for misspelling the name of Heinrich Wieting's ship, the *Gauss*, as well as the name of the Captain himself. Those were details that belonged to the past that was being rewritten.

35. "... in the following order: Social Mounted Club, German Hussars, The Fusilier Band, Carolina Rifle Club, Charleston Riflemen, Washington Artillery, Sumter

Rifle Club, Palmetto Guard, Washington Light Infantry, Wagener Artillery, Irish Volunteer Rifle Club, Color Guard, National Zouaves, Irish Volunteers, German Fusiliers, Montgomery Guards, Guard of Honor, the chariot containing the eagle target. Then the various carriages: in the second carriage behind the eagle target rode Major Melchers, editor of the Zeitung, and Ex-Kings Melchers, Dunnemann and Bequest, of the Charleston Schutzen Club, and visiting Schutzen in citizens' dress.... The streets through which the pageant passed were thronged with spectators, who occupied windows, balconies and the sidewalks," *News and Courier,* April 21, 1874. The Germans would have been prominent participants in any of the annual parades.

36. See Lloyd A. Hunter, "The Immortal Confederacy: Another Look at Lost Cause Religion," in *The Myth of the Lost Cause and Civil War History,* ed. Gary W. Gallagher and Alan T. Nolan (Bloomington: Indiana University Press, 2000), 186.

37. In 1889, for example, the Fusiliers were called up to quell a "disturbance" in Mount Pleasant. See *Post and Courier,* August 24, 1889.

38. Andrea Mehrländer, *The Germans of Charleston, Richmond, and New Orleans during the Civil War Period* (New York: DeGruyter, 2011), 79.

39. Holden, "Is Our Love for Wade Hampton Foolishness?" 81.

40. Hunter explores the "religion" of the Lost Cause throughout "The Immortal Confederacy: Another Look at Lost Cause Religion."

WORKS CITED

Capers, Ellison. *South Carolina.* Vol 5 of *Confederate Military History: A Library of Confederate States History,* edited by Clement A. Evans. 12 vols. Atlanta: Confederate Publishing Co., 1899.

Clark, Thomas D. "The Furnishing and Supply System in Southern Agriculture since 1865." *The Journal of Southern History* 12, no. 1 (February 1946): 22–44.

Coker, P. C. *Charleston's Maritime Heritage 1670–1865: an Illustrated History.* Charleston: CokerCraft Press, 1987.

Encyclopedia of the Reconstruction Era. Vol 1: A–L, edited by Richard Zuczek. Westport, CT: Greenwood Press, 2006.

"An Eye Witness Account of the Occupation of Mt. Pleasant: February 1865." *The South Carolina Historical Magazine* 66, no. 1 (January 1965): 8–14.

Foner, Eric. "Redemption and After." In *A Short History of Reconstruction: 1863–1877,* edited by Eric Foner, 238–249. New York: Harper & Row, 1990.

Fraser, Walter J., Jr. *Charleston! Charleston! The History of a Southern City.* Columbia: University of South Carolina Press, 1991.

Friedrichs, Erika, and Klaus Friedrichs, eds. *Das Familienbuch des Kirchspiels Geestendorf (heute Bremerhaven-Geestemünde), 1689 bis 1874,* Bd. 1. Bremerhaven, Germany, 2003.

Holden, Charles J. "'Is Our Love for Wade Hampton Foolishness?': South Carolina and the Lost Cause." In *The Myth of the Lost Cause and Civil War History,* edited by Gary W. Gallagher and Alan T. Nolan, 60–88. Indianapolis: Indiana University Press, 2000.

Hunter, Lloyd A. "The Immortal Confederacy: Another Look at Lost Cause Religion." In *The Myth of the Lost Cause and Civil War History*, edited by Gary W. Gallagher and Alan T. Nolan.

McCandless, Amy, ed. *The Historic Landscape of Mount Pleasant: Proceedings of the First Forum on the History of Mount Pleasant*. Mt. Pleasant, SC, 1993. https://www.tompsc.com/DocumentCenter/View/569/MTP_First_Historic_Forum_1993?bidId=.

Mehrländer, Andrea. *The Germans of Charleston, Richmond, and New Orleans during the Civil War Period*. New York: DeGruyter, 2011.

Rogers, George C., Jr., and C. James Taylor. *A South Carolina Chronology 1497–1992*. 2nd ed. Columbia: University of South Carolina Press, 1994.

Strickland, Jeffery. "Frederick Wagener, 1832–1921." *Immigrant Entrepreneurship: German-American Biographies 1720 to the Present*, 2015. www.immigrant entrepreneurship.org.

———. "How the Germans Became White Southerners: German Immigrants and African Americans in Charleston, South Carolina, 1860–1880." *Journal of American Ethnic History* 28, no. 1 (2008): 52–69.

Intervening in Jim Crow

The Green Book *and Southern Hospitality*

Cherish Thomas and Meredith A. Love

In July 1956, Miss O. J. Ragland of Oxford, North Carolina, was planning a visit to Florence, South Carolina, and wrote the following letter to the Florence Chamber of Commerce [misspellings were in the original text]:

> Dear Sir:
> I plann to be in Flornce during the week of July 30, 1956. I would like to know if there are any "first-class" Hotels for Negroes, and also the rates of the hotel or motel.
>   Looking to hear from you soon concerning this matter.
> Yours truly,
> (Miss) O. J. Ragland"

In response to her letter, Ragland received the following reply:

> Dear Miss Ragland:
> According to our city directory there are only two hotels for Negroes in Florence:
>   Alphonso's Hotel, 257 N. Dargan Street
>   Lincoln Hotel, 130 S. Church Street
> You will have to write the manager of the two hotels concerning rates. This is in response to your July 19 inquiry.
> Very truly,
> (Miss) Beverly Brown
> Office Assistant"[1]

The plight of identifying, investigating, and locating acceptable accommodations in 1950s America was not unique to Black women such as O. J. Ragland. Although writing ahead to destinations was one way to make plans, it was nearly impossible for Black travelers to take a road trip with any kind of spontaneity, as they could not leave it up to chance that they would find safe overnight accommodations and the comforts of hospitality when traversing the Jim Crow–era landscape. Although the respondent, Beverly Brown, refers to the city directory in Florence, South Carolina, to answer Ragland's query, we know that there were other resources available at that time; specifically, travel guides, designed for the very purpose of aiding Black Americans facing discrimination on the road. In this article, we focus on one such guide—*The Negro Motorists Green Book* (*Green Book*) published by US postal worker Victor Green from 1936 to 1966. To begin, we explicate the struggles that Black travelers faced during this period and then focus our discussion on the *Green Book* sites in Florence, South Carolina. In doing so, we demonstrate that the *Green Book* was a rhetorical force, a text that rejected and resisted racist practices and attitudes and instead helped to foster a culture of hospitality.

In a brochure published some time around 1956, the South Carolina State Development Board "invites you to spend your vacation leisurely and pleasurably in her state of gay and friendly people . . . in South Carolina you will find the finest in hotels, tourist courts, and tourist homes. Many ultramodern hotels have been built in recent years, and of course there are still the older hotels which have acquired reputations for fine hospitality and real Southern cooking."[2] Although "fine hospitality" was promised, the reality was that this hospitality, this "Southern hospitality" was limited; when considered in terms of "true" or "unconditional" hospitality, it is, as American Studies scholar Andrew Szczesiul terms it, a "mythic hospitality." Szczesiul explains that Southern hospitality is a fiction, "an essential, foundational narrative within the larger national project of southern exceptionalism—the persistent belief that the South is a distinct, unique, and separate culture with the larger United States."[3] Furthermore, it cannot be defined as "true" hospitality, because this welcome is not extended unconditionally. And although it can be argued that unconditional hospitality is near impossible to achieve, the conditions that limited Southern hospitality were real and problematic. In the Jim Crow South, in particular, white-owned businesses welcoming only other whites constituted a version of hospitality that was exclusionary; thus, it failed to be hospitable at all.[4] Black travelers, as we will show, were often treated with hostility, and "were unwelcome strangers and aliens to this invented image of the South as a hospitable tourist destination."[5]

Victor Green published the *Green Book* from 1936 to 1966 in an effort to, quite literally, extend the reach of hospitality nationwide so that Black travelers were included. Green's travel guide listed, state by state and city by city, a variety of establishments—boarding houses, restaurants, gas stations, and hotels—that were hospitable to Black clients and often owned by Black businesspeople. The guide cost twenty-five cents in its first year of publication and was sold in locations such as Esso gas stations, a major company that hired Black executives and employed Black franchisees.[6] What began as a sixteen-page pamphlet eventually grew into a 128-page book, and although there were other travel guides published specifically for Black travelers during this period, the *Green Book* was in print the longest.[7] In the 1956 edition—the same year when Miss Ragland was inquiring about accommodations in Florence—Green states, "The White traveler has no difficulty in getting accommodations, but with the Negro traveler it has been different. He, before the advent of a Negro travel guide, had to depend on word of mouth, and many times accommodations were not available."[8] But perhaps a more bluntly worded phrasing of Green's statement would be, "and many times accommodations were not available to the Black traveler." For the white traveler, of course, there would have been no need to write to the Florence Chamber of Commerce and inquire about lodging; white accommodations were the default and always available. Only a year before Ragland's inquiry, there existed thirty-nine boarding accommodations for whites in Florence as compared with eight boarding accommodations for Blacks. This included boarding houses, furnished rooms, hotels, motels, and tourist homes and courts.[9] Furthermore, this same disproportionate ratio of white-to-Black accommodations is also found a year later in the 1957 Florence Business Directory.[10]

It seems fitting to have Florence as the focus for an article about hospitality, for the area is now home to over five thousand hotel rooms and is often colloquially referred to by residents as a "hospitality hub." Florence's relationship with the hospitality industry began in 1852 with the arrival of the railroad. As Florence grew in both population and influence, it adopted the titles of "magic city" and "Gate City to the South," which contributed to its "rapid development" and "unprecedented prosperity."[11] According to the website for the City of Florence, "by the 1870's Florence had a population of about 700 but, due to ever-expanding railroad activity, an emerging middle class more than doubled the town's population by the end of the decade." The town was chartered in 1871, and in 1888, the new county of Florence was created from portions of Darlington, Marion and Williamsburg counties.[12]

Nationally, the golden age of the railroad began to decline during the mid-20th century, but transportation still played a vital role in the continued growth and development of Florence. Instead of rail, priority shifted toward the development of roads. Conveniently located midway between New York and Miami, as well as between Washington, DC, and Jacksonville, Florida,

Florence became a popular stopover for tourists along Highway 301. Additionally, the arrival of two major interstates, I-95 in 1969 and I-20 in 1975, further bolstered Florence's economy and lent way to the development of a "hospitality district" at the junction of these two interstates.

Within a city that has historically placed such an emphasis on tourism (and by extension, hospitality), little consideration was given to the Black traveler, as evidenced by the terse response given to Miss Ragland's inquiry by Miss Brown at the Chamber of Commerce, and the incommensurate lodgings noted in the city directory. Unlike the mainstream hospitality industry of the Jim Crow era, the *Green Book* presented the opportunity for lived experiences of real, alternative hospitality for Black patrons, both those traveling through and those living in the Florence community. Rather than simply accepting poor treatment and fear, businesses that were listed in the *Green Book*, and the publishers themselves, were pushing back against a racist system that was inhospitable and treacherous. Although it is common to think about a text such as a travel guide as neutral or apolitical, the *Green Book* was a form of resistance, as much a part of the fight for civil rights as other texts published during this time.

The story of the *Green Book* begins with the story of the American auto industry. With the assembly line and the mass production of cars in 1913 came a boom in car ownership that changed travel in the United States. By 1967, there were nearly eighty million cars on the road. In terms of Black car owners, Gretchen Sorin, author of *Driving While Black: African American Travel and the Road to Civil Rights*, notes, "By the 1940s and 1950s, all of the studies indicated a significant increase in the number of Black American households with a car parked out front or in the driveway. One study estimated that 475,000 Black families owned at least one car, with half of these purchased new."[13] Not surprisingly, as cars became more affordable and more common, and more roads were built, there was also a proliferation in travel-related industries—gas stations, hotels, and restaurants popped up all along these new interstates as families went on vacation. The South, in particular, attempted to draw visitors looking for Southern hospitality and a taste of history, inviting them to a South that kept its Black citizens in the role of helper or servant in hotels and restaurants. Black customers in restaurants or guests in hotels did not fit within the "good ole' Southern hospitality" narrative; therefore, they were not welcome. Although Black families owned automobiles and traveled on the same roads as their white counterparts, the businesses that constituted the hospitality industry were overwhelmingly not welcoming of the Black tourist. Even whites who were sympathetic to the plight of Blacks were often not welcome in establishments for their own race. G. L. Ivey, a tavern owner in Florence and president of the local chapter of the National Association for the Advancement of White People (NAAWP), a political organization dedicated to maintaining segregation, made this message abundantly clear by hanging a sign overhead the dining room that read, "If You Are A Negro Sympathizer, Get Lost Fast!"[14] Black travelers "were unwelcome strangers and aliens to this invented image of the South as a hospitable tourist destination."[15] Another example may be found in a speech (titled "The Human Factor") given by James A. Rogers at a gathering of approximately seventy Florence community leaders at Litchfield Beach, South Carolina, in November of 1963. Rogers, the editor of the *Florence Morning News*, called for an open discussion of race issues and told the group a story about three Black visitors who were on a business trip to Florence: "They were here on a business trip to consider another investment which would be very beneficial to the city. While conferring on this business matter in the lobby of a local hotel, their presence was noted. Soon the rumor was widespread that the hotel where they had been seen had been integrated, and nasty anonymous telephone calls were reaching the hotel operator. Whether these men applied for rooms in any local hotel or motel, I am not certain, but they spent the night at the home of a local Negro."[16]

In addition to the observable hostilities, Isabel Wilkerson, in her book *The Warmth of Other Suns*, notes that there was also an "invisible hand" that was at work from state to state and town to town. For example, in Calhoun City, Mississippi, there were "colored" and "white" parking spaces, yet they were unmarked—"it was just the work of the invisible hand."[17] At intersections, Black motorists were expected to let white motorists go first and were not permitted to pass even the slowest of cars if they were driven by white motorists.[18] This invisible hand applied to pedestrians and even children, as well. For instance, in Florence in 1950, a white man named Ellis Snelling flogged a young Black girl named Mary Joe Washington, believing her to be the same girl who allegedly bumped into his daughter on the way to school.[19] Historian Leon Litwack notes, "The 'unwritten law' in the rural South dictated that a white resident must be able to vouch for the character of all Negroes unknown to the mass of the community. That meant that a Black stranger could be stopped anywhere at any time and forced to state his business to the satisfaction of the white questioner; if the stranger provided the wrong answer or replied in a manner less than deferential, he or she was likely to be arrested or forcibly removed."[20] Apparently, this may have been the case for one man in Florence in 1954. T. H. Miller, vice president of the

Columbia

★MOTEL SIMBETH..............................U. S. No. 1, 8 miles north of city
"Rest for the Weary on this Side of the Jordan"
Quiet, Beautiful—Ideal for Honeymooners, Rt. 3, Box 988 Tel. 4-9189

Y.W.C.A. ....1429 Park St.
Nylon Hotel ....918 Senate St.
Mrs. Irene B. Evans Tourist Home ....1106 Pine St.
College Inn Tourist Home ....1609 Harden St.
Mrs. S. H. Smith Tourist Home ....929 Pine St.
Mrs. H. Cornwell Tourist Home ....1713 Wayne
Mrs. W. D. Chappelle Tourist Home ....1301 Pine St.
Beachum Tourist Home ....2212 Gervais St.
Mrs. J. P. Wakefield Tourist Home...................816 Oak St.
Green Leaf Restaurant......................................1117 Wash. St.
Savoy Restaurant ....Old Winnsboro St.
Cozy Inn Restaurant ....1509 Harden St.
Mom's Restaurant...1005 Washington St.
Waverly Restaurant..2515 Gervais St.

Darlington

Mable's Motel ....U. S. 52

Florence

★EBONY GUEST HOUSE ....712 North Wilson St.

Richmond Tourist Home ....108 S. Griffin St.
John McDonald Tourist Home ....501 S. Irby St.
Mrs. B. Wright Tourist Home ....1004 E. Cheeve St.
Ace's Grill ....1109 E. Chenes St.
Wright's Restaurant..802 Chenes St.

Georgetown

Mrs. R. Anderson Tourist Home ....424 Broad
Mrs. D. Atkinson Tourist Home ....811 Duke
Jas. Becote Tourist Home ....118 Orange
Mrs. A. A. Smith Tourist Home ....317 Emanuel

Greenville

Dr. Gibbs Tourist Home ....914 Anderson Rd.
Miss M. J. Grimes Tourist Home ....210 Mean St.
Fowlers Restaurant ....16 Spring St.

Mullins

E. Calhoun's Tourist Homes...........................535 N. Smith St.

Myrtle Beach

Fitzgerald's Motel ....Carver St.

Orangeburg, S. C.

★JOHNSON'S TOURIST HOME...............Calhoun Drive (U.S. 301)

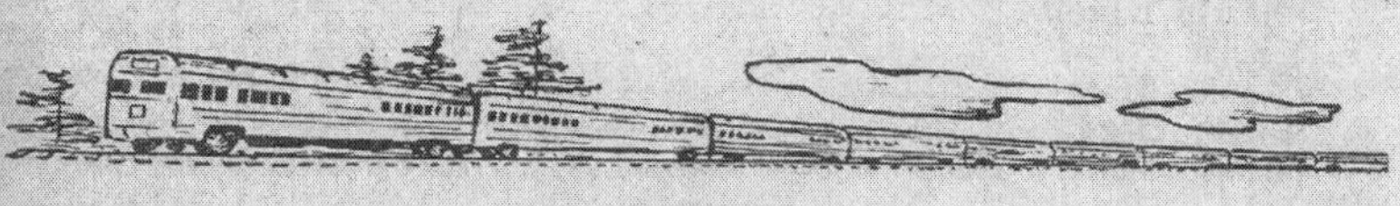

Figure 6. Detail from *The Negro Travelers' Green Book*, 1957.

local chapter of the NAAWP, allegedly antagonized a young Black cyclist by following him down the road and then started a fight with him over his riding of the bicycle.[21]

Sundown towns—"all-white communities inside and outside the South that barred minorities after dark"—were also of grave concern and were avoided by Black travelers.[22] Mark Foster recounts the experiences of Black travelers in his article "In the Face of 'Jim Crow': Prosperous Blacks and Vacations, Travel and Outdoor Leisure." One tourist noted that "as the afternoon wears on, it casts a shadow of apprehension on our hearts and sours us a little." The spontaneous detours and off-the-beaten-path excursions enjoyed by so many tourists were denied Black travelers, who were understandably worried about reaching safe overnight accommodations before nightfall.[23]

In *Lemon Swamp and Other Places: A Carolina Memoir*, Karen Fields describes her family's trips from Washington, DC, to Charleston in the 1920s as "voyages to another country where Black people were relegated to separate (although not always equal) spaces."[24] The car, she notes, had to be "self-sufficient," packed with food, lemonade, and even water for the radiator, if needed.[25] Fields writes:

> Our parents made our "capsule" self-sufficient because we would make no pause for refreshment, not from the time we passed the whites-only Marriott Hotel, just across the Potomac, to the time we at last turned off U.S. 1 toward Charleston. . . . my father planned ahead where to stop for gas. . . .We could not break up the 550-mile trip in some scenic places to sleep in a roadside motel. . . .We carried detailed maps for the same reason that we carried so much food and drink: a determination to avoid insult, or worse. I remember the anxiety of my parents when we had to stop once, in the middle of a Southern nowhere, to change a flat tire.[26]

In recounting traveling with his family in North Carolina, George Kenneth Butterfield Jr. testified to the agility required of Black travelers. As a family who traveled often, they knew how to find overnight accommodations in Southern towns where there were no hotels. On entering a town, they would "find a black community, and we would find the local boarding house and that's where we would stay."[27] He continues:

> When you live in the South and have been in the South all your life, you could find [places to eat and sleep] instinctively. . . . Southern towns are laid out in the same fashion, basically, and you could use your senses

and sense where you are and where you're not. And if you keep driving, you can see the quality of the housing decreasing and blight setting in— abandoned cars and people hanging on the streets and then you can begin to see blacks. You know you are getting closer to the black community, and you can just go right in and find it. You may have to stop and ask someone: "Where's the boarding house?" And you may be a block or two from it. It wasn't hard to find. You can find it instinctively.[28]

Despite these dangers and hassles, Black people in America wanted and needed to travel—to see the country, visit family, or travel for work. For some, public transportation was often the only option available; however, its use came with its own challenges. For instance, in February 1945, four Black women aboard a train en route to Florence were arrested after a dispute over seating arrangements within the coach.[29] Even famous Black Americans such as renowned writer W. E. B. Du Bois; Clarence Mitchell, director of the Washington bureau of the National Association for the Advancement of Colored People (NAACP); and pop singer Jackie Wilson were not exempt from unequal treatment when traveling. In 1929, Sarah "Sadie" Harrison, the Secretary of the New London, Connecticut, chapter of the Negro Urban League received a letter from Du Bois asking for a recommendation for a "colored boarding house" for an upcoming trip.[30] In 1956, Clarence Mitchell and Reverend Horace Sharper were both arrested, also at the train station in Florence, for entering the "whites-only" waiting room, despite the fact that no segregation signs were posted (yet another example of the "invisible hand" of racism at work) and despite the 1955 ban on segregation imposed on interstate buses, train lines, and their waiting rooms by the Interstate Commerce Commission.[31] In 1967, Jackie Wilson, bandmate Jimmy Lee Smith, and two white women, Brenda Louise Britt and Janet Linda Fay Barfield, were all arrested in their motel rooms in Columbia, South Carolina, and charged with immoral conduct, each for entertaining the companies of the other (Britt and Barfield were additionally charged with disorderly conduct).[32]

Of course, these types of incidents were common across the American South and in other regions of the country as well. Sorin notes that the privacy of travel by car was often preferred, as it was not subject to the rules imposed on travelers on rail and bus; it was, for many Black travelers, a way to resist restrictions and reclaim agency.[33] Additionally, there was a patriotic dimension to car travel, as "seeing America" was perceived as a means of participating in the "American experience." Geographers Derek Alderman and Joshua Inwood point out that, "The right to move across space on one's own terms and to resist efforts to constrain one's mobility has long been part of the African-American struggle for equality and justice—from escaping slavery to the post-emancipation Great Migration out of the South, from the freedom rides of the Civil Rights Movement to more recent transportation justice campaigns."[34]

Although mistreatment of Black travelers was common, it should not be understood as "normal" or in any way normalized. As Sorin notes, "The emotional and psychological effects of continual racist encounters—day in and day out, on buses, trains, and other public conveyances—exerted an emotional toll that was both exhausting and long lasting."[35] Furthermore, we argue that printed texts had the potential to be traumatizing as well. Signage such as "Whites Only," the labeling of individuals or groups as "Negro" or "Colored" that pervaded newspaper articles, city directories, and, of course, the official written laws that denied rights on the basis of skin color, all reinforced exclusionary racist practices and perpetuated a sense of otherness. Seen in these terms, interventions into this system were necessary to improve the well-being of Black citizens in our country; therefore, it is important that we see the *Green Book* as more than a quaint historical curiosity. Rather, the *Green Book* allowed travelers to "mock Jim Crow."[36] For *Green Book* businesses, the deliberate act of advertising in the *Green Book* was a political move, an attempt to alter the course and pave a safe road for Black travelers, despite attempts to intimidate and incite fear.

Before Green's publication of the *Green Book*, Sadie Harrison and Edwin Henry Hackley published one of the very first guides for the Black traveler, *Hackley & Harrison's Hotel and Apartment Guide for Colored Travelers* (published in 1930 and 1931). In its first issue, the guide included listings in three hundred cities, twenty-six of which were located in six South Carolina counties[37] Another such guide was *A Directory of Negro Hotels and Guest Houses*, published by the US Department of the Interior National Park Service in 1939, itself noteworthy because it stands as evidence that the government was aware of the limitations to and dangers of travel. The Travel Bureau wanted to "develop the nation's physical, economic, and social welfare by encouraging more Americans to travel in their own county," and included three sites in South Carolina.[38] Musician Billy Butler published another guide, *Travelguide*, from 1947 to 1957, pointing travelers to sites identified through his network of traveling musicians. Other such publications include *Grayson's Travel and Business Guide*, *The Go Guide to Pleasant Motoring*, and *Smith's Tourist Guide*.[39]

As for the *Green Book*, in the 1948 edition, Green commented on several inspirations for publishing his travel guide:

> With the introduction of this travel guide in 1936, it has been our idea to give the Negro traveler information that will keep him from running into difficulties, embarrassments and to make his trips more enjoyable. The Jewish press has long published information about places that are restricted [non-Kosher vs. Kosher establishments] and there are numerous publications that give the gentile whites all kinds of information. But during these long years of discrimination, before 1936 other guides have been published for the Negro, some are still published, but the majority have gone out of business for various reasons.[40]

It is important to note that not every Black-owned business located within a particular city and state was included within the *Green Book*.[41] Early on in its publication, Green writes that "Advertisers have been selected with care and are always the best representative and responsible in their field."[42] To help accomplish this, Green enlisted the help of fellow postal workers as well as *Green Book* readers. By the 1941 edition, however, Green included a disclaimer on page four: "We have given you a selection of listings that you might choose from, under no circumstances do these listings imply that the place is recommended."[43] Perhaps the guide was growing too fast to guarantee, with individual visits and firsthand knowledge, the quality of individual establishments. Regardless, Green also made a point to encourage readers to openly communicate any dissatisfactions or complaints against *Green Book* businesses, as well as errors within the guide.

The first edition of the *Green Book* to include listings outside of Green's home state of New York was published in 1938 and included twenty-four entries across South Carolina in Aiken, Charleston, Columbia, Florence, Georgetown, and Spartanburg. The following year, travelers found sixty South Carolina listings in the *Green Book*. Anderson, Darlington, Greenville, "Mullens," and Sumter were included, as were listings for barbers, drug stores, and other businesses. Businesses in South Carolina routinely appeared in the *Green Book* over the nearly thirty annual editions. Columbia, as the centrally located capital, routinely had several listings, whereas towns such as Anderson, Myrtle Beach, and Darlington, for example, were represented with fewer businesses; some, however, are still serving customers today.[44]

Figure 7. The private residence that was previously the Ebony Guest House. Photograph by Cherish Thomas.

One such extant building listed in the *Green Book* was a tourist home by the name of the Ebony Guest House in Florence. Built in the 1920s and located at 712 North Wilson Street, the Ebony Guest House first opened its doors to Black travelers on May 30, 1949.[45] Geraldine Barkley, granddaughter of Mary Holmes, who was the owner and operator of the Ebony Guest House, fondly remembers her childhood years growing up with her grandparents and living next door to the guest house: "She [Mary Holmes] always had a business mind ... she always had some little kinda business going on, you know, she used to do cooking and sell sandwiches to the people who worked on the railroad ... she always had something going on ... She seen the need for it [the guest house] ... because Black people, when they came to town, they couldn't stay in the hotel."[46]

For roughly twenty-five years, Black travelers from all over the nation came to the Ebony Guest House for its hospitality, modern conveniences, and ideal location. Moreover, because of its close proximity to the American Legion Stadium (now Dr. Iola Jones Park, located at the corner of Oakland Avenue and East Maxwell Street), various celebrities stayed at the Ebony

Guest House when performing at the stadium or as a resting stop while on tour. Such celebrities included Jackie Wilson, Sam Cooke, Mahalia Jackson, Buddy Johnson, Ike and Tina Turner, Ray Charles, Fats Domino, The Shirelles, Amos and Andy, The Marvelettes, Shirley Caesar, Ruth Brown, Sister Rosetta Tharpe, and Shirley and Lee, among others.[47]

As children, Barkley and her siblings often helped their grandmother perform various chores at the guesthouse. When asked of her experiences with the celebrities who stayed there, she explained: "We used to take them their meals and sheets to put on the bed. . . . I liked Fats Domino because he was funny, but the majority of them [the celebrities] I liked . . . they stayed right here at the Ebony Guest House. . . . I remember one time my grandmother gave me a whipping because I was on the side of the guest house and peeping through the window, and I think it was . . . Shirley and Lee . . . when I peeped in the window—I guess they were making love to each other— and they looked up and seen me and they told my grandmother that one of the grandkids was peeping in the window and my grandmother wanted to know which one . . . when they described the one that had the pigtails in her hair . . . then my grandmother knew it was me!"[48]

Another site of hospitality for Black travelers in Florence was the Richmond Tourist Home (Richmond Rest). It appeared in the *Green Book* in 1953, but the popular tourist home, located at 108 South Griffin Street and owned by Lillie Richmond, had been in operation since at least 1948.[49] In their book, *Notable Blacks of the Pee Dee Section of South Carolina*, Daniel Lane and Roy Cunningham wrote this of Richmond Rest: "Richmond's Rest was a home away from home for many black railroad men. At this Griffin Street home, Mrs. Richmond was like a mother to many community persons and to the railroad men who stayed overnight or longer. These railroad workers always felt that they were coming home. Her meals were tasty, well balanced, and served in a wholesome environment. Her rates were kept in balance with those of the times."[50] Aside from housing railroad workers, Richmond also played host to several minor league baseball players in the 1950s, all of whom were en route to Myrtle Beach where they were to train at the farm of the Boston Braves. These players included Roy White (pitcher, Eau Claire Bears), Pablo Bernard (second baseman and shortstop, Denver Bears), and Fernando Alberto Osorio (pitcher, Ventura Braves).[51]

Because the majority of intrastate newspapers of the time catered to a white audience, Richmond found it necessary to outsource advertisements of her business, often cleverly woven into local society columns in out-of-state newspapers such as Baltimore's *Afro-American* and Norfolk's *New*

Journal and Guide; the latter employed her son, E. P. Broome, as a correspondent. When new guests arrived, Richmond informed her son, who would then submit the news for publishing. This news often read simply, "Henry Davis who resides at . . . Boston, Mass., stopped over at Richmond Rest, 108 S. Griffin St. last Wednesday evening."[52] Yet it was, nevertheless, an effective means of advertising and a contributing factor to the long-term success of Richmond Rest.

Before opening her tourist home, Richmond was the proprietor of Richmond Café, located at 323 East Evans St., which she successfully managed for approximately twelve years.[53] On Richmond's death in July 1966, her obituary read that she was, "a member of Trinity Baptist Church . . . a voting citizen . . . and always participated in any project for the good of the community."[54]

Little is known about the tourist home of John and Alcess McDonald, once located at 501 South Irby Street (the current site of South Carolina Federal Credit Union). By trade, John was a blacksmith, and Alcess was a dressmaker and insurance agent. Alcess likely inherited the property and the house that became the tourist home from her parents, and she began offering "furnished rooms" during the 1930s. After Alcess died of cancer in 1942, John continued in his regular line of work as a blacksmith for several years. From 1942 to 1946, it is unclear whether the tourist home was operational, but by 1947, the name and address of John McDonald had been added to the list of Florence tourist homes included in the *Green Book*. In 1952, the McDonald Tourist Home was emphasized by an advertisement in the *Green Book*. However, by 1960, McDonald Tourist Home was no longer listed in the *Green Book*, and a year later in 1961, John McDonald died.

Sadly, much is left to the imagination as to the sort of lives lived by both the McDonalds and the various lodgers of the McDonald Tourist Home. The names of Nickolas Briscoe, Creasie Sanders, Beulah Robinson, Randolph Howe, James Carter, Daniel Scott, Sam and Virginia Harrison Jr., and Carl and Amie Bonapart are all on record as residing at the McDonald Tourist Home at various times between 1930 and 1950, but our knowledge of their stories largely ends there.[55] One is left curious to know more about the people who passed through the halls of the tourist home. Where did they come from? Where were they heading? What became of them once they left? The documentation of the lodgers' names signifies their tangible yet transient existence in a place that has been all but forgotten in memory and a landscape during a time that is all too painfully recalled today.

Even less is known about the two matriarchs of *Green Book* tourist homes in Florence—C. E. Godbold (Catharine Godbold; listed as C. C. Godbold in the *Green Book*) and Bertha Wright. Godbold's tourist home (227 East Marion Street) and Wright's tourist home (1004 East Cheves Street) were the first Florence businesses to be featured in the *Green Book*, appearing alongside each other in the 1938 edition as the only two tourist homes for Black travelers in Florence. Both businesses first appeared in Hackley and Harrison's guide, paving the way for future businesses of Black hospitality.[56] Godbold's tourist home was advertised in the *Green Book* until 1940, and Wright's tourist home was featured until 1960.[57]

Although the stories of many of these listings remain a mystery, the inclusion of these listings testifies to the long-standing entrepreneurship and ingenuity of women proprietors such as Mary Holmes, Lillie Richmond, Alcess McDonald, and others. During an era in which few economic opportunities were available to women—let alone Black women—the women of the *Green Book* were ambitious and challenged the societal norms for women of their time. For boarding house proprietors in particular, the act of opening up one's own home was a resourceful measure that provided *Green Book* businesswomen and their families with a source of income, a necessity for single or widowed *Green Book* businesswomen, as many Florence proprietors were. Aside from running operations at the Ebony Guest House, Holmes was also responsible for the care of twenty-two children (her own, plus her grandchildren and several nieces and nephews). Lillie Richmond and Bertha Wright both operated eating establishments for several years in conjunction with managing their tourist homes. And although she did not live to meet all of whom walked through the doors of her tourist home, Alcess McDonald left the legacy of a safe haven in the care of her husband, John, which he dutifully stewarded for seventeen years after her death. Candacy Taylor, author of *Overground Railroad: The Green Book and the Roots of Black Travel in America*, points out that, over the course of its publication, almost nine hundred beauty shops were listed in the *Green Book*, which were often owned by women who were "pillars of the community"; moreover, some of these businesses "served as headquarters for community development, especially during the birth of the civil rights movement."[58] Furthermore, had Alma Green, wife of Victor Green, and her all-female staff not taken over publishing of the *Green Book* after Green's death in 1960, the popular and influential travel guide may not be as widely remembered as it is today. Likewise, without the influence of Black women—more specifically, Black

South Carolinian women and Black Florentine women—the representation of Black businesses in the *Green Book* for both South Carolina and Florence would have been severely lacking.

In addition to helping the traveler, the *Green Book* sites were often places of gathering for locals in the community, for Black citizens were often not permitted to enjoy meals or company with their fellow white counterparts. Rather than being the recipients of Southern hospitality, they were often relegated to back rooms, balconies, and spaces that were separate but, of course, not on par with the facilities reserved for "whites only." In 1963, for example, in the city of Greenville, South Carolina, it was against city code for white and Black customers to eat in the same room. There was also a stipulation that there should be "[s]eparate eating utensils and separate dishes for the serving of food, all of which shall be distinctly marked by some appropriate color scheme."[59] These utensils and dishes were also cleaned in a separate area of the kitchen. It was this sort of ill and unequal treatment of Black customers that sparked a movement of civil disobedience across the South in the 1960s. In Florence, in March of 1960, junior high and high school students, and members of the local youth chapter of the NAACP held a sit-in at the S. H. Kress & Co. Department Store lunch counter to protest the similarly unfair treatment of Black customers. Police were summoned on the second day of the protest, and forty-eight people (many of whom were minors) were arrested on charges of parading without a permit. The Kress lunch counter closed after the protest but later reopened in the 1970s and eventually began serving Black customers.[60] Additional protests took place in Nashville, Tennessee; Greensboro, North Carolina; and Rock Hill, South Carolina, among others.

Until the fullness of integration was secured, Blacks needed their own spaces within their own communities, and *Green Book* businesses were often the businesses that served this purpose. Moreover, depending on the type of establishment (restaurants, barbershops, beauty parlors, and drugstores) as well as the location, it is likely that certain businesses were frequented more so by locals rather than by travelers. Such businesses provided a kind of neighborly hospitality that helped to support community and served as "black counter-public spaces," which recognize a rich history of African Americans claiming place of racial segregation as their own and transforming them into locations where Black identities, cultural traditions, and political debate could flourish separate from and in opposition to the white-dominated public sphere."[61]

The College Inn (listed from late 1940s through the 1960s editions) in Cheraw (about fifty miles north of Florence) is, in fact, one such business. When it opened, it was next door to the Coulter Academy, a school for Black students. David Sides, the director of Tourism and Community Development for Cheraw, notes that "during the days of Coulter Academy, this establishment was the only place in town where Blacks were welcomed to sit and enjoy a hamburger and a shake."[62] Down in Florence, Ace's Grill was another such place. Ace's opened in Florence on the corner of East Cheves and Kemp Street around 1948 and appeared in the *Green Book* the following year as the first Florence restaurant to be featured. Co-owned by George and Luretha Dennison and Walter and Juanita Alston, Ace's was arguably the most popular *Green Book* site for Florence locals and was well known throughout town for its Southern American staples such as fresh pit-cooked barbeque, fried chicken, and "He-man" hamburgers. The dance floor, jukebox, pool tables, and pinball machine at Ace's were all added bonuses. Even renowned journalist and civil rights activist John H. McCray made mention of Ace's Grill in his 1957 article "Roving About Car'lina."[63]

Throughout its history, Ace's became a hub for many civic and community groups. In 1950, three Florida-based representatives of the International Association of Railway Employees came to Florence for the purpose of unionizing train porters and locomotive firemen of the Atlantic Coast Line Railroad. The Florence meeting was held at Ace's Grill as part of a larger campaign to organize Black railway workers across the southeastern United States.[64] In the 1970s, Ace's became the regular meeting spot for the alumni of Wilson High School, the Spaulding Heights Community Association, and American Legion Post #228.[65] After roughly forty-five years of business and many changes in management, Ace's Grill closed its doors in the mid-1990s, likely in part because of the expansive development of McLeod Regional Medical Center in east Florence. In 1996, the Alston family sold the property to McLeod, and in 2011, McLeod sold it to PDN Properties, LLC. Pee Dee Nephrology (1100 East Cheves Street) is now situated on the lot where Ace's Grill once stood.[66]

First appearing in the *Green Book* in 1963, Spring Valley Motel and Restaurant was a ten-room establishment located on US Highway 301 North (now 4001 East Palmetto Street) where the Florence Flea Market now stands. The motel was originally owned and operated by James Miller and his wife, Marian, but after James's death, the motel restaurant was taken over by another *Green Book* business owner, Paul Wright.[67] According to Reverend William

Thompson, owner of Thompson's Barber Shop in Florence, Paul Wright owned and operated the 400 Club on North Dargan Street (listed simply as "Wright's" in the *Green Book*) for several years in the 1950s and early 1960s before moving his business out to the Spring Valley Motel & Restaurant.[68] In *Notable Blacks of the Pee Dee*, Lane states, "city and county residents looked forward to going to the 400 Club on Saturday. 'Doc' Wright always created an atmosphere equaled to no other establishment. First, in the 200-block of North Dargan Street, he operated an 'elegant' supper club and speakeasy. He later moved his business to the out-skirts of town to the Spring Valley Motel." Once established at the Spring Valley Motel & Restaurant, "[Wright] continued the tradition of serving fine foods to small and large groups in his restaurant. Once, he bragged of serving five busloads of people."[69]

Mable's Chicken Shack, also known as Mable's Motel in Darlington (about ten miles northwest of Florence) is another example of a tourist pit stop and a local hot spot. Business began during the early 1940s, when Mable Robinson erected what her adopted brother Hubert Boatwright referred to as "a one room hot dog stand during tobacco season" on the lot that is now Blackmon Memorials, located at 1717 South Main Street in Darlington. According to Boatwright, Mable's was the only place around where you could get a decent hot dog or hamburger at the time. Later, when Mable expanded the business and began adding more seating, she also began offering fried chicken and gave the restaurant the name, "Mable's Chicken Shack."[70]

Through the years, Mable's attracted local youths from both Darlington and Florence. Roosevelt Scott, a Darlington brick mason who described himself as "growing up" at Mable's, said that Mable was famous for her chicken sandwiches and fries and described Mable as being strict with the kids. Along with food and soft beverages, Mable's served alcohol, but, despite their best efforts, Mable made sure that none of the kids were ever served any beer if they were underage, according to Scott. Once the restaurant was established, Mable began adding rooms behind the building. Finally, there were between twenty and thirty rooms, enough to warrant the name Mable's Motel, as it is listed in the *Green Book*. The motel was first listed in the 1956 edition and was one of only two Darlington listings ever to be included in the guide.[71]

Another site that embodies both the notion of neighborly hospitality and traveler hospitality was located in Columbia—the Motel Simbeth (listed from 1956 to 1961). The Motel Simbeth provided "Rest for the Weary on this side of the Jordan"[72] and was co-owned by civil rights activist Modjeska Monteith Simkins, who taught history and civics at Benedict College in Columbia and advocated for better salaries and transportation for teachers,

among other pursuits.[73] *Historic Columbia* notes that, "despite the intermit-
tent violence and covert visits by civil rights figures with proverbial targets
on their backs (Martin Luther King, Jr. once visited during the 1950s), the
motel was also an oasis. Its only known depiction, which appeared in postcard form and in advertisements, shows a main structure set amongst pines
and surrounded by cabins, with signage designating it as a space for Black
guests."[74]

The Civil Rights Act in 1964 outlawed segregation on a national scale;
however, by this time, the market for the *Green Book* was already in decline.
The number of listings featured in each edition began to drop in 1956, which
was likely due to a number of factors, including post–World War II industrialization, increased costs associated with retail merchants' associations, the
Great Migration, and fallout over the continued struggle over civil rights
in the United States.[75] Green himself once prophesied that, "there will
be a day sometime in the near future when this guide will not have to be
published. That is when we as a race will have equal opportunities and
privileges in the United States."[76] With selfless regard for his life's work,
Green went on to say with hopeful longing that, "it will be a great day for
us to suspend this publication for then we can go wherever we please, and
without embarrassment."[77] Sadly, having died in 1960, Green did not live to
see his longing fulfilled. Perhaps sensing a shift in society's attitudes toward
integration, the word "Negro" was omitted from the title of the 1960 edition
of the *Green Book*. In 1966, the final *Green Book* was published, bearing the
name *Travelers' Green Book: International Edition*.

After 1964, as Black people were beginning to be welcomed into new
places and spaces that were once withheld from their patronage, a question
quietly arose: What was to become of the hundreds of small businesses that
were promoted and nourished by the *Green Book*? Some, such as the Ebony
Guest House, Ace's Grill, the Spring Valley Motel & Restaurant, The College Inn, and Mable's Motel, outlasted the double-edged sword of integration
and remained open. But what of those that didn't? Arthur Lawrence, a Black
Charlestonian who lived through decades of the Jim Crow and civil rights
eras, boldly stated in a 2019 interview with the Historic Charleston Foundation that "integration was a bad thing for the Black community . . . in the time
I was growing up, we had everything we needed. You had Black businesses.
You had the stores. You had the restaurants, filling stations, taxicabs, lawyers,
doctors, everything. But when integration came about, people forgot about
what they had, and they'd want to go out and sample other people's venues
and left their venue behind. So their venue died."[78] Although Lawrence's

statements are not representative of the entire Black community, many Black businesses were unable to withstand the competition of the newly available, formerly "whites-only" businesses and services. As more and more Black customers moved up the socioeconomic ladder and into other communities, their time, money, and resources went with them. The social and communal network that once upheld these businesses, either by association or proximity, began to wither and shrink. A vacuum was left behind, one that is still visible today in the growing urban decay of once flourishing Black communities.

Take, for example, Florence, the case study of this article. When walking the streets of downtown Florence, one reaches the railroad tracks intersecting North Dargan Street, a visceral yet unofficial boundary line of "historic downtown."[79] By this point, one might assume that there is nothing left worth seeking out. Of course, seasoned Florentines know that the 200 and 300 blocks of North Dargan Street once housed Florence's thriving Black business district.[80] Historically, from the birth of the city through the civil rights movement, Black Florentines lived and worked in either the northern or eastern portions of Florence in which most of Florence's *Green Book* sites were located.

Yet, Florence, like other southern cities of the time, was also affected by mid-twentieth century industrialization, although it is unclear how many of these new industries were willing to employ Black workers and pay them a living wage. Nevertheless, in 1962, many young Black Florentines began leaving town and traveling north in pursuit of greater opportunities after becoming increasingly frustrated by unemployment and low wages. As more Blacks moved out of Florence, more whites moved in.[81] Today, in north Florence, a handful of surviving businesses (e.g., barber shops, a funeral parlor) along with dilapidated residences and a vague historical marker are all that is left, entrusted with the complex and infeasible task of regaling the small-town grandeur of Black Florence, all of which have also historically and quite literally been located on "the wrong side of the tracks." Although a few relics of a bygone era of Black industry remain in north Florence, the blocks of the once tightly knit Black residential communities of east Florence have, by and large, been completely eradicated—the land purchased and many of the homes and businesses vacated and razed to make way for the expansion of McLeod Regional Medical Center. The few pockets of homes that remain in East Florence are marred with blight, dotted along poor or unpaved roads, and tucked away along alleys and dead ends. Florence is not unique in this sense. One can drive across America—not only South Carolina or the South—and find that there exist parts of north and east Florence in every metropolis, city, and town, for the gatekeepers of "urban planning" and "revitalization" have often been inhospitable to Black communities at the cost of their history and culture.

Arguably before, but assuredly since the onset of integration, historically hospitable Black spaces have been gradually left to die. "A recent survey of the locations of the *Green Book* sites by ethnographer Candacy Taylor found that of the thousands of *Green Book* sites on record, only 5 percent are still in operation and more than 75 percent are gone."[82] Nevertheless, there are many still standing, testaments to the will and strength of the innovation and hospitality of Black citizens. Today, some of these extant sites are being documented, added to historical registers and are receiving historical markers.[83] As Nsenga Burton of *The Root* suggests, "If tourists and history buffs are willing to recreate Civil War battles or trace the Trail of Tears, then it would also seem worthwhile to spend some time finding out which locales in *The Green Book* are still standing or which establishments have taken their place."[84]

Moreover, today's modern, integrated public spaces can, at times, still be inhospitable to Blacks. Two dichotomies can be true: During its day, the *Green Book* and other Black travel guides were vital tools for Black Americans, despite critics later claiming that they encouraged the continuity of segregation. Integration was a moral and ethical good for both Black and white America, despite Black businesses' suffering as a result. The present-day quandary is twofold. First, we must work to maintain the integrity of historically Black spaces by keeping them hospitable (i.e., operational, visually appealing, structurally sound, technologically current, inviting, and welcoming).[85] Second, we must become better, more conscientious stewards of the hospitality that should be freely conferred *by all* persons *upon all* persons regardless of race, within the public sphere. For history has already suffered and will continue to suffer for the failure of the former, and past, current, and future generations have suffered and will continue to suffer for the failure of the latter.

Meredith A. Love is professor of English at Francis Marion University. She was a founding director of Center of Excellence for College and Career Readiness and is currently preparing a collection of essays related to South Carolina *Green Book* businesses.

Cherish Thomas is the registrar of the Florence County Museum. Her research interests include local history and the social, political, and religious culture of the American South. She is wife to Nick, and mom to eight cats: Elsa,

Sundae, Tony, Taffy, Simon-Pierre, Stormcloud, Bullseye, and Pharaoh Qingdao-Rameses III.

NOTES

1. "Miss O. J. Ragland to Florence Chamber of Commerce," July 19, 1956, Chamber of Commerce Collection, Florence County Museum.
2. State Development Board Tourism Promotional Brochure, circa 1955, S 149013, South Carolina Department of Archives and History, Columbia, South Carolina.
3. Anthony Szczesiul, *The Southern Hospitality Myth* (Athens: University of Georgia Press, 2017), 2–3.
4. *Ibid.*, 181.
5. *Ibid.*, 185
6. Candacy Taylor, *Overground Railroad: The "Green Book" and the Roots of Black Travel in America* (New York: Abrams Press, 2020), 65–66.
7. Jerry T. Mitchell and Larianne Collins, "The Green Book: 'Safe Places' from Place to Place," *The Geography Teacher* 11, no. 1 (2014): 30.
8. Victor H. Green, *The Negro Travelers' Green Book* (Victor H. Green & Co., 1956), 3
9. See, "Florence South Carolina Business Directory," in *Florence South Carolina City Directory* (Charleston, SC: Nelsons' Baldwin Directory Company, 1955), 12, 29–30, 35, 47, 64.
10. See, "Florence South Carolina Business Directory," in *Florence South Carolina City Directory*, (Charleston, SC: Nelsons' Baldwin Directory Company, 1957), 13, 31, 37, 50, 69. Within the directory, both Black businesses and Black residents alike were denoted with a small letter "C" enclosed in a circle beside their name. The symbol, ©, signified to all readers that the accompanying resident name or business was "colored." The demarcation of white and Black was a common practice of city directories during the years of segregation, having been evident in some form of symbolism within the Florence directories since at least 1892, and continuing until the late 1960s. The 1957 Florence city directory goes so far as to say that "the publishers are very careful in using this [symbol], but do not assume any responsibility in case of error." Nelsons,' *Florence South Carolina City Directory*.
11. G. L. Luhn, "Florence: The 'Magic City' of South Carolina," *Sea Side Thoughts*, January 1894, 3.
12. City of Florence, "Our History: About Florence," www.cityofflorence.com/.
13. Gretchen Sorin, *Driving While Black: African American Travel and the Road to Civil Rights* (New York: Liveright Publishing, 2020), 55.
14. Ivey's Tavern, postcard, no date, Florence County Museum. This postcard further states, "We are believers in constitutional government and racial integrity. Are you?"
15. Szczesiul, *The Southern Hospitality Myth*, 185.
16. Typescript speech of "The Human Factor" by James A. Rogers, November 1963, James A. Rogers Collection, Special Collections, The Arundel Room, M-17, Box 20, James A. Rogers Collection, Francis Marion University, Florence, SC.
17. Isabel Wilkerson, *The Warmth of Other Suns: The Epic Story of America's Great Migration* (New York: Random House, 2010), 31.

18. *Ibid.*, 44.

19. E. P. Broome, "Florence Man Charged With Flogging Colored Child," *New Journal and Guide* (Norfolk, Virginia), January 21, 1950, ProQuest Historical Newspapers: Black Newspaper Collection. The flogging of thirteen-year-old Mary Joe Washington by Ellis Snelling led to a two-month-long city and county-wide boycott of The Merita Bread Company by local Black citizens. Snelling was an employee of Merita and the boycott ended once he was fired. See also, "Flogging Suspect Fired, Citizens Lift Bakery Boycott," *Afro-American* (Baltimore, Maryland), April 8, 1950, ProQuest Historical Newspapers: Black Newspaper Collection

20. Leon F. Litwack, *Trouble in Mind: Black Southerners in the Age of Jim Crow* (New York: Vintage Books, 1998), 239.

21. John McCray, "New Hate Group Picks Warren for its Target," *Afro-American*, July 31, 1954, ProQuest Historical Newspapers: Black Newspaper Collection.

22. Derek H. Alderman and Joshua Inwood, "Toward a Pedagogy of Jim Crow: A Geographic Reading of *The Green Book*," in *Teaching Ethnic Geography in the 21st Century*, edited by Lawrence E. Estaville, Edris J. Montavo, and Fenda A. Akiwumia (Washington, DC: National Council for Geographic Education, 2014), 70.

23. Mark S. Foster, "In the Face of 'Jim Crow': Prosperous Blacks and Vacations, Travel and Outdoor Leisure, 1890-1945," *Journal of Negro History* 84, no. 2 (Spring, 1999): 142.

24. Mamie Garvin Fields, with Karen Fields, *Lemon Swamp and Other Places: A Carolina Memoir* (New York: The Free Press, 1983), xiii.

25. *Ibid.*, xiii–iv.

26. *Ibid.*, xiv.

27. William H. Chafe, Raymond Gavins, and Robert Korstad, eds., *Remembering Jim Crow: Africa Americans Tell About Life in the Segregated South* (New York: The New Press, 2001), 113.

28. *Ibid.*, 113.

29. "S.C.'s NAACP Prexy Chased At R.R. Depot: Sought To Protest Jim Crow of 4 Women; Gets Bum's Rush Via Cops," *New York Amsterdam News*, February 17, 1945, ProQuest Historical Newspapers: Black Newspaper Collection.

30. Clay Williams, "The Guide for Colored Travelers: A Reflection of the Urban League," *Journal of American and Comparative Cultures* 24, nos. 3–4 (2001): 71.

31. "NAACP Official Jailed In South", *Daily Defender*, February 29, 1956, ProQuest Historical Newspapers: Black Newspaper Collection. The case against NAACP president Clarence Mitchell and Rev. Horace Sharper was decided within three minutes; Mitchell and Sharper were exonerated, and *interstate* passengers were (in theory) no longer subjugated to illegal segregation practices at the Florence railroad station. *Intrastate* passengers were still required to abide by local segregation policies and laws, regardless. The lunchroom at the Florence railroad station allegedly remained unconditionally segregated. See, "Bluff called, so Florence gives in," *Afro-American*, March 10, 1956, ProQuest Historical Newspapers: Black Newspaper Collection; "Mayor Promises New Policing Policy in ACL Waiting Rooms," *Florence Morning News*, February 29, 1956, Newspapers.com; and John McCray, "Rail Station J.C. 'Back In Business,' *Afro-American*, August 10, 1957,

ProQuest Historical Newspapers: Black Newspaper Collection." After the case
was adjourned, Mitchell, Sharper and a large crowd of Black citizens made their
way to the train station and ceremoniously entered through what had formerly
been the "whites-only" entrance. Segregation signs were reposted over the rail
station waiting rooms, nineteen months after the case was decided, supposedly for
the purpose of directing *intrastate* passengers. Nevertheless, the case and its aftermath made national headlines, appearing in newspapers such as *Daily Defender,
Pittsburgh Courier, New Journal and Guide, Afro-American,* and *Los Angeles Sentinel.*
The Mitchell-Sharper case is also thought to have attributed to the integration of
the Charleston, SC railroad station in December 1956. See, Staff Correspondent,
"Charleston opens mixed RR station," *Afro-American,* December 22, 1956, Pro-
Quest Historical Newspapers: Black Newspaper Collection.

32. "Jackie Wilson Jailed in Raid," *The Journal Herald,* April 12, 1967, Newspapers.com.
33. Sorin, *Driving While Black,* 40–1.
34. Alderman and Inwood, "Toward a Pedagogy of Jim Crow," 72.
35. Sorin, *Driving While Black,* 30.
36. Alderman and Inwood, "Toward a Pedagogy of Jim Crow," 73.
37. Edwin H. Hackley, and Harrison, *Hackley & Harrison's Hotel and Apartment
Guide for Colored Travelers* (Philadelphia: Hackley & Harrison Publishing Company, 1930), 41. See also, Edwin H. Hackley, and Harrison, *The Travelers Guide
For Colored Travels* (Philadelphia: Hackley & Harrison Publishing Company,
1931), 41.
38. Ellen Terrell, "A 'Reliable Source' for the Assurance of Adequate Accommodations," *Inside Adams* (blog), February 8, 2018, https://blogs.loc.gov/inside_adams.
39. Taylor, *Overground Railroad,* 60–61.
40. Green, *The Negro Motorist Green Book,* 1948 ed., 1
41. Neither Alphonso's Hotel nor the Lincoln Hotel, the two Florence establishments
which Brown recommended to Ragland, were listed in the *Green Book.*
42. Green, *The Negro Motorist Green Book,* 1938 ed.
43. Green, *The Negro Motorist Green Book,* 1941 ed., 4.
44. While a complete listing of extant *Green Book* sites has yet to be published, Taylor's *Overground Railroad* offers a "sampling" of sites, including several photographs. Researchers associated with the Institute for Advanced Technology in
the Humanities at the University of Virginia are working to compile a complete
digital database of *Green Book* sites which can be viewed at https://community
.village.virginia.edu/greenbooks/. Additionally, many issues of the *Green Book*
have been digitized by the New York Public Library Digital Collections and
are available for viewing at https://digitalcollections.nypl.org/collections/the
-green-book.
45. "Ebony Guest Home Has Formal Opening," *New Journal and Guide,* June 18, 1949,
ProQuest Historical Newspapers: Black Newspaper Collection.
46. Cherish Thomas, unpublished interviews with Geraldine Barkley, September 6,
2019
47. *Ibid.*
48. *Ibid.*

49 1948 was the first year Lillie Richmond was listed in the Florence business directory as offering "furnished rooms." See "Baldwin's Florence South Carolina 1948 Business Directory," in *Baldwin's Florence South Carolina City Directory* (Charleston, SC: Baldwin Directory Company, Inc., 1948), 536

50. Daniel A. Lane, *Notable Blacks of the Pee Dee Section of South Carolina: Past and Present* (Columbia, SC: Cunningham-Lane Publishing, 1997), 298–9.

51. For Roy White, see E. Broome, "Ernest Gary's Death Robs Florence of Good Citizen," *New Journal and Guide*, April 1, 1950, ProQuest Historical Newspapers: Black Newspaper Collection. For Pablo Bernard and Fernando Alberto Osorio, see E. Broome, "Field Scout Leader Speaks in Florence," *New Journal and Guide*, April 8, 1950, ProQuest Historical Newspapers: Black Newspaper Collection.

52. E. Broome, "Florence, S.C. Business Woman Taken By Death," *New Journal and Guide*, March 12, 1949, ProQuest Historical Newspapers: Black Newspaper Collection.

53. Lillie Richmond is listed in the Florence city directory as operating an "eating house" (Richmond Café) on East Evans Street from 1933 until 1943. In 1945, James Jones is listed as the owner of Richmond Café. By 1948, Lillie Richmond is listed as offering "furnished rooms" and is no longer listed as being associated with Richmond Café. The address at which Richmond Rest had been located (323 East Evans) is now listed as being occupied by Parnell Furniture Company. This information was extracted by the authors from various editions of the Florence city directories, 1933–1948, courtesy of the Florence County Museum and the South Carolina Room of the Drs. Bruce and Lee Foundation Library.

54. "Mrs. Richmond, proprietor, dies," *Afro-American*, July 30, 1966, ProQuest Historical Newspapers: Black Newspaper Collection.

55. Nickolas Briscoe is listed as a "boarder" in the household of John McDonald on the 1930 US Census. See, 1930 US Census, Florence, Florence County, South Carolina, digital image s.v. "John McDonald," https://www.familysearch.org/en/. Creasie Sanders is listed in the 1936 Florence city directory as residing in the "rear" of 501 S. Irby. Beulah Robinson is listed in the 1938 Florence city directory as residing in the "rear" of 501 S. Irby. Randolph Howe and James Carter are both listed as "lodger[s]" in the household of John McDonald on the 1940 United States Census. See, 1940 United States Census, Florence, Florence County, South Carolina, digital image s.v. "John McDonald," https://www.familysearch.org/en/. Daniel Scott is listed in the 1940 Florence city directory as residing in the "rear" of 501 S. Irby. Sam and Virginia Harrison Jr., and Carl and Amie Bonapart are listed on the 1950 census as residing at 501a and 501b South Irby Street, respectively. See, 1950 US Census, "Florence, Florence County, South Carolina, Enumeration District 21-27," https://1950census.archives.gov/.

56. Listings for two other Florence boarding houses also appeared alongside Mrs. Wright and Mrs. Godbold on page 41 of both the 1930 and 1931 editions of *Hackley & Harrison's Hotel and Apartment Guide for Colored Travelers*—Mrs. Julia Irvin, 221 North Church Street, and Mrs. S. Bacote (Sallie Bacote), 411 East Evans Street. Advertisements for neither Mrs. Irvin's nor Mrs. Bacote's boarding houses transitioned over to the *Green Book*.

57. There is some speculation as to whether Catharine Godbold was truly the proprietor of a boarding house at 227 East Marion Street. From 1900 to 1930, there is no record in the Florence city directories or the US Census of Catharine Godbold operating a boarding house. Her documented occupations from 1900 to 1930 were dressmaker, teacher, seamstress, and census enumerator. Furthermore, Catharine Godbold died in 1932, yet her alleged boarding house was advertised in the *Green Book* until 1940, despite a new resident (Reverend Andrew Hill) occupying the address after her death. However, from 1920 to 1943, a neighbor of Godbold's, Catherine Ryan, operated an eating house on Marion Street. In the 1924–25 Florence city directory, Ryan's home, located at 226 East Marion Street, was listed in the Florence business directory under "boarding houses." Ryan died in 1944.

58. Taylor, *Overground Railroad.* 235–36.

59. *Peterson v. City of Greenville,* 373 U. S. 244, 246–47 (1963); quoted in Alberto B. Lopez, "The Road To, and Through, *Heart of Atlanta Motel*," *Savanna Law Review* 2, no. 1(2015): 61.

60. "Civil Rights Sit-Ins in Florence, SC," *The Green Book of South Carolina,* https://greenbookofsc.com.

61. Alderman and Inwood, "Toward a Pedagogy of Jim Crow," 72.

62. "The College Inn," *SC Picture Project,* www.scpictureproject.org.

63. John McCray, "Roving About Car'lina: He's A Nice Guy," *Afro-American,* September 14, 1957, ProQuest Historical Newspapers: Black Newspaper Collection.

64. E. P. Broome, "Train Porters On ACL Will Be Organized," *New Journal and Guide,* March 4, 1950, ProQuest Historical Newspapers: Black Newspaper Collection.

65. Wilson (aka "Jillson") was the first public school located within city limits of Florence that was attended by Black students.

66. Florence County, South Carolina, Deed Books A472, 1605; B336, 0976.

67. James Miller was also longtime principal of Holmes School, Florence's first school established specifically for Black elementary school students. His wife, Marian, was a longtime teacher and librarian of Wilson High School.

68. From 1953 to 1962, Wright's is listed in the *Green Book* as being located at each of the following addresses: 110 S. Griffin Street; 802 E. Chenes [Cheves] Street; 711 Lynch Street; and 244 N. Dargan Street. On cross-referencing each address with other sources such as the Florence city directories, Florence telephone books, and local newspaper articles and ads, we conclude that it is unlikely that Wright operated a business out of each location listed. Instead, it is possible that the Griffin, Chenes [Cheves], and Lynch addresseses that are listed were Wright's places of residence at various times.

69. Lane, "*Notable Blacks of the Pee Dee Section of South Carolina,*" 299.

70. Dwight Dana, "Chicken Shack Memories Remain," *Morning News,* October 17, 2005.

71. *Ibid.* Mable's Motel was listed in the *Green Book* from 1956 to 1966. The only other Darlington business to be listed in the *Green Book* was the service station of M. L. Caungton, 715 South Main Street, which was listed only in 1939.

72. Katharine Allen, "Searching for Motel Simbeth," *Historic Columbia,* www.historiccolumbia.org.

73. Taylor, *Overground Railroad.* 247.

74. Allen, "Searching for Motel Simbeth."

75. Nsenga K. Burton, "How Did Blacks Travel During Segregation?" *The Root*, https://www.theroot.com/how-did-blacks-travel-during-segregation-1790892293.

76. Green, *"The Negro Motorist Green Book,"* 1.

77. *Ibid.*, 1.

78. Historic Charleston Foundation, interview with Arthur Lawrence, March 20, 2019, Lowcountry Digital Library, https://lcdl.library.cofc.edu/lcdl.

79. The railroad had once employed much of Florence's Black workforce, yet cutbacks in the 1960s relegated many to farming or domestic work. See, James Booker "Racial Overtones In South Carolina Riots: The Riot Act," *New York Amsterdam News*, October 20, 1962, ProQuest Historical Newspapers: Black Newspaper Collection.

80. According to text from a historical marker erected on North Dargan Street by the City of Florence: "The 200 and 300 blocks of N. Dargan St. were once the center of a thriving African American business district in Florence. A number of Black-owned businesses operated here, including restaurants, barber shops, funeral parlors and pharmacies. These businesses provided services to African American customers who were often denied access to white-owned businesses. By the first decades of the 20th century North Florence had become the principal African American residential district as patterns of racial segregation became more fixed. The shops located on N. Dargan St., just north of the Atlantic Coast Line Railroad, served the predominantly African American residents who lived and worked here." See, "Locations: Historic Downtown African American Business District (Florence, SC)," *The Green Book of South Carolina*, https://greenbookofsc.com.

81. Booker, "Racial Overtones In South Carolina Riots: The Riot Act"

82. National Park Service, "Green Book Historic Context and AACRN Listing Guidance (African American Civil Rights Network)," www.nps.gov.

83. Currently, local interest groups are making an effort to further document and commemorate Florence's *Green Book* sites. The first of these sites to be publicly recognized on a national and local scale is the Ebony Guest House, which was added to the National Register of Historic Places in January 2021 and was approved for a state historic marker in May 2022. The marker was installed and dedicated in spring 2023. For more information, contact the National Park Service, nps.gov; and Universities Studying Slavery at Francis Marion University, www.fmarion.edu/uss.

84. Burton, "How Did Blacks Travel During Segregation?"

85. At the time of writing there are some signs of hope evident for the preservation and revitalization of Florence's historically Black business district. The Streater Building (located on the corner of Dargan and Darlington Streets) "is the northernmost remaining architectural landmark of the historically African American downtown business district" and is currently being renovated and modernized for use by local medical group Hope Health. For more information, see Florence County Museum, "The Streater Building – A Historical Summary," www.flocomuseum.org. Additionally, a Save-A-Lot grocery store opened on this same street corner in October 2021, providing locals access to fresh fruit, vegetables,

and meat in a community that had previously been deemed a "food desert." See Lacey Lee, "Florence man opens his own grocery store after 20 years of dreaming," *WBTW*, October 28, 2021. www.wbtw.com. At 218 North Dargan Street, a community mural is currently in production to honor the business contributions the Thompson family has made to downtown Florence as well as "to amplify our African-American businesses downtown." See Matthew Robertson, "Volunteers flock to help paint Downtown Florence Mural" *SCNow*, July 9, 2022. www.flochamber.com. Many other veteran and newly established Black-owned businesses exist in other parts of downtown Florence.

WORKS CITED

Alderman, Derek H., and Joshua Inwood. "Toward a Pedagogy of Jim Crow: A Geographic Reading of *The Green Book*." In *Teaching Ethnic Geography in the 21st Century*, edited by Lawrence E. Estaville, Edris J. Montavo, and Fenda A. Akiwumia, 55–72. Washington, DC: National Council for Geographic Education, 2014.

Allen, Katherine. "Searching for Motel Simbeth." *Historic Columbia*. www.historiccolumbia.org.

Baldwin's Florence South Carolina City Directory. Charleston, SC: Baldwin Directory Company, 1948.

Burton, Nsenga K. "How Did Blacks Travel During Segregation?" *The Root*. https://www.theroot.com/how-did-blacks-travel-during-segregation-1790892293.

Chafe, William H., Raymond Gavins, and Robert Korstad, eds. *Remembering Jim Crow: Africa Americans Tell About Life in the Segregated South*. New York: The New Press, 2001.

City of Florence. "Our History: About Florence." www.cityofflorence.com/our-history-about-florence.

"Civil Rights Sit-Ins in Florence, SC." *The Green Book of South Carolina*. https://greenbookofsc.com.

"The College Inn." *SC Picture Project*. www.scpictureproject.org.

Fields, Mamie Garvin, with Karen Fields. *Lemon Swamp and Other Places: A Carolina Memoir*. New York: The Free Press, 1983.

"Florence South Carolina Business Directory." In *Florence South Carolina City Directory*. Charleston, SC: Nelsons' Baldwin Directory Company, 1955.

"Florence South Carolina Business Directory." In *Florence South Carolina City Directory*. Charleston, SC: Nelsons' Baldwin Directory Company, 1957.

Foster, Mark S. "In the Face of 'Jim Crow': Prosperous Blacks and Vacations, Travel and Outdoor Leisure, 1890–1945." *Journal of Negro History* 84, no. 2 (Spring, 1999): 130–149.

Green, Victor H. *The Negro Travelers' Green Book*. New York: Victor H. Green & Co., 1956.

Hackley, Edwin H., and Harrison. *Hackley & Harrison's Hotel and Apartment Guide for Colored Travelers*. Philadelphia: Hackley & Harrison Publishing Company, 1930.

————. *The Travelers Guide For Colored Travels*. Philadelphia: Hackley & Harrison Publishing Company, 1931.

Lane, Daniel A. *Notable Blacks of the Pee Dee Section of South Carolina: Past and Present*. Columbia, SC: Cunningham-Lane Publishing, 1997.

Lawrence, Arthur, interview with Charleston Historical Society, March 20, 2019. Lowcountry Digital Library. https://lcdl.library.cofc.edu/lcdl.

Litwack, Leon F. *Trouble in Mind: Black Southerners in the Age of Jim Crow*. New York: Vintage Books, 1998.

"Locations: Historic Downtown African American Business District (Florence, SC)." The Green Book of South Carolina. Accessed September 14, 2022. https://greenbookofsc.com.

Lopez, Alberto B. "The Road To, and Through, *Heart of Atlanta Motel*." *Savanna Law Review* 2, no. 1 (2015): 59–72.

Luhn, L. "Florence: The 'Magic City' of South Carolina." *Sea Side Thoughts*, January 1894.

Mitchell, Jerry T., and Larianne Collins. "The Green Book: 'Safe Places' from Place to Place." *The Geography Teacher* 11, no. 1 (2014): 29–36.

National Park Service. "Green Book Historic Context and AACRN Listing Guidance (African American Civil Rights Network)," www.nps.gov.

Ragland, O. J. "Miss O. J. Ragland to Florence Chamber of Commerce," July 19, 1956. Chamber of Commerce Collection, Florence County Museum, Florence, SC.

Rogers, James. A. "The Human Factor." November 1963. James A. Rogers Collection, Special Collections, The Arundel Room, M-17, Box 20. James A. Rogers Collection, Francis Marion University, Florence, SC.

Sorin, Gretchen. *Driving While Black: African American Travel and the Road to Civil Rights*. New York: Liveright Publishing, 2020.

State Development Board Tourism Promotional Brochure, circa 1955. S 149013. South Carolina Department of Archives and History, Columbia, South Carolina.

Szczesiul, Anthony. *The Southern Hospitality Myth*. Athens: University of Georgia Press, 2017.

Taylor, Candacy. *Overground Railroad: The "Green Book" and the Roots of Black Travel in America*. New York: Abrams Press, 2020.

Terrell, Ellen. "A 'Reliable Source' for the Assurance of Adequate Accommodations." *Inside Adams* (blog). February 8, 2018. https://blogs.loc.gov/inside_adams.

Williams, Clay. "The Guide for Colored Travelers: A Reflection of the Urban League." *Journal of American and Comparative Cultures* 24, nos. 3–4 (2001): 71.

Wilkerson, Isabel. *The Warmth of Other Suns: The Epic Story of America's Great Migration*. New York: Random House, 2010.

Junior and High School Student Voices

The Influence of Youth Activists during the Civil Rights Movement in South Carolina

Kerington B. Shaffer and Erica Johnson Edwards

The civil rights movement was a fight to end racial discrimination, segregation, and injustice in the United States through peaceful demonstrations. Americans memorialize this movement every year and continue to remember prominent figures such as Dr. Martin Luther King Jr. and W. E. B. Du Bois for their leadership and dedication. The sit-in movement was a significant part of the civil rights movement. It consisted of student-led, peaceful protests at segregated lunch counters throughout the South, particularly at F. W. Woolworth and S. H. Kress department stores.[1] Youth involvement influenced the civil rights movement significantly. This study of two consecutive days of protests carried out in 1960 by Wilson High School (WHS) students and the youth branch of the National Association for the Advancement of Colored People (NAACP) in Florence, South Carolina, highlights these impacts.[2] The students' protests ended in arrests, mishandlings by the police and Florence courts, and a 1962 South Carolina Supreme Court case. The demonstrations led by WHS students and the NAACP youth branch were the spark that initiated necessary changes in Florence's racial dynamics. The students' agency influenced Black community members and increased involvement in the fight for desegregation and radical changes in race relations in Florence that continues today.

Led by Vice President John Wesley Miller Jr., Florence's NAACP youth branch staged two days of protests at the S. H. Kress store. On March 3, 1960, students performed a sit-in at the segregated lunch counter until the police arrived and forced them to leave. The following day, students marched two blocks from Trinity Baptist Church to Kress to perform another sit-in, but police forces halted the demonstration and arrested forty-eight students on charges of "parading without a permit."[3] The Florence magistrate court convicted thirty-four students on the charges, but the decision of the 1962 South Carolina Supreme Court case, *City of Florence v. George*, overturned the convictions.

Coinciding student-led protests conducted in Florence and other South Carolina cities, particularly in Darlington and Charleston, provide context for the 1960 events. Furthermore, other incidents in Florence, such as a 1942 riot over racial discrimination in the military; the 1956 arrest of NAACP Washington Bureau Director Clarence M. Mitchell Jr., and Rev. Horace Sharper of Sumter, South Carolina; and the 1969 riots over racial discrimination at Charles Smith's Little Farmer's Market provide an understanding of the city's past racial dynamics. Several committees, groups, and organizations also influenced Florence's race relations. These included the NAACP, the White Citizens' Council (WCC), the Ku Klux Klan (KKK), and the Community Relations Committee.

Historiography

Junior and high school students organized and conducted boycotts, sit-ins, pickets, and other forms of protests during the civil rights movement. The Library of Congress's Civil Rights History Project has several oral histories of youths from Alabama, Oklahoma, and Virginia who took part in the movement. There is one account from South Carolina, that of Cleveland Sellers, organizer of an NAACP youth chapter in Denmark.[4] The Kress demonstrations in Florence are significant, however, because they represent the earliest involvement of youths anywhere in the South. Despite the available primary sources, few scholars have written about youth activists. Jon Hale is one historian who recognizes youth involvement. He indicates that student involvement was not limited to college campuses, but the literature on the civil rights movement largely overlooks high school student involvement.[5] Similarly, Aldon Morris analyzes youth involvement during the sit-in movement in South Carolina and other US cities. Works by Christopher W. Schmidt and William C. Hine reference youth efforts in Rock Hill and Orangeburg, South Carolina.[6] Although these events made national news, the demonstrations in Florence did not. Consequently, scholars have omitted them from even the most recent studies of the civil rights movement in South Carolina.[7]

Methodology

It was not until 2011 that research on the Florence demonstrations began in earnest. Stephen Motte, curator of Interpretation and Collections at the Florence County Museum, carried out this research when creating a civil rights movement exhibit in the museum. His efforts also led to a commemorative plaque placed in front of the former Kress store location honoring the students. Motte studied the riot in 1942, Mitchell's and Sharper's arrest in 1956, the 1960 demonstrations, and the 1969 incident at the Little Farmer's Market. His research involved conversations with Florence residents who recollected these incidents and the city's racial dynamics. He also accessed newspaper articles, NAACP documents, police and court records, and documents referencing integration in Florence schools.[8] This initial research has opened the doors for further in-depth study of the civil rights movement and past race relations in Florence.

Our research includes recently recorded interviews with Wilson Junior High and WHS students. These oral histories provide interpretations of the 1960 Kress demonstrations, race relations in Florence, and civil rights demonstrations throughout the country. Our interview with student leader John Miller describes the formation of the NAACP youth branch, the planning and carrying out of the Kress demonstrations, the student's jail and court experiences, and the demonstration's effect on the community.[9] Similarly, Ann Nelson recounts her experiences as the youngest participant and student arrested. Nelson spoke of the events on March 4, the arrests and jail experience, and segregation in Florence compared with other cities throughout the country.[10] In addition to Miller's and Nelson's accounts, our interview with Allie Brooks, a Florence native and student at Wilson Junior High School in 1960, offers an understanding of race relations, segregation, and the media's effect on white communities throughout the civil rights movement.[11] Likewise, in the Francis Marion University African American Faculty and Staff Coalition Cultural Conversations Series, Florence native Joseph Heyward presents the changing race relations, the 1960 Kress demonstrations, the Community Relations Committee in Florence founded in 1963, and the 1969 incident at the Little Farmer's Market.[12] Although Brooks and Heyward did not participate in the 1960 demonstrations, their insights are instrumental in contextualizing the Kress demonstrations and understanding race relations in Florence.

Oral histories are invaluable to studying and understanding youth involvement in the civil rights movement. They provide direct accounts of segregation, changing race relations, and the changing dynamics in Florence. Moreover, they provide detailed descriptions of the activists' goals and experiences. These accounts add to the historical record and explain both race relations and the impact of youth activists. In addition to oral accounts, primary documents also offer information regarding racial incidents and the media's portrayal of those incidents. Multiple US and South Carolina Supreme Court cases offer legal documentation and decisions regarding racial matters. The *Florence Morning News* and *The State* reported on KKK activities in South Carolina, the 1942 riot, Mitchell and Sharper's arrests in 1956, the 1960 events at Kress, the 1969 Little Farmer's Market incident, and the Community Relations Committee.

Background of Florence's Racial Dynamics

The oppression and unjust treatment of Blacks in the United States dates to the country's founding, and Florence provides evidence of this inequity. Slavery was prevalent in South Carolina for centuries, and many enslaved people worked on Florence plantations, including the Gregg Plantation, the current location of Francis Marion University's main campus. After the Civil War and the abolition of slavery through the Thirteenth Amendment, the formerly enslaved people continued to work the land as sharecroppers and tenant farmers. During the Reconstruction Era (1865–1877), there was progress toward equality for Black people. For example, the Pee Dee region sent the country's first Black congressman, Joseph H. Rainey of Georgetown, to Washington in 1870.[13] Nevertheless, racial discrimination, segregation, and oppression continued throughout the North and South.

The 1896 *Plessy v. Ferguson* US Supreme Court ruling allowed segregation if the racially separated facilities were considered to be of equal quality.[14] Florence, along with other cities, strongly enforced segregation. Railroad tracks separated the Black businesses on North Dargan Street from the white businesses on South Dargan Street.[15] Despite the US Supreme Court ruling, the facilities were never equal, and racial inequality is evident when studying segregated facilities. Customary segregation measures included "whites-only" lunch counters, doors, bathrooms, water fountains, schools, libraries, seating areas, parks, tennis courts, and swimming pools. When Black people disregarded the segregation, they faced consequences imposed by white community members, such as arrest or losing their jobs.[16] A pernicious dynamic developed in these communities. White civic leaders and business owners built enticing facilities and then punished Black people who wanted to use them.[17] Segregated facilities disadvantaged Black Americans and restrained them from opportunities widely accessible to the white community. African Americans violated segregation codes to overcome inequities to access public amenities, such as lunch counters and recreation areas.

Segregation had a significant impact on African-American education. Although there was an increase in the number of Black high schools in South Carolina following *Briggs v. Elliott*, from eighty in 1951 to one hundred forty-five in 1957, school districts did not spend equal amounts of money on supplies for Black students.[18] For instance, Florence County spent twice as much on white high school libraries, even though there were not twice as many white high school students.[19] Furthermore, instead of supplying the school with funds to buy school books, the Florence school district provided WHS's Black students with second-hand school books from McClenaghan High School, a white high school. Additionally, before 1962, many Black students had to walk to school because the buses only transported Black students who lived outside city limits and white students.[20]

In addition to legal segregation practices, the KKK began demonstrations in the area during the 1920s. On January 31, 1924, seven hundred Klansmen performed a "meeting of the Pee Dee Klansmen" march in Florence. The following year, Klansmen received an invitation to the Pee Dee Fair to host the KKK Conclave.[21] Expected in attendance were over fifteen thousand Klansmen, including Hiram Wesley Evans, the Imperial Wizard of the KKK. The weather prevented the event from happening, so the Klansmen attended the fair's pageant to shoot fireworks during the Reconstruction Era scene. The Klan attended the event dressed in robes and riding horses. They intended to intimidate and instill fear in the Black community. However, the *Florence Morning News* portrayed the robes and horses as stimulating interest in the pageant.[22] One month after the pageant, Klansmen left threats and burning crosses on two doors along North Dargan Street.[23] The Klan also made efforts to ally with law enforcement so vigilante Klansmen could report certain crimes in the city. Other Klan marches occurred in Florence during the 1940s, '50s, and '60s. Their demonstrations were in full force as late as May of 1978, and the Klan attempted to perform rallies in 2010.[24] The KKK's activities prove that racial tensions continued throughout the area, and white supremacists perpetually sought to taunt Black Americans in Florence.

During World War II, Florence and other cities faced riots over racial discrimination.[25] In 1942, the army stationed service members in Florence while utilizing the airport for the Florence Army Airfield base.[26] On November 7, 1942, Florence police responded to a call about a fight. When one Black soldier reportedly resisted arrest, a riot broke out along North Dargan Street. The unrest involved as many as fifteen hundred participants, including two hundred service members. The Sheriff's office, fire department, highway patrol, and military police aided in restoring peace. They deployed tear gas on the crowd. Multiple civilians and soldiers suffered injuries, and the police arrested over twenty-five rioters.[27] The following day, officers supposedly recognized two Black soldiers, Charles Williams and Lando Guin, and arrested them for their involvement the previous night.[28] After the war, individuals and organizations like the NAACP worked to end racial discrimination throughout the South.

At the Florence Atlantic Coast Line train station in February of 1956, police arrested Clarence M. Mitchell, director of the NAACP Washington Bureau, and Rev. Sharper of Sumter for attempting to enter a "whites-only" waiting room.[29] However, there was no sign indicating that it was a white waiting room. In fact, in January of that year, the station took the signs down because the Interstate Commerce Commission ordered their removal. Patrolman Bruce Buffkin and three other officers arrested Mitchell and Sharper for disorderly conduct. Assuming that the charges would not hold up, Buffkin changed the charges to "interfering with a police officer" before the trial. The following day, Judge Wylie H. Caldwell heard the case.[30] Attorneys William W. Bennett, Elliott D. Turnage, and Lincoln C. Jenkins Jr. represented Mitchell and Sharper.[31] Judge Caldwell requested the dismissal of the charges because they were not sufficient for convictions, and the court dismissed the charges.

Two Florence Federal Bureau of Investigation agents investigated the incident to determine whether the arrests violated any civil rights laws. Chief of Police Julian Price was a director of Florence's WCC.[32] WCCs began in Indianola, Mississippi, after *Brown v. Board of Education of Topeka* in 1954. They quickly spread from Mississippi into Texas, Arkansas, Alabama, and South Carolina, fighting against the integration of public spaces.[33] Florence's WCC published an advertisement in the *Florence Morning News* in February 1956, only a few weeks before the incident with Mitchell and Sharper. The recruiting advertisement proudly stated, "Maybe your community has had no racial problems! This may be true; however, you may not have a fire, yet you maintain a fire department.... The Citizen's Council is the South's answer to the mongrelizers. We will not be integrated! We are proud of our white blood and our white heritage of sixty centuries. If we are bigoted, prejudiced, un-American, etc., so were George Washington, Thomas Jefferson, Abraham Lincoln and other illustrious forebearers who believe in segregation."[34] Chief Price's membership suggests that there may have been racial prejudices within the police force. The arrests generated so much attention in Florence that community members filled the courtroom in support of Mitchell and Sharper. The community viewed the incident's outcome as the first big win for desegregation in Florence, and local interest in the NAACP increased.

Florence NAACP Youth Branch Formation

The demonstrations carried out by the WHS students and Florence NAACP youth branch were the first organized protests in Florence. Before the Kress protests, the 1942 riot on North Dargan Street was the only demonstration in Florence. Mitchell's arrest in 1956 captured the attention of community members and involvement increased in the NAACP. Nevertheless, neither of these incidents was planned, and people were still hesitant to protest out of the fear of repercussions from white supremacist groups. Possible ramifications for participating in the Civil Rights Movement in the South included job loss, arrest, harassment, torture, and even murder at the hands of whites.[35] These consequences limited early involvement in the civil rights movement. However, by 1960, things were ramping up in the civil rights movement throughout the Southern states, and the sit-in movement was getting underway.

John Miller, a Florence native, was the first vice president of the Florence NAACP youth branch and the lead organizer of the Kress demonstrations. Three WHS students—Miller, Marilyn Miller (John Miller's sister), and Cecil Gunter, neighbor and friend of the Millers—attended an NAACP conference held in Greenville, South Carolina, in late December 1959. Reverend Sharper, state president of the NAACP and pastor of Trinity Baptist Church, brought the three WHS students to the conference. The South Carolina NAACP adult branches, along with youths throughout the state, attended the conference. The conference's focus was to train the youth how to organize youth branches and carry out sit-ins and protests. The youths learned the correct way to conduct nonviolent protests and to refrain from doing things such as yelling.[36]

Shortly after the students returned to Florence, they began to establish a youth branch, and many students were interested in joining. Rev. Edward Thomas was the branch's first advisor. Per NAACP guidelines, a senior in high school would be president of a youth branch, and a junior in high school would be vice president. Warren James, a senior at WHS, became president, and John Miller, a junior at WHS, served as vice president.[37]

As protests occurred throughout the United States and the sit-in movement began, the Florence NAACP youth branch became eager to conduct a demonstration. After the training received at the Greenville conference and the example set forth by the "Greensboro Four," the Florence youth branch, under Miller's leadership, organized a sit-in at the S. H. Kress lunch counter on the corner of West Evans and South Dargan Street on March 3, 1960.[38]

Although James was the president of the youth branch, Miller led the demonstrations. Miller's parents were business owners, which afforded the family more freedom to act. James's parents worked for white employers, so their
son's involvement could have resulted in them losing their jobs.[39]

1960 Kress Demonstrations

After school on March 3, around thirty students met at Trinity Baptist
Church and prepared to carry out the initial Kress demonstration. Before
the group left the church, one student, Cecil Gunter went to the Kress lunch
counter to scope things out. Because he had a lighter skin tone, the other
students hoped that there was a chance the counter would serve Gunter, but
when he arrived, the workers behind the counter would neither serve him
nor let him stay. Gunter reported back to Trinity Baptist to inform the group
of his denial, and on hearing the news, the branch members decided to move
forward with the sit-in. Around twenty-five students walked two blocks from
the church to Kress and entered through the Dargan Street door.[40] On entry,
the workers behind the counter made comments such as, "Here they come,"
and "Clear the counter. We're not serving you."[41] The workers likely anticipated a demonstration because of the reporting on sit-ins at many other
Kress and Woolworth stores.[42]

There were only a small number of unoccupied chairs at the counter,
resulting in most of the students standing. The workers at the lunch counter
did not serve the students, and when asked to leave, the students refused.
Soon after their arrival, the store manager called the police and turned off
the store lights. Chief of Police Melvin D. Adams and City Manager Aaron
March arrived at the lunch counter and told the students that the store had
closed, and they had to leave. The students went back to Trinity Baptist, but
they decided to go back later that day to see if the store had reopened. They
arrived back at the store to find it still closed, but trash cans had taken the
place of the chairs the students had sat in earlier that day.[43]

The outcome of the sit-in prompted the students to regroup and conduct
another demonstration. They made plans to march and picket the front of
Kress on the following day, March 4. On the second day of the demonstrations, over seventy students participated. They were mostly fifteen-, sixteen-,
and seventeen-year-olds, but the youngest participant was twelve-year-old
Ann Nelson. The students constructed handwritten signs and pinned them
to their shirts. Their placards stated slogans, including "Full service or none,"
"Our money is the same," and "Give us equality."[44]

As the students marched from Trinity Baptist Church to Kress, they split into two groups, each going to different store entrances. One group found the door barricaded, so it rerouted to join the other group. Before the protestors could enter Kress, police forces intervened and arrested forty-eight students on charges of "parading without a permit."[45] The students had their signs taken from them, and those who pinned their signs onto themselves had their clothing ripped. Onlookers began name-calling, but the students remained peaceful. In pairs, the police took the students to the Florence jail, which was located behind the store.

Customers at the lunch counter on the first day of the demonstrations did not react to the students. The only people who spoke to the students were the female server, the store manager, and Chief Adams. However, on the second day of the demonstrations, onlookers responded to the students by calling them names, taking their signs, and throwing projectiles.[46] Their antagonistic responses paralleled those of other communities. In Charleston, for example, "white patrons cleared the premises, and bystanders circulated rumors of a bomb threat" when Burke High School students performed a sit-in at a Kress store.[47] While the students in Florence endured derogatory remarks and physical confrontations, the police and court caused the brunt of their mistreatment.

When the students arrived at the jail, the police conducted body searches on each student, took their pictures, and questioned them. Twelve-year-old Ann Nelson said the police made her take off her dress when they conducted her body search. Nelson also described how the students passed word to one another to drop their heads when the officers tried to take their pictures. Nelson and Miller were among the students questioned. Nelson explained that the police chief asked her who told her to demonstrate. She responded, "My mind told me to come down here."[48] Furthermore, five police officers took sixteen-year-old Miller into an interrogation room and questioned him without a parent present. One officer became frustrated and said, "Ain't no need in talking to him. He's not going to change his mind."[49]

The only parent the police called to the jail was Nelson's mother.[50] Instead of calling the other students' parents, the police called WHS's Black principal, Dr. Gerald A. Anderson, and requested his presence at the jail to identify the students.[51] Principal Anderson arrived and claimed that he did not recognize any of the students.[52] His denial suggests either that he hoped to dissociate himself from the students and any further civil rights demonstrations or that he was trying to resist cooperating with the police. The police separated the students and placed the girls in adjacent cells and the boys in a different part of the jail. Officers gave each student a hamburger and a soda, but the jail cells were so filthy that some students, including Nelson, could not bear to eat the food. After holding them for many hours, the police released the students around one o'clock in the morning of March 5, on a combined bond of one hundred dollars.[53]

The Florence Recorder's Court set the first trial for March 7, but the students' attorney, William Bennett, requested a continuance.[54] April 18 was the next scheduled court date, but the court granted a second continuance.[55] On April 20, the Florence court heard the case, and Bennett, Jenkins, and Matthew Perry represented the students.[56] Like Mitchell's trial, the courtroom was at total capacity. Community members were eager to support the students, so they filled the courtroom and gathered in crowds outside the courthouse. Judge Charles C. McDonald heard the case, and he convicted thirty-four students on the charges of "parading without a permit" and sentenced them each to pay a thirty-dollar fine.[57] At the time, Article 5, Section 47 of the Ordinances of the City of Florence only allowed parades after obtaining a permit from the Chief of Police.[58]

The demonstrators appealed their conviction, and the South Carolina Supreme Court overturned it. The wrongful convictions by Judge McDonald led to the 1962 South Carolina Supreme Court case, *City of Florence v. George*. Attorneys Bennett, Perry, and Jenkins represented the students. Ten students, including Nelson, had their cases transferred to the Children's Court because they were under the age of sixteen at the time of their arrests. Chief Melvin D. Adams and multiple other officers as well as several of the accused students testified before the court. Perry made a motion to dismiss the charges, citing the First and Fourteenth Amendments. The South Carolina Supreme Court determined that the convictions of the remaining twenty-four students were wrongful because the students were not simply marching; they "were proceeding to a designated place in the City of Florence, to give public expression to their grievances," and the Court overturned Judge McDonald's ruling.[59]

Although the South Carolina Supreme Court reversed the students' convictions, the charges were not immediately dropped. Students arrested in 1960 still had charges on their records as late as 2014 and 2020.[60] As if Florence's authorities had not already caused enough suffering, they made no efforts to expunge the students' charges and completely disregarded the resolution reached by the state court. Additionally, instead of following desegregation efforts like other Woolworth and Kress stores, Florence's Kress chose to close the lunch counter instead of desegregating. Kress did not reopen the counter until the mid- to late 1970s.[61] The incident sheds light on the lengthy measures Florence took to sustain its deeply rooted segregation practices.

Aftermath and Effects on the Community

Further youth-led protests occurred in Florence after the March 3–4 demonstrations. For two days, WHS students boycotted milk provided by the school cafeteria. Coble Dairy manufactured the milk, and the NAACP sent orders to boycott the company's products because of its practices of racial discrimination.[62] After the first day of boycotting, Principal Anderson threatened the students with punishment if they continued refusing the milk. Despite the threats, the students reworked their plan and boycotted the milk for an additional day.[63] Like the WHS students, around fifty students at Darlington's Mayo High School also boycotted Coble Dairy products. However, instead of threatening the students with punishment, Mayo's principal expelled four students for the protest.[64] The incident resulted in two 1960 South Carolina Supreme Court cases, *Byrd v. Gary* and *Stanley v. Gary*.[65] In addition to the milk boycotts, the NAACP adult and youth branches picketed in front of Florence's Kress on August 13, 1960.[66]

The demonstrations led by the Florence students influenced Black community members, and their involvement in the fight for civil rights increased. The community recognized the efforts of its Black members. Equal numbers of white and Black residents established the Florence Community Relations Committee in 1963. Mayor David H. McLeod pushed for the committee, hoping it would serve as a bond between the Black and white communities and lead to Florence becoming a unified community. A goal of the committee was for Florence to "set an example of social concern, job opportunity, and human relations . . . and contribute to progress and freedom in the world society."[67] Notably, the Florence community formed the committee before the Civil Rights Act of 1964.

Over the next several years, community members came together to focus on the racial relations in Florence, and Mayor McLeod was in the middle of the efforts. In 1969, an incident occurred at the Little Farmer's Market after people accused the white owner, Charles Smith, of racial discrimination and threats with a gun. Smith operated his farmer's market in a predominantly Black neighborhood. With the support of the Southern Christian Leadership Conference, around two hundred Black community members picketed the market in August of 1969. Mayor McLeod and local Black faith leaders encouraged the protestors to remain peaceful. However, there was some property damage, and the police arrested some demonstrators. Smith ultimately closed the farmer's market after Mayor McLeod and other city officials urged him to do so.[68]

The community heavily focused on school desegregation, as schools in surrounding areas had started integration efforts years before. In 1965, Florence allowed the first student to integrate McClenaghan High School Marvin Gunter, the brother of Cecil Gunter, who took part in the Kress demonstrations.[69] A few other Black students integrated after Gunter, and it led to a 1970 US Department of Justice order for Florence to provide an acceptable school desegregation plan. However, Florence School District 1 did not present a suitable desegregation plan to the Department of Justice until 2017.[70] Although the plan satisfied the Department of Justice, a degree of segregation is still evident in Florence schools. The demographics of Florence schools in the 2009–2010 academic year shows that WHS continues to have the most significant percentage of Black high school students compared with West and South Florence High Schools. Even with three hundred more students, West Florence had thirty-three percent fewer Black students than Wilson had during 2009–2010. The Department of Justice may consider Florence schools desegregated on the basis of the 2017 plan, but demographics prove that Florence schools have not achieved integration.[71] Therefore, in the coming years, it remains critical to focus on school desegregation and equal opportunities among students.

Conclusion

During the civil rights movement, youth activists were leaders whose efforts were undeniably effective. They withstood violent treatment and other ramifications such as police brutality and imprisonment for conducting peaceful protests. The demonstrations led by the WHS students were inspiring and motivational to Black community members in Florence. Black people were fully aware of the city's racial issues, but they mostly refrained from speaking out because of the fear of repercussions. However, seeing junior high school and senior high school students use their voices in the fight for change was the needed encouragement that drove the Black adults in the community to include themselves in the fight.

The junior high school and senior high school students' demonstrations were successful. They sparked an eagerness in the community and led to changes in Florence's race relations. Although negative consequences held back many Black people from participating early during the civil rights movement, the support at both Mitchells' and the students' court hearings showed that the community wanted to see change. The students' desire to make a difference in racial dynamics motivated the Black community to unite and further the fight. The student-led demonstrations also led to the engagement of white members in the fight for racial equality through efforts such as creating the Community Relations Committee.

Youth participation during the civil rights movement shows awareness of racial inequality and an understanding of necessary action in fighting for radical changes. Miller states that the students' demonstrations "generated awareness and stirred people to action."[72] The arrest and conviction of the forty-eight students generated the needed awareness in both the Black and white communities. Although the police arrested the students for their demonstrations, the community heard their voices. Although they lost the court case in Florence, they won in the South Carolina Supreme Court, which triggered awareness throughout the country, not just in Florence.

There has been progress toward ending institutional racism, yet its prevalence continues today. Recent racial issues prove that the battle is not over and that resistance to equity and justice continues today. Therefore, we cannot be content with where we stand. Further progress is necessary, and it is our duty, as Americans and humans, to uphold the voices of youth activists. Each person, young and old, has a responsibility to continue pushing for radical changes in America's racial dynamics.

Erica Johnson Edwards is associate professor of history and faculty coordinator for Universities Studying Slavery at Francis Marion University. Her current research is into the influence of the Haitian Revolution across the US South during Reconstruction and into the early twentieth century.

Kerington B. Shaffer is a 2021 graduate of Francis Marion University's history department. She completed an internship at the Marion County Museum and is a member of Phi Alpha Theta. She currently works in the motion picture industry.

NOTES

1. For more on the F. W. Woolworth and S. H. Kress department stores, see Jean Maddern Pirone, *F. W. Woolworth and the American Five and Dime: A Social History* (Jefferson, NC: McFarland, 2003) and Charlotte C. Egerton, "More than Nickels and Dimes: S. H. Kress Stores in the New South" (MA thesis, University of North Carolina Wilmington, 2012).

2. Wilson High School was a Black high school.

3. "Negroes Jailed at 2 SC Cities," *The State*, March 5, 1960, 1, 10.

4. See Library of Congress, "Youth in the Civil Rights Movement," www.loc.gov. See also Cleveland Sellers, interview by John Dittmer, directed by John Bishop, Civil Rights Project, Library of Congress, March 21, 2013, www.loc.gov (accessed June 7, 2022).

5. Jon Hale, "'The Fight was Instilled in Us': High School Activism and the Civil Rights Movement in Charleston," *South Carolina Historical Magazine* 114, no. 1 (2013): 4–28.

6. Aldon Morris, "Black Southern Student Sit-in Movement: An Analysis of Internal Organization," *American Sociological Review* 46, no. 6 (1981): 744–67; William C. Hine, "Civil Rights and Campus Wrongs: South Carolina State College Students Protest, 1955-1968," *The South Carolina Historical Magazine* 97, no. 4 (1996): 310–31; Christopher W. Schmidt, "Why the 1960 Lunch Counter Sit-Ins Worked: A Case Study of Law and Social Movement Mobilization," *Indiana Journal of Law and Social Equality* 5, no. 2 (2017): 280–300.

7. See for example, Claudia Smith Brinson, *Stories of Struggle: The Clash over Civil Rights in South Carolina* (Columbia: University of South Carolina Press, 2020).

8. Stephen Motte, Research on the civil rights movement in Florence, SC, Florence County Museum, 2011–14.

9. John Miller, interview by Erica Edwards and Kerington Shaffer, Zoom, March 3, 2021.

10. Ann Nelson, interview by Erica Edwards and Kerington Shaffer, directed by Larry Falck, Francis Marion University, March 23, 2021.

11. Allie Brooks, Jr., interview by Erica Edwards and Kerington Shaffer, Zoom, February 17, 2021.

12. Joseph Heyward, "Changes in African American Race Relations in Florence," Francis Marion University African American Faculty and Staff Coalition Cultural Conversations Series. YouTube Video, 1:38, November 6, 2020, https://www.youtube.com/watch?v=1zSQMRaWgak (accessed June 7, 2022).

13. For more on Rainey, see William C. Hine, "Joseph Hayne Rainey," *South Carolina Encyclopedia* (Columbia: University of South Carolina Press, 2006), www.scencyclopedia.org.

14. *Plessy v. Ferguson*, 163 US 537 (1896).

15. Miller, interview; Brooks, interview.

16. Miller, interview.

17. Nelson, interview.

18. *Briggs v. Elliott* was a case in Clarendon County, South Carolina. Twenty African-American parents sued for equal education opportunities for their children. For more see, Delia B. Allen, "The Forgotten *Brown* Case: *Briggs v. Elliott* and Its Legacy in South Carolina," *Peabody Journal of Education* 94 (2019): 442–67; and Wade Kolb III, "*Briggs v. Elliot*: A Study in Grassroots Activism and Trial Advocacy from the Early Civil Rights Era, *Journal of Southern Legal History* 19 (2011): 123–75.

19. *Eighty-Eighth Annual Report of the State Superintendent of Education, State of South Carolina, 1955–1956* (Columbia, SC: State Budget and Control Board, 1956), 234, 242.

20. Brooks interview; John Miller interview.
21. Called a "klonklave" within the KKK, a conclave was originally a secret session of the KKK. See A. V. Dalrymple, *Liberty Dethroned: An Indictment of the Ku Klux Klan Based Solely upon Its Own Pronouncements, Philosophy, and Acts of Mob Violence* (Philadelphia, PA: Times Publishing Company, 1923), 14.
22. "KKK Conclave at Pee Dee Fair is Talk of Day," *Florence Morning News*, November 8, 1925; "Historical Pageant will be the Big Feature of Program for Closing Day of the Show," *Florence Morning News*, November 13, 1925.
23. "Klansmen Get Busy on Case Long Standing," *Florence Morning News*, December 12, 1925.
24. Miller Recorded Interview; Traci Bridges, "Klan Rally Coordinator Cancels Planned Florence Event," *Florence Morning News*, August 14, 2010.
25. For other examples, see "Arizona Negro Soldiers Riot," *The State*, November 28, 1942, 11; Harvard Sitkoff, "Racial Militancy and Interracial Violence in the Second World War," *The Journal of American History* 58, no. 3 (1971): 661–81; Ann V. Collins, *All Hell Broke Loose: American Race Riots from the Progressive Era through World War II* (Santa Barbara, CA: Praeger, 2012), 87–114; and Nikki L. M. Brown and Barry M. Stentiford, eds., *Jim Crow: A Historical Encyclopedia of the American Mosaic* (Westport, CT: Greenwood, 2014), 440–41.
26. J. D. Lewis, "South Carolina – Military Airfields in World War II," *Carolana*, www.carolana.com/SC/Transportation.
27. "Near Riot by Negro Soldiers Quickly Quelled," *Florence Morning News*, November 8, 1942.
28. "3 More Negroes are Arrested," *Florence Morning News*, November 9, 1942.
29. Fred Andersen, "Test of Racial Law Nol Prossed in the City," *Florence Morning News*, February 29, 1956.
30. *Ibid.*
31. William W. Bennett was from Lane, South Carolina. In 1953, he earned his law degree from South Carolina State University, a law school for Black students from 1947 to 1966. In addition to representing Mitchell, he represented a group of parents in a case to desegregate Florence schools in 1955, the Kress student demonstrators in 1960, and college student demonstrators in Orangeburg in 1960. At the time of his death in 1969, he was a trustee at Allen University and director of the Florence County Antipoverty Agency. From Darlington, Elliott D. Turnage earned his law degree from Harvard in 1954. He worked with Bennett on the school desegregation case in 1955. He also represented Darlington students who had been expelled over a milk boycott in 1960. Lincoln C. Jenkins Jr. was from Columbia. He completed his law degree at Howard in 1949. For more on these lawyers, see W. Lewis Burke, *All for Civil Rights: African American Lawyers in South Carolina, 1868–1968* (Athens: University of Georgia Press, 2017).
32. "Thurmond Hits Possible FBI Council Probe," *Florence Morning News*, January 2, 1956; and "What IS the Citizens' Council?" *Florence Morning News*, February 11, 1956.
33. Harold C. Fleming, "Resistance Movements and Racial Desegregation," *The Annals of the American Academy of Political and Social Science* 304 (1956): 46–47.
34. "What IS the Citizens' Council?"

35. For more on the ramifications, see James M. Fendrich, "Keeping the Faith or Pursuing the Good Life: A Study of the Consequences of Participation in the Civil Rights Movement," *American Sociological Review* 42, no. 1 (1977): 144–57; Anthony J. Blasi, *Segregationist Violence and Civil Rights Movements in Tuscaloosa* (Lanham, MD: University Press of America, 1980); and Wayne A. Santoro, "The Civil Rights Movement and the Right to Vote: Black Protest, Segregationist Violence and the Audience," *Social Forces* 86, no. 4 (2008): 1391–1414.

36. Miller interview.

37. Miller interview.

38. For more on the Greensboro Four, see Iwan Morgan, *From Sit-Ins to SNCC: The Student Civil Rights Movement in the 1960s* (Gainesville: University Press of Florida, 2012).

39. Miller interview; Nelson interview.

40. "Negroes Stage First Sitdown at Florence," *The State*, March 4, 1960, sec. D.

41. Miller interview; Nelson interview.

42. See for example, "Negro Students Denied Service Again in NC," *The State*, February 4, 1960, 8; "Seating Row Spreads to 2 More Cities," *The State*, February 9, 1960, 1; "Rock Hill Praised in Negro Cases," *The State*, February 27, 1960, 3; and "Lunch Counter Pressure Eases in Three North Carolina Cities," *The State*, February 22, 1960, 2.

43. "Negroes Stage First Sitdown in Florence," *The State*, March 4, 1960, 1.

44. *City of Florence v. George*, 241 S.C. 77 (1962). Stephen Motte, Research on the Civil Rights Movement in Florence, SC, *Florence County Museum*, 2011–2014.

45. "Negroes Jailed at 2 SC Cities," *The State*, March 5, 1960, 1, 10.

46. Miller interview; Nelson interview.

47. Hale, "'The Fight was Instilled in Us,'" 4.

48. Nelson interview.

49. Miller interview.

50. Nelson interview.

51. Anderson had been principal at WHS for 24 years (1942–1966) when he resigned to become assistant coordinator of the state-wide adult basic education program. See "Wilson High's Principal Had Dreams Fulfilled," *Florence Morning News*, December 12, 1965, 1.

52. Miller interview.

53. Nelson interview.

54. "48 Negroes Win Delay in Hearings," *Florence Morning News*, March 8, 1960, 2.

55. "Trials Set on April 18 for Negroes," *Florence Morning News*, March 26, 1960.

56. "48 Demonstrators to be Tried Today," *Florence Morning News*, April 20, 1960, 2. Matthew J. Perry was from Columbia. He earned his law degree at South Carolina State in 1953. He became the chief counsel of the South Carolina NAACP. For more on Perry, see Matthew J. Perry, Recorded interview by Joseph Mosnier, Civil Rights Project, Library of Congress, June 7, 2011, www.loc.gov.

57. "In 'Parading' Case, Negro Youths Found Guilty as Charged," *Florence Morning News*, April 21, 1960.

58. *City of Florence v. George*.

59. *City of Florence v. George*.

60. Miller interview; Nelson interview.
61. Miller interview.
62. Hine, "Civil Rights and Campus Wrongs," 316.
63. Miller interview; Nelson interview.
64. "Expelled for Boycotting Milk, S.C. Students File Suit," *Jet Magazine*, April 21, 1960, 23; "Negro Youth," *Florence Morning News*, May 7, 1960.
65. *Byrd v. Gary*, 184 F Supp. 388 (D.S.C. 1960); *Stanley v. Gary*, 237 S.C. 237 (1960). See also "Mayo Students' Petition Denied by U.S. Court," *Florence Morning News*, May 20, 1960.
66. Isaiah DeQuincey Newman, "Picketing of S. H. Kress and F. W. Woolworth Stores in South Carolina," *Special Report #3*, August 13, 1960. Stephen Motte, Research on the Civil Rights Movement in Florence, SC, Florence County Museum, 2011–14.
67. Community Relations Committee, "A Statement of Support: Believing These Things, We Voice our Individual and Collective Support," 1963. Stephen Motte, Research on the Civil Rights Movement in Florence, SC, *Florence County Museum*, 2011–14.
68. Larry Falck, "James A. Rogers, Progressive Editor, and the 1969 Racial Disturbances in Florence, SC," (unpublished manuscript, May 2016). For more on the SCLC, see Adam Fairclough, "The Preachers and the People: The Origins and Early Years of the Southern Christian Leadership Conference, 1955–1959," *The Journal of Southern History* 52, no. 3 (1986): 403–40; and *To Redeem the Soul of America: The Southern Christian Leadership Conference and Martin Luther King, Jr.* (Athens: University of Georgia Press, 1987).
69. Essie Gunter Gross, Conversation with Stephen Motte, Florence County Museum, March 4, 2014; Miller interview.
70. *United States of America v. Florence County School District 1*, Civil Action no. 70-609 (2017).
71. Florence County Public School Statistics / Demographics, Public Schools K12, "Wilson High School, West Florence High School, and South Florence High School," https://publicschoolsk12.com/high-schools/sc/florence-county/.
72. Miller interview.

WORKS CITED

Allen, Delia B. "The Forgotten *Brown* Case: *Briggs v. Elliott* and Its Legacy in South Carolina." *Peabody Journal of Education* 94 (2019): 442–67.

Blasi, Anthony J. *Segregationist Violence and Civil Rights Movements in Tuscaloosa.* Lanham, MD: University Press of America, 1980.

Brinson, Claudia Smith. *Stories of Struggle: The Clash over Civil Rights in South Carolina.* Columbia: University of South Carolina Press, 2020.

Brown, Nikki L. M., and Barry M. Stentiford, eds. *Jim Crow: A Historical Encyclopedia of the American Mosaic.* Westport, CT: Greenwood, 2014.

Burke, W. Lewis. *All for Civil Rights: African American Lawyers in South Carolina, 1868–1968.* Athens: University of Georgia Press, 2017.

Collins, Ann V. *All Hell Broke Loose: American Race Riots from the Progressive Era through World War II*. Santa Barbara, CA: Praeger, 2012.

Dalrymple, A. V. *Liberty Dethroned: An Indictment of the Ku Klux Klan Based Solely upon Its Own Pronouncements, Philosophy, and Acts of Mob Violence*. Philadelphia, PA: Times Publishing Company, 1923.

Egerton, Charlotte C. "More than Nickels and Dimes: S. H. Kress Stores in the New South." MA thesis, University of North Carolina Wilmington, 2012.

Eighty-Eighth Annual Report of the State Superintendent of Education, State of South Carolina, 1955–1956. Columbia, SC: State Budget and Control Board, 1956.

Fairclough, Adam. "The Preachers and the People: The Origins and Early Years of the Southern Christian Leadership Conference, 1955–1959." *Journal of Southern History* 52, no. 3 (1986): 403–40.

———. *To Redeem the Soul of America: The Southern Christian Leadership Conference and Martin Luther King, Jr.* Athens: University of Georgia Press, 1987.

Fendrich, James M. "Keeping the Faith or Pursuing the Good Life: A Study of the Consequences of Participation in the Civil Rights Movement." *American Sociological Review* 42, no. 1 (1977): 144–57.

Fleming, Harold C. "Resistance Movements and Racial Desegregation." *The Annals of the American Academy of Political and Social Science* 304 (1956): 46–47.

Hale, John. "'The Fight was Instilled in Us': High School Activism and the Civil Rights Movement in Charleston." *South Carolina Historical Magazine* 114, no. 1 (2013): 4–28.

Heyward, Joseph. "Changes in African American Race Relations in Florence." Francis Marion University African American Faculty and Staff Coalition Cultural Conversations Series. YouTube. 1:38. November 6, 2020. https://www.youtube.com/.

Hine, William C. "Civil Rights and Campus Wrongs: South Carolina State College Students Protest, 1955–1968." *The South Carolina Historical Magazine* 97, no. 4 (1996): 310–31.

———. "Joseph Hayne Rainey." *South Carolina Encyclopedia* (Columbia: University of South Carolina Press, 2006), www.scencyclopedia.org.

Kolb, Wade III. "*Briggs v. Elliot:* A Study in Grassroots Activism and Trial Advocacy from the Early Civil Rights Era." *Journal of Southern Legal History* 19 (2011): 123–75.

Lewis, J. D. "South Carolina—Military Airfields in World War II." *Carolana*. https://www.carolana.com/SC/Transportation/aviation/.

Library of Congress. "Youth in the Civil Rights Movement." www.loc.gov.

"Matthew J. Perry." Interview by Joseph Mosnier. Civil Rights Project, Library of Congress. June 7, 2011. www.loc.gov.

Morgan, Iwan. *From Sit-Ins to SNCC: The Student Civil Rights Movement in the 1960s*. Gainesville: University Press of Florida, 2012.

Morris, Aldon. "Black Southern Student Sit-in Movement: An Analysis of Internal Organization." *American Sociological Review* 46, no. 6 (1981): 744–67.

Pirone, Jean Maddern. *F. W. Woolworth and the American Five and Dime: A Social History*. Jefferson, NC: McFarland, 2003.

Santoro, Wayne A. "The Civil Rights Movement and the Right to Vote: Black Protest, Segregationist Violence and the Audience." *Social Forces* 86, no. 4 (2008): 1391–1414.

Schmidt, Christopher W. "Why the 1960 Lunch Counter Sit-Ins Worked: A Case Study of Law and Social Movement Mobilization." *Indiana Journal of Law and Social Equality* 5, no. 2 (2017): 280–300.

Sellers, Cleveland. Interview by John Dittmer, directed by John Bishop. Civil Rights Project. Library of Congress. March 21, 2013. www.loc.gov.

Sitkoff, Harvard. "Racial Militancy and Interracial Violence in the Second World War." *The Journal of American History* 58, no. 3 (1971): 661–81.

McKrae Game and the Christian Closet

Conversion Therapy in South Carolina

Esther Liu Godfrey

In June 2021, Columbia's city council passed an ordinance that created the first restrictions within South Carolina on conversion therapy, banning licensed therapists from using the approach on minors within the city limits. Although twenty states, the District of Columbia, and many cities and municipalities across the country have already passed legislation making conversion therapy for minors illegal, and President Biden signed an executive order in June 2022 that limits federal funding for conversion therapy, the four-to-three Columbia city council vote revealed how closely contested the practice remains in South Carolina—even in the state's capital, which houses the flagship university. *Conversion therapy*, also known as reparative therapy, promises to identify and "heal" the causes of a person's same-sex attractions, often through prayer and sometimes through the "casting out" of demons. Allegedly, through conversion therapy, a person could become "ex-gay" and pursue a heterosexual life. Many professional organizations, including the American Medical Association, the American Psychological Association, and the American Academy of Pediatrics, have denounced the practice as harmful and unethical, but the Williams Institute of the University of California, Los Angeles, estimates that 698,000 individuals have received conversion therapy in the United States.[1] Religious organizations and counselors remain immune from existing bans.

The long-term negative effects of this practice have begun to attract national attention through works such as the *New York Times* bestselling memoir by Garrard Conley, *Boy Erased*, which became a major motion picture, and the 2021 Netflix documentary *Pray Away*.[2] The human consequences in South Carolina are unavoidably tragic and, at the same time, an intrinsic element of the culture of lesbian, gay, bisexual, transgender, queer/questioning, plus other (LGBTQ+) individuals in the South. An examination of the life of McKrae Game, an "ex-ex-gay" Spartanburg native who appears as both villain and victim in the history of conversion therapy, demonstrates how complex the journey to personal acceptance can be.[3]

McKrae was born in Spartanburg in 1968 into what seemed to be a typical white Southern family. His sister, Maria, was popular and competed in dance competitions. His father sold real estate and then had several business ventures. His mother was a housewife. They all attended the First Baptist Church in downtown Spartanburg, where McKrae has happy memories of church potlucks and where he was baptized. McKrae remembers playing for hours with Legos in his parents' basement or, whenever the weather was nice, exploring the neighborhood's creeks. The appearance of normalcy was carefully crafted by his mother, who only left the house in perfectly styled wigs and matching pantsuits and who obsessively cleaned and managed their home. Any inclination that McKrae expressed toward anything "abnormal," like the time he came home wearing a necklace he had borrowed from another boy at school, was quickly corrected. "You look like a goddamn fucking faggot," his mother screamed at him.

He also remembers trying on his sister's ballerina costume and the red-hot shame he felt when he was discovered. Easily distracted, McKrae struggled in school, eventually being held back a grade. His parents later moved Maria, and then him, to the private Spartanburg Day School. There, other students promptly dubbed him "McGay," a slur that was both confusing and uncomfortable to the prepubescent McKrae. His parents divorced when he was in his teens, but McKrae later thrived in high school. After mowing a few neighborhood lawns, McKrae bought equipment, hired some friends, and created a sizable lawn care service. Returning to the public high school, McKrae found himself to be popular: He had plenty of pocket money from his lawn care business, his sister was a popular cheerleader at the public high school, and his father let him throw raucous parties for his friends in his home. McKrae dated girls and had sex with them. He didn't tell anyone that he often thought about rock stars like Bon Jovi and Adam Ant, whom he had seen on MTV, when he slept with girls.

Life changed for McKrae when he turned eighteen, graduated from high school, and moved into a house across the street from his mother. A clever businessman, McKrae rented the house and then sublet a separate upstairs apartment to offset his own rent. His mother helped him show the apartment after he placed an ad, and when he met the prospective renter she had found, he laughed and told her, "Mama, that man is gay." His mother shook her head in skeptical disbelief. "Mama," he said, "he just asked me to have the windows cleaned. He said they are *filthy*. He's gay." Doubtfully, his mom shrugged her shoulders and brushed it off. McKrae rented out the apartment.

The upstairs tenant quickly picked up on McKrae's repressed attraction, and McKrae had his first gay sexual experience with the tenant. He began traveling several times a week from Spartanburg to Greenville, where, in the late 1980s, a private nightclub called The Castle catered to an LGBTQ+ clientele.[4] McKrae had never been around openly gay people before, and the experience was liberating. Feeling a mixture of fear and belonging, McKrae kept his membership card to The Castle in his wallet, even though he largely restricted his open displays of attraction to men to gay-friendly areas in Greenville and, eventually, Atlanta. For his family, friends, and clients, McKrae maintained a heterosexual identity, even when he began dating men and entering longer term relationships. Once, his mother walked in on him kissing his boyfriend in his living room. After hearing the news, his father asked him to go for a drive. "I understand that you like guys," his father said, "But you like girls too, right?" McKrae shook his head no. "I really wish you would reconsider and stay open to women. I just think it will be a much more difficult life for you being gay and only being with men, rather than being with a woman and just having sex with men." This advice was not what McKrae expected to hear from his father, and, many years later, after his father had remarried and divorced again, McKrae learned that his father had himself engaged in affairs with men. For many in the South, being gay was tolerated as long as it was not flaunted and, ideally, remained concealed within an outward-facing heterosexual marriage. McKrae found ways to prevent his mother from unexpected drop-ins, and despite what his mother had seen, he realized that maintaining the façade of traditional heterosexuality was enough to satisfy his family.

For three years, McKrae enjoyed life as a young, gay man. While he refrained from fully embracing his identity in Spartanburg, he was active in the Greenville gay community and eventually fell in love. Growing closer to his boyfriend's family in Greenville, McKrae began to experience relationships that did not require hiding one's sexual orientation. Around his boyfriend's family, the young couple and their displays of affection were not merely tolerated but treated like any other healthy relationship. However, this source of stability abruptly ended when McKrae's boyfriend was sentenced to prison for a DUI charge that had happened years prior. Tragically, while in prison, McKrae's boyfriend learned that he was HIV positive. Although McKrae's family had stopped attending church regularly when he was a young teen, he now feared that God was punishing him. The social structures and teachings of Evangelical Christianity remained deeply engrained in his thinking. McKrae started to hear what he believed were direct messages from heaven. Watching the weekly drag show at The Castle, McKrae thought he heard a voice say, "This is not where you are supposed to be." Today, when McKrae looks back at his younger self, he sees a man conflicted: "My mind was telling me one thing. My body was telling me another."

Another landscaper in Spartanburg invited McKrae over for dinner, then to church, and eventually to a meeting about an exciting business opportunity. Feeling lost, McKrae enjoyed the attention of this man, who was a bit older and had all of the things that signaled a traditional Southern family: a successful business, a nice home, and a pregnant wife. At this man's invitation, McKrae attended an information session at a local hotel about selling Amway products. McKrae left the Amway meeting with a one-hundred-seventy-five-dollar startup kit and halfheartedly persuaded his mom to buy some plastic wrap and dishwashing detergent. Selling Amway products did not really matter that much to McKrae, but being accepted and encouraged by this new set of friends did. For a short period, McKrae vacillated between these two different worlds, having dinner with his new Amway friends before driving to The Castle later that evening and joining his friends for Sunday morning worship service after a late night at the club. "Don't you want to have a family one day, McKrae?" probed the wife of his friend. When McKrae thought about it, he knew he did want kids, but in the early 1990s, gay marriage or adoption were not realistic possibilities.

The lifestyles of his Amway friends appeared to be the only way to create a loving family, something McKrae deeply wanted. A few months later, his new friends invited him to an Amway convention in Tampa, Florida. Researchers have classified Amway as a "quasi-religious organization" because of the shared spiritual beliefs of its core community.[5] Because Amway operates under a multilevel marketing, or "direct sales," model, the growth of the organization is predicated on the personal recruitment and mentoring efforts of its members. Existing Amway "independent business owners" identify others who might be receptive to the brand's worldview. Thus, Amway's conventions offered seminars and motivational speeches to its tens of thousands of attendees, but they also incorporated Christian music, testimonials, and sermons, packing football stadiums like large tent revivals. Throughout the convention, McKrae found himself more and more emotional, weeping uncontrollably at times. On the final day, McKrae had a conversion experience, going to the altar onstage at the stadium floor. This "coming to Jesus" moment went hand-in-hand with a renunciation of

McKrae's identity; when the speaker asked the audience to repent from their sins, McKrae only thought about life with his gay friends. When his friends from Spartanburg gathered around him in celebration, McKrae blurted out in a tearful confession, "I've been living as a homosexual." His friend's wife hugged him and patted him on the back. "We know. We've been praying for you," she said.

Although McKrae had not been attending church for many years, the religious component of his internalized homophobia was strong.[6] One of his first thoughts was, "Now I can go to heaven and not to hell." But Christianity offered protection here on Earth, not just in the afterlife, by outwardly reinforcing compulsory heterosexuality and conventional gender roles and by providing a "Christian closet" in which to hide his sexual orientation.[7] On returning to Spartanburg after the Amway conference, McKrae solicited the advice of a local pastor, who told him to join a large congregation with an active singles program. McKrae returned to First Baptist Church of Spartanburg, the church of his youth, and threw himself into a new circle of friends and activities. His friends from The Castle tried to contact him for a while, leaving exasperated messages on his answering machine warning that he had been brainwashed, but he ignored them. Eventually, those calls stopped. McKrae did not share with everyone at First Baptist that he had recently enjoyed life as a gay man, but he did tell church leaders. When he was eventually tapped to become a leader in their youth ministry program, church leaders gave him clear instructions. First, he had to promise to stop drinking. Second, if he ever returned to his former "lifestyle," he had to leave the church and promise not to come back. Filled with a new sense of belonging and acceptance, McKrae readily agreed to both.

As part of his new Christian identity, McKrae stopped listening to rock music and started listening to contemporary Christian radio. His landscaping business in Spartanburg continued to grow, and he was driving his truck between job sites when he heard a radio advertisement for "people who are homosexual but don't want to be." The advertisement announced a one-day conference in Greenville. McKrae did not want anyone to know that he was still attracted to men, and, once again, Greenville promised some degree of anonymity. This conference was small, with thirty or forty men and women in a small church on the outskirts of town. After praise and worship, the organizer, Dan, explained that there was hope for change and that therapy could get at the sources of same-sex attraction, which stemmed, according to Dan, from childhood family dynamics or abuse. At the end of the day, McKrae met Dan and bought the book *You Don't Have to Be Gay*, by Jeff

Konrad. He told his parents about the conference, and his mother offered to pay for weekly individual and group counseling sessions with Dan.

Group therapy was refreshing for McKrae because, now that he was no longer going to The Castle, he no longer had a community of gay friends. Even though the individuals in group therapy were, like McKrae, trying to stop being gay, McKrae felt connected by their shared experiences. Each week, group members would share their personal triumphs and setbacks, and McKrae could see that he was not the only person who was trying—and failing—to repress his sexual attractions. Individual therapy began with confessions. McKrae confided in Dan his childhood fascination with his sister's clothes, his former relationships, and his fears of being alone. Dan told McKrae to keep a prayer journal, which McKrae dutifully did, highlighting the parts each week that he wanted to discuss with Dan. Part of Dan's approach involved repairing failures in parenting from McKrae's childhood by recreating aspects of the parent–child relationship, so during some weeks they would spend the session playing with Legos on the floor. Dan encouraged McKrae to think about the small things that made him attracted to men. Was it the clothing? Was it the man's hair? Dan suggested that pinpointing and resolving whatever was triggering could dismantle the same-sex attraction. Dan's approach was not purely psychological. As months progressed, sessions also incorporated Dan's prayerful laying of hands on McKrae, speaking in tongues, and the casting out of evil spirits.

On many levels, the conversion seemed to be working. Pushing through great anxiety, McKrae arranged through his family doctor to be privately screened for HIV. McKrae tested negative, which he took as a sign that God was pleased with his renunciation of his sexual orientation. He signed up for a dating service and was paired with a young Evangelical woman whose father was a pastor. Within six months, they were engaged to be married. McKrae's parents were thrilled and openly expressed their relief: "McKrae, please put this behind you and live your life. No one has to know." But McKrae felt compelled to openness. Traveling by bus with a men's group from First Baptist Church to a Promise Keepers convention in Boulder, Colorado, McKrae stood up in the aisle of the bus on the long drive home and testified to the men on the bus.[8] He confessed to living a former sinful life and thanked God for delivering him from temptation. Although McKrae was fearful before the testimonial, which he felt God called him to do, he was immediately rewarded. Many men on the bus were in tears by the end of his story, and they praised him for his honesty and bravery. Buoyed up by their approval, McKrae began to feel more comfortable with identifying as "ex-gay." He told his fiancée about his past, and they worked together to plan a large wedding. He continued to go to individual and group therapy. Another young man from church approached him and admitted that he "used to be gay too." Together, they began attending an additional conversion therapy group in Charlotte.

In some ways, group therapy normalized the "falls" that ex-gays experienced. Each week, members confessed to lapses into same-sex fantasies or even real-life hookups. McKrae often masturbated to *Men's Exercise* magazine, the closest thing he could find to male pornography at the grocery store. McKrae alternated between feelings of guilt and pride. For all outward appearances, he was succeeding in his goals to be ex-gay. He was engaged to be married. He had stopped drinking and going to gay clubs. He was leading a Christian life. Momentary "falls" were evidence of the Devil's continued temptation to sin. They were to be expected, experienced, and then confessed. For many months, McKrae felt in control of this cycle and his desires. His wedding announcements went out. His fiancée had her bridal shower. Then, without any premeditation, he began having sex with his new friend from church, sometimes before they drove to Charlotte for group therapy. Riddled with shame, he told his fiancée not long before their wedding date. Despite his promises that it would never happen again, she ended the relationship. The wedding was cancelled.

The fallout from this experience was painful, although it could have had even more serious consequences. When McKrae told his friend that he was ending their sexual relationship, his friend was devastated and attempted suicide. After seeing that his friend got additional support, McKrae left First Baptist for another large Baptist church in Spartanburg, First North. McKrae was able to transition quickly from one religious social circle to another. Wanting to limit her own exposure to negative gossip, McKrae's ex-fiancée did not publicly expose the reason for calling off the wedding. As he turned twenty-seven, McKrae began to feel some relief that the wedding did not happen. Although he still wanted to get married, he questioned whether his former fiancée was the right person for him. McKrae did not question the conversion therapy message. He believed that he had simply been tempted by the Devil and had made a mistake—one he would not make again.

McKrae made friends quickly at First North. Within months, he was asked to teach Sunday School. Unlike at First Baptist, McKrae did not share that he was ex-gay. He joined the adult singles group and became roommates with another man from church. Through these connections, he met soon met Julie, a beautiful blonde woman in her early thirties. Within a year of breaking off his first engagement, McKrae and Julie were dating. He told Julie about his prior engagement but not the reason the wedding was called off. Before he proposed marriage, however, he told Julie that he needed to tell her something about his past. "It's not really bad," he said in preparation, "but it's not really good." Without going into many details, he told Julie that he used to be gay. She let out a sigh of relief and laughed. "Gosh, McKrae, I thought you were going to tell me that you used to be addicted to drugs or something."

Despite knowing the reasons for the failure of the first engagement, McKrae's therapist, Dan, now viewed McKrae as a success story. In Spartanburg and Greenville, the Evangelical fight against equality of LGBTQ+ people was escalating, and the ex-gay movement participated openly in efforts to shut down "the gay agenda." In Greenville, there were efforts to prevent a group home for people with AIDS, and plans were blocked for a gay-affirming church to remodel and occupy a former school. In the summer of 1996, both Spartanburg and Greenville County Councils introduced resolutions that claimed "gay lifestyles" were in opposition to community standards. The International Olympic Committee threatened to refuse the Olympic torch to be carried through any county that adopted such a position, as it had done with Cobb County in Georgia three years prior.[9] Evangelical churches took issue with this punishment, claiming that they were forced to accept an immoral and anti-Christian lifestyle. Pastors, including the pastor at First North, spoke from the pulpits in favor of the resolutions. McKrae was asked to speak before Greenville County Council, where hundreds of citizens gathered, mostly in favor of the resolution. McKrae pleaded, "I used to be gay. That lifestyle almost destroyed my life. It almost destroyed me. Thankfully, I was saved by our Lord Jesus Christ. I'm here to tell you that no one has to be gay. Our county has to take up a stance against this lifestyle. We should never condone it. For the good of the children. For the good of us all." McKrae received thunderous applause and cheers and was later quoted in local news stories. Ultimately, the Spartanburg resolution was passed but then rescinded, but the Greenville resolution passed and held. The Olympic torch did not go through Greenville County.

This time, the wedding went off as planned, and McKrae and Julie were married. McKrae describes the early years of their relationship as ideal. They were best friends, and, although McKrae was not sexually attracted to her, he felt sincerely in love with her. Although he had had sex with other women in high school, he would have to fantasize about men to be aroused. With Julie, this was not the case, at least not in the beginning, and their emotional bond supported a sexual relationship. In the early years of their marriage, they went to the movies. They went out to dinner. They moved from the singles group at church into the married groups for men and women. Only when they began trying to conceive a child did sex become formulaic and, as McKrae describes, like "work." As the couple struggled with fertility issues, McKrae became more and more tempted by gay fantasies. He found a convenience store that sold gay porn magazines, and he would impulsively buy one, only to burn it a few days later. Late at night after Julie had fallen asleep, he began calling the phone sex numbers advertised in the magazines. When Julie caught him, first with the magazines, and then with the phone bill, he apologized and prepared himself for her to leave him. Each time she did not react angrily but said that, when he was tempted, he needed to call her and that she would pray with him. McKrae was grateful for Julie's response and would control his behaviors temporarily, but as the stress of infertility grew, McKrae would return to gay outlets. It was during this period of stress that McKrae engaged in his first extramarital affair, a spontaneous encounter with a repairman. He hid this one-time slip from Julie for months, but he was riddled with guilt. When he did confess what had happened, Julie again forgave him.

Julie's unconditional love inspired McKrae to try harder to repress his desires. He learned, through Dan, that there was a larger organization for ex-gay individuals called Exodus International. With Julie, he attended his first Exodus conference in Massanetta Springs, Virginia. Although he had attended the Amway conference in Florida and the Promise Keepers conference in Colorado, this trip was his first exposure to the size and scope of the ex-gay world. The conference days were organized around thematic workshops on topics like "Sex Addiction" and "Pornography" and were divided for men and women. Praise and worship gatherings were for everyone, and meals were served family style. Julie attended some of the workshops but often went back to their room to rest. "This is your thing," she told McKrae, "not mine. You like talking about your feelings and everything. I don't." But she was also encouraging. "I think this is good for you," she said. McKrae had never been around so many ex-gay people, and this was just a regional conference. When he heard others talking about the national conference that was coming up in Seattle, he knew he wanted to go. The conference in Virginia also gave McKrae a new sense of calling. After he heard one participant give testimony, he felt like he had another direct message from God. The man explained the need for more ex-gay individuals to go public with their stories: "So many people walk away from homosexuality and never tell anyone. That's why so many people take this journey alone." Similar to his experience at The Castle, McKrae believed that he heard a voice in his head saying, "This is what I've called you to do."

At this point, McKrae had been attending conversion therapy for over six years with Dan. Within group sessions, he became something of a leader, and, when someone would miss several weeks or disappear from group, McKrae would call them to encourage them to come back. Eventually, some group members began calling McKrae to express frustrations or to receive encouragement. At times, Dan seemed to support McKrae as a leader within the group; at other times, he seemed to resent it. That summer, McKrae and Julie flew to Seattle to attend the Exodus International national conference, and McKrae became more familiar with the structure of the organization. Back in South Carolina, Dan invited McKrae to assist him in a six-week workshop, at a church, for heterosexual people who wanted to understand LGBTQ+ people. This church was not what would be called gay affirming, but it did embrace a "love the sinner, hate the sin" view of sexuality. As Dan led each workshop with the premise that people did not choose to be gay, he explained to the participants, many who had friends, children, or relatives who were gay, that same-sex attraction stemmed from childhood trauma and failed parent–child relationships. After Dan's lecture and a short break, McKrae would provide a firsthand narrative from an ex-gay perspective. He would talk about his parents' divorce and the lack of attention he received as a child. He detailed his years living as a young gay man and then his religious conversion that led to a new ex-gay life. When he proudly declared that he was happily married and that they were hoping to have a baby, he fulfilled the ex-gay narrative, and participants praised him for renouncing his former lifestyle and doing the right thing. As with the Greenville County Council, McKrae found himself as a poster boy for what could be. He was proof that no one had to remain gay.

McKrae's position in the ex-gay world began to rise. At Dan's suggestion, he traveled to Promise Keepers conventions and set up booths for Exodus International. Some attendees of this Evangelical men's group were resistant to the display, because they found even the recognition of gay people offensive, but McKrae experienced a lot of positive feedback as well. Through this work, McKrae also met others involved with Exodus International, some of whom were surprised and curious about this new rising star in ex-gay ministry. Back at home, another significant development happened. Dan let him read a letter, handwritten in blue ink on white copier paper, from a sixteen-year-old boy. The teenager lived in Spartanburg and had no way of getting to Greenville or money to pay for therapy, but he was asking Dan for help to stop being gay. McKrae knew what Dan was going to say before he said it. "Why don't you see if you can help him?" Dan asked. Later that week, McKrae picked up the teenager from his mother's trailer and took him out to eat. At the end of the meal, the boy asked in earnest, "So, do you think you can fix me?" McKrae smiled reassuringly back, "Well, you know, I used to be gay."

Life began to change quickly for McKrae. His landscape business was thriving, and Julie became pregnant. They bought their first home. With Julie's support, McKrae formed a board of directors and organized a non-profit organization to create his first conversion therapy ministry: Truth Ministry. Because McKrae had never gone to college, his father gave him the money that he had set aside for his tuition to fund the ministry's initial startup. He purchased radio ads on the local Christian station, His Love Radio, and they featured a story about him. Driving around Spartanburg, McKrae grew fond of hearing himself on the radio, "Hi, I'm McKrae Game, and I used to be gay. For those of you out there who are struggling with homosexuality or have someone close to them, perhaps a friend or a family member, who is struggling, I want you to know that God has a plan. No one has to give in to homosexuality. There is another path, made possible by faith in Jesus Christ our Savior. To find out more about freedom from sexual sin, visit www.truthministry.org." McKrae started the process of becoming an affiliate member of Exodus International, and he stopped seeing Dan, who now expressed regret for encouraging McKrae into leadership and counseling positions. Never someone who could be considered a shy person, McKrae nevertheless signed up for a Dale Carnegie course to improve his skills in public speaking. He read and reread books like Joseph Nicolosi's *Restorative Therapy for Male Homosexuality*, highlighting and taking notes as he went.[10] Meanwhile, his client base grew. Clients signed a form acknowledging that he was not a professional counselor, and they paid by voluntary donation. McKrae's church, First North, sponsored him and gave him a monthly stipend to speak at churches and conferences in the area. He attended the annual Southern Baptist Convention, which officially endorsed Truth Ministry and recommended it to their members. Soon, McKrae sold his landscaping business so that he could focus on the ministry full time, and he was promoted to be director of the South Atlantic region for Exodus International. Julie became pregnant with their second child, and they both felt like God was rewarding them for the way they were living their lives.

As momentum grew in the early 2000s for the South Carolina legislature to amend the state constitution and define marriage as between one man and one woman, the Southern Baptist Convention donated five thousand dollars to Truth Ministry for McKrae to travel to churches and community organizations across the state and speak in favor of the amendment. The ministry grew and hired more employees. McKrae purchased billboards along the highways and interstates of the Upstate, some with his face on them. The billboards declared, "I Questioned Homosexuality. Change is Possible. Discover How." Truth Ministry opened satellite offices around the region in Greenville, Charleston, Savannah, and Asheville, and a team of twenty leaders moderated online support groups. After Barack Obama was elected, McKrae was part of a larger effort to push back against legislation supporting LGBTQ+ equality, flying to Washington, DC, to speak against the Matthew Shepard and James Byrd Jr. Hate Crimes Act.[11] Eventually, Truth Ministry became the largest member organization within Exodus International. McKrae became a featured speaker at the national Exodus conferences, and he developed a workshop based upon his own experiences. Without irony, he called the workshop "The Transparent Life."

Despite all of these successes, a loving wife and two beautiful children, McKrae continued to struggle. Gay pornography and masturbation were constant temptations, but, at least for some conversion therapy leaders, this was an expected part of the daily struggle against sin. A message that is consistent throughout "The Transparent Life" is a recognition and acceptance of the endless fight. McKrae had not had an extramarital affair since their struggles with infertility, but he thought incessantly about men. As a group leader himself, he knew that his desires were, even in the ex-gay world, normal. Unlike some conversion therapy leaders, McKrae did not promise that same-sex attractions would stop but that they could be redirected so that people could maintain a Christian lifestyle. Same-sex attraction and its theoretical opposite, heterosexuality, became more a question of choices and actions rather than feelings and longings. Proponents of conversion therapy were not united on this position, however, and as years passed, rifts began to form within ex-gay ministry about their stance and messaging regarding same-sex desire and the LGBTQ+ community at large. Alan Chambers, the president of Exodus International, began advocating for Christianity to be more welcoming to gays and lesbians. At this point, Chambers still held that same-sex relationships were sinful but began to suggest that it was no greater a sin than behaviors such as drinking or gambling. Chambers eventually met with the leader of the Gay Christian Network, and rumblings grew from within Exodus International that the organization was becoming too "gay friendly."

McKrae felt torn. Exodus International was the largest conversion therapy network in the country, and he was one of its most prominent leaders. When some members proposed breaking off into a new organization that focused more intently on the idea that same-sex relationships were sinful, they invited McKrae to join them. Yet McKrae also understood the evolution of Chambers's views and was not entirely opposed to the more tolerant vision that he had for Exodus International. Although McKrae had aggressively lobbied against the 2009 Hate Crimes Prevention Act, now that it had passed, he could see that it was positive, and he questioned why he had been so vehemently opposed to it. Most important, McKrae realized that he sided with Chambers on the issue of same-sex desire. Both Chambers and McKrae were becoming clearer in their statements that they could not change sexual attractions—that conversion therapy really centered on changing behaviors. In 2013, sensing growing resistance to a more inclusive message from within Exodus International, Chambers emailed the board of directors, copying McKrae, and informed them of his decision to close the ministry. The next month, Chambers appeared on *Our America with Lisa Ling* and publicly apologized for his role in conversion therapy. Exodus International was over.[12]

Chambers's decision to copy McKrae on the email gave him advance notice of the folding of Exodus; the official announcement came at the annual Exodus national conference, which was held during the same week when the episode featuring Lisa Ling's interview with Chambers aired. To McKrae, it seemed as if Chambers was passing the baton to him intentionally. Although Chambers had disavowed the practice of conversion therapy, he seemed to be suggesting that, if it was going to continue, he wanted to encourage the more lenient factions within the ministry. Seeing the collapse of Exodus as an opportunity, McKrae was poised and ready to elevate Truth Ministry as the new Exodus International. McKrae used the month between the private email announcing the closing of Exodus and the national conference to rebrand Truth Ministry as Hope for Wholeness, a new national ex-gay ministry. Many former Exodus affiliate ministries transitioned directly from the old organization into Hope for Wholeness. A rival organization, Restored Hope Network, formed to represent the members who wanted to return to a less tolerant message.[13] But McKrae was now in charge of the nation's largest conversion therapy ministry.

Hope for Wholeness held its first national conference in 2013 at the First Presbyterian Church in downtown Greenville. Stephen Baldwin was the keynote speaker. Realizing that many people did not live near an affiliate ministry, Hope for Wholeness launched a DVD conversion therapy curriculum that could be purchased by individuals or checked out from church libraries. Production of the curriculum was fraught with difficulties, as sessions with instructors would have to be pulled when, one by one, the instructors themselves came out as gay or lesbian. When finally published, the curriculum was successful, further cementing Hope for Wholeness as the leader in the world of ex-gay ministry. McKrae transformed his former workshop into a book, *The Transparent Life*.[14] Momentum for the ministry continued to grow, but so did McKrae's doubts. He texted Alan Chambers, "Do you think homosexuals will go to hell?" This question had been an important part of McKrae's own conversion: When he had promised to leave behind his life as a young gay man at that Amway conference, his first thought had been, "Now I can go to heaven." Eventually, Chambers responded to McKrae's question, "I don't know." Finally, after decades of working in conversion therapy, McKrae felt relief. "I don't know" opened the door to a possibility other than damnation. "I don't know" was liberating.

Additionally, with the elevated national profile, McKrae began to experience increased scrutiny from his board of directors. What may have been considered within ex-gay circles as one's private struggles with extramarital or same-sex desire became normalized as topics for discussion at monthly board meetings. The board questioned McKrae about his consumption of pornography, his sex life with Julie, and his masturbation. The board sent McKrae and Julie to marriage counseling; they ordered McKrae to private counseling; and, by majority vote, they made him attend Sex Addicts Anonymous. Since the birth of their children, McKrae and Julie had long enjoyed a companionate, mostly sexless marriage. McKrae still considered Julie his best friend, and although she agreed to go to counseling, they both shook their heads in confusion. McKrae was forced to explain to his board, "My wife doesn't want to have sex. She doesn't care if I masturbate," but the board held firm in its decision. Hope for Wholeness may have been more open than the rivaling conversion therapy groups, but the central premise of the organization remained the ongoing scrutiny of personal sexual matters, and McKrae was not immune to this fact. When McKrae found a therapist who would accept his insurance, he was dismayed to find that the therapist was gay affirming. He immediately told the board of directors, but they dismissed his concerns, stating that they saw sex addiction as more of his problem than sexual orientation. When he told the therapist that he led an ex-gay ministry, the therapist told him it would be fine: "Don't worry, McKrae. I won't make you gay."

McKrae started to experience severe physical symptoms. Some days, he could not get out of bed. Migraine headaches became debilitating. While walking across a parking lot to his car one day, he had to call Julie crying. He could see his car, it was only a couple of spaces away, but he could not walk to it. He went to the doctor for tests, but there did not appear to be anything medically wrong. "Stress," the doctor suggested, "Get some rest." That Christmas, the board of directors gave him a gift certificate to Cataloochee, a ski resort in Western North Carolina. McKrae had not been skiing in years, but the experience was liberating, so far removed from the world in which he was typically immersed. McKrae slowly transitioned away from group and individual therapy into a more detached role within the ministry, writing the weekly newsletter and overseeing operations. There was nothing in his contract with Hope for Wholeness that dictated his schedule, and he gradually decreased his hours there from sixty- and seventy-hour workweeks to a more moderate schedule. He began spending less time in the office, and his health slowly improved. Then, while skiing with his teenage son at another resort, Sugar Mountain in Banner Elk, North Carolina, he was invited to try out for ski patrol. McKrae gleefully accepted a part-time position with the resort, working there on weekends, and traveling back to Spartanburg for the week. Julie was supportive. "I think it'll be good for you," she said.

Although Banner Elk, or even the nearby college town of Boone, is hardly an area known for its progressive spirit, the culture of ski patrol was a new world for McKrae, who had not had close friends outside of the Evangelical Christian community in over twenty years. No one there knew him as a leader in ex-gay ministry, and, although none of the other patrollers identified as gay, the general sentiment among both male and female patrollers was LGBTQ+ friendly. McKrae started working ten- and twelve-hour days on the slopes on Saturdays and Sundays, crashing on friends' couches in exchange for buying dinner. When ski season ended, he stayed in touch with his new friends, and the group even met up over the summer at the beach for a get together. McKrae's world was expanding.

Back in Spartanburg, however, tensions within Hope for Wholeness were growing. McKrae's book made clear his ongoing struggles with pornography, and the board of directors was not pleased with this public confession from the organization's president. Some of McKrae's positions in the weekly newsletter also drew ire from the board. In one essay, McKrae compared masturbation to eating Snickers bars. Having one every now and then is not that bad for you, he argued. When McKrae left for an annual retreat with ministry leaders, the organization's secretary asked him to leave his laptop, saying that she needed it to print postage. After he returned from the trip, things began to unravel. His business credit cards were declined. One of his insurance claims for therapy failed to go through. He asked several people what was going on, but he received only noncommittal answers. Within weeks, two members of the board flew in and, without notice, announced that they had found gay pornography on McKrae's laptop and fired him from the organization that he built and escorted him from the building. McKrae drove directly to the school where Julie worked as a receptionist, bawling hysterically. Julie listened to him until his breathing calmed and his tears subsided. "I know you don't see this right now, but this is a blessing," she said. "They did you a favor."

For a couple of months, McKrae drifted. He picked up work as a caterer, and he asked the director of ski patrol if he could work full time during the ski season. That winter, his schedule was reversed, and instead of working weekends and returning to Spartanburg for the week, he did ski patrol for most of the week, visiting Julie and the kids on weekends. McKrae gravitated toward the female ski patrollers, and they coaxed him toward a new understanding of himself. Without challenging him or asking him if he was gay, they would say things like, "I just want you to be happy," and "You need to stop living for everybody else." As McKrae drove the two-and-a-half hours back and forth from Sugar Mountain to Spartanburg, he had time to reflect on his life. Slowly, he realized that he wasn't ex-gay, he was gay. For over twenty-six years, he had been living in a fantasy world that he had helped to construct.

Coming out still took McKrae several more months. McKrae eventually created an account on the gay dating app Grindr and, with the encouragement of some male patroller friends, had his first gay sexual experience in decades. McKrae told Julie, who was more concerned about preserving the structure of the marriage, their house, and lifestyle than the details of the affair. McKrae had a large social media following, and he began to make more LGBTQ+-affirming statements online. He did not yet intend to make a public statement, but when one follower questioned, "McKrae, are you now pro-gay?" he responded, "I don't know. I know I'm not anti-gay. I am gay."

McKrae tried to stay off social media, off Grindr, and out of the public eye, but several media outlets picked up on the story. *The Post and Courier* ran a story in August 2019 about McKrae, who, by this time, had developed serious misgivings about the practices of the ex-gay ministry that he had himself founded.[15] Subsequent news outlets followed suit. *People, CBS News, Time, The Guardian, The Washington Post, BBC News*, the *New York Post*, and multiple other outlets spread the word. In multiple sources, McKrae has acknowledged the harm he has caused others through his work in ex-gay ministry.[16] In a Facebook post from August 25, 2019, McKrae declared, "I'll take advantage of any opportunity I get to share my experiences, and my belief that exgay ministry and conversion therapy IS HARMFUL." He apologized, "I WAS WRONG! Please forgive me!" For some, the narrative of an ex-gay minister coming out as gay elicited eyerolls and knowing chuckles. For others, McKrae was a bitter reminder of the hypocrisy and pain that conversion therapy caused for hundreds of thousands of people. He received death threats. Others told him he should kill himself. And there were still others who welcomed McKrae with open arms into the LGBTQ+ community. Deb Foreman, the president of the local chapter of PFLAG, messaged McKrae and invited him to lunch.[17]

McKrae's status as villain or victim in the larger history of LGBTQ+ individuals in South Carolina has yet to be determined. In an interview with McKrae in 2020 for Logo TV, Garrard Conley, the author of *Boy Erased*, expressed mixed feelings about McKrae's new position in the gay community.[18] When McKrae described that he was enjoying the opportunity to be "authentic," Conley responded, "That's kind of hard to hear, a little bit, just because it's not as if I'm not happy that you've reached a place of authenticity. It's that I wished when I walked away, I had that kind of self-assurance. You can see how those words can trigger people and upset them, right?" Conley's response is fairly typical. Many commenters found McKrae "disgusting," "insufferable," and "shameless." Some viewers acknowledged that McKrae also experienced the effects of conversion therapy, but most were reluctant to forgive his contributions to a practice that wrecked so many lives.

The past two years have brought a lot of change to McKrae's life. Exploring his sexuality as a fifty-year-old man in a pandemic was not easy. Several of McKrae's friends have noted the difference in his real age and his "gay age," pointing to the fact that he seems to have regressed to his mid-twenties, to the period when he stopped living as his true self. McKrae's social media posts are full of seductive selfies with him sporting rainbow tank tops, earrings, painted nails, and even Speedos. He now talks openly about his attraction to men, and he has had a series of short-lived relationships. McKrae and Julie are still on good terms and technically married, although he has moved out of their family home and into a rental. Since coming out, McKrae has spoken out publicly against the practice of conversion therapy, lobbied for efforts to ban the practice, and has advocated for LBGTQ+ advocacy groups like The Trevor Project. In the winters, McKrae continues to work on ski patrol at Sugar Mountain.

Esther Liu Godfrey is professor of nineteenth-century British literature at the University of South Carolina Upstate. She has published on issues of gender, race, and critical aging studies. Her current project examines various forms of problematic marriages in the nineteenth century.

NOTES

1. "Conversion Therapy and LGBT Youth." The Williams Institute. June 2019. https://williamsinstitute.law.ucla.edu/publications.
2. Garrard Conley, *Boy Erased: A Memoir of Identity, Faith and Family* (New York: Riverhead Books, 2016); *Pray Away*, directed by Kristine Stolakis (Multitude Films, 2021), www.netflix.com.
3. The biographical information on McKrae Game originates in personal interviews with the author and appears with Mr. Game's permission.
4. The Castle was a fixture in the local gay scene for decades. It closed in the early 2010s.
5. For more information about how Christian Evangelicalism was incorporated into Amway's business model, see Claudia Groβ's "Spiritual Cleansing: A Case Study on how Spirituality Can Be Mis/used by a Company," *Management Revue* 21, no. 1 (2010): 60–81.
6. J. Lock defines internalized homophobia as "the self-hatred that occurs as the result of being a socially stigmatized person." See "Treatment of Homophobia in a Gay Male Adolescent," *American Journal of Psychotherapy* 52, no. 2 (1998): 202.
7. I use the term "Christian closet" with a nod to Michael Messner's exploration of "the athletic closet" and the ways in which many competitive sports have contributed to gay men's performance of heterosexuality. See "Becoming 100 Percent Straight" in *Inside Sports*, ed. Jay Coakley and Peter Donnelly (New York: Routledge 1999), 97–104.
8. For more information about the Promise Keepers, see Rhys H. Williams, "Introduction: Promise Keepers: A Comment on Religion and Social Movements," *Sociology of Religion* 61, no. 1 (2000): 1–10.
9. Because the city of Greenville wanted nothing to do with the County's resolution, the torch was carried within the city limits. See Pete Iacobelli, "Olympic Torch Run in S.C. Tinged with Controversy, Compromise," *AP News*, June 25, 1996, https://apnews.com/article/e8e1782adfb8b51727862228597d5dae.
10. Joseph Nicolosi, *Reparative Therapy of Male Homosexuality: A New Clinical Approach* (Pasadena, CA: Liberal Mind Publishers, 1991).
11. For more information on this legislation, see the US Department of Justice, "The Matthew Shepard and James Byrd, Jr., Hate Crimes Prevention Act of 2009," www.justice.gov/crt/.

12. There are many excellent resources about the closure of Exodus International. See, for example, Jonathan Merritt's "The Downfall of the Ex-Gay Movement," *The Atlantic*, October 6, 2015.

13. Restored Hope Network avoids the term *conversion therapy* in favor of *ex-gay ministry* but continues to practice even as more states and cities ban conversion therapy. In 2020, Facebook removed Restored Hope Network from their platform.

14. McKrae Game, *The Transparent Life: Learning to Live Without a Mask* (Arlington, TX: Touch Publishing, 2015).

15. See Michael Majchrowicz, "Conversion Therapy Leader for Two Decades, McKrae Game Disavows Movement He Helped Fuel," *Post and Courier*, August 30, 2019.

16. See examples in Marisa Iati's "Conversion Therapy Center Founder Who Sought to Turn LGBTQ Christians Straight Says He's Gay, Rejects 'Cycle of Self Shame,'" *Washington Post*, September 5, 2019; and Mahita Gajanan's "'I Was a Religious Zealot That Hurt People.' After Coming Out as Gay, a Former Conversion Therapy Leader Is Apologizing to the LGBTQ Community," *Time*, September 4, 2019.

17. For more information on PFLAG (formerly Parents, Families, and Friends of Lesbians and Gays), see https://pflag.org/.

18. See "Face to Face: Conversion Therapy," from February 20, 2020, on Logo TV, available on YouTube, https://www.youtube.com/watch?v=mdGlfD3v8ac.

WORKS CITED

Conley, Garrard. *Boy Erased: A Memoir of Identity, Faith and Family*. New York: Riverhead Books, 2016.

"Conversion Therapy and LGBT Youth." The Williams Institute. June 2019. https://williamsinstitute.law.ucla.edu/publications.

Gajanan, Mahita. "'I Was a Religious Zealot That Hurt People.' After Coming Out as Gay, a Former Conversion Therapy Leader Is Apologizing to the LGBTQ Community." *Time*, September 4, 2019.

Game, McKrae. *The Transparent Life: Learning to Live Without a Mask*. Arlington, TX: Touch Publishing, 2015.

Groβ, Claudia. "Spiritual Cleansing: A Case Study on How Spirituality Can Be Mis/used by a Company." *Management Revue* 21, no. 1 (2010): 60–81.

Lock, J. "Treatment of Homophobia in a Gay Male Adolescent." *American Journal of Psychotherapy* 52 no. 2 (1998): 202–14.

Logo TV. "Face to Face: Conversion Therapy." YouTube video, 2:26. February 20, 2020. https://www.youtube.com/.

Merritt, Jonathan. "The Downfall of the Ex-Gay Movement." *The Atlantic*, October 6, 2015.

Messner, Michael. "Becoming 100 Percent Straight," in *Inside Sports*, edited by Jay Coakley and Peter Donnelly, 97–104. New York and London: Routledge, 1999.

Nicolosi, Joseph. *Reparative Therapy of Male Homosexuality: A New Clinical Approach*. Pasadena, CA: Liberal Mind Publishers, 1991.

Stolakis, Kristine, dir. Pray Away. Multitude Films, 2021. Online. www.netflix.com.

US Department of Justice. "The Matthew Shepard and James Byrd, Jr., Hate Crimes Prevention Act of 2009." https://www.justice.gov/crt/matthew-shepard-and -james-byrd-jr-hate-crimes-prevention-act-2009-0.

Williams, Rhys H. "Introduction: Promise Keepers: A Comment on Religion and Social Movements." *Sociology of Religion* 61, no. 1 (2000): 1–10.

Inclusive Placemaking

A Study of the Joseph Vaughn Plaza at Furman University

Whitni Simpson, Chiara Palladino, Benjamin K. Haywood,
Sarah Adeyinka-Skold, Alyson Farzad-Phillips, Brandon Inabinet,
Claire Whitlinger, John A. McArthur, and James Engelhardt

In 2021, among its ongoing initiatives to reckon with a historical connection to slavery, Furman University in Greenville, South Carolina, designed, constructed, and dedicated "a place for reflection and celebration of those who helped to make the university a more equitable and inclusive place."[1] The Joseph Vaughn Plaza resides in the main academic quad just in front of the university's central James B. Duke library and bears a bronze statue of Furman's first African-American undergraduate student. Vaughn enrolled at the university in January 1965 and graduated in 1968 *cum laude* with a degree in English. Dedicated in April 2021, the plaza is a central gathering site for campus events and community conversation.

The coauthors approach this monumental space as members of the Furman University faculty and student community who are interested in how spaces make possible more inclusive communities. Furman's campus, like much of the state of South Carolina and the southern United States, served mostly to celebrate achievement on battlefields and in board rooms. Given historical exclusions as to who could participate in these cultures and as to which sides of conflict get celebrated, the predominantly white campus left out African Americans and persons of color completely. These were often unconscious, implicit decisions by those in power—also mostly white men. Thus, Vaughn Plaza marks a significant shift in commemorative placemaking—toward social justice and equity in the campus landscape.

We praise this achievement to honor a more diverse set of social actors. Who we honor matters for identity construction. However, we also want to investigate this space more critically, understanding how the official need to communicate and celebrate inclusion comes with unintended consequences. In particular, the statue within the context of its use signifies exposure (when centrality to Furman might have been intended), solitude (when engagement with daily university life might have been intended), and subversion (when reflective celebration may have been intended).

Still, rather than thinking of this as a rejection of the plaza's commemorative successes, which do phenomenal work for campus life, equity, and social justice in the landscape, we use these as an invitation to explore placemaking for inclusivity more deeply. Such a critique invites us to look into design, student opinions, commemorative activities, and daily life on the plaza. By exploring the space within all of these, we better understand the difficult work of creating a more inclusive landscape—a landscape that constructs a society where all are welcome and honored, despite the racist past and racist landscapes of the United States that exist today.

Placemaking in Social Geographies of Race

To complete this analysis, the coauthors of the article review the plaza from a mixed methodological perspective. Four coauthors engaged in ethnographic observation and reflection, guided by Ronald Lee Fleming in *The Art of Place-making*.[2] As Vaughn Plaza represents a public art installation on an already busy campus space, Fleming's four-part framework is apt. It suggests that well-designed spaces for public engagement incorporate an attention to orientation, connection, direction, and animation. Fleming's work focuses on redesigned spaces that visitors visit by necessity—much like Vaughn Plaza is impossible to avoid in Furman's central campus footpaths. Placemaking aims to amplify already high-traffic, public space to attract, bring economic development, build community, and shape identity. Moreover, "deep placemaking," as Jon Spayde calls it, goes even further to embed art within experiences, reminding those who enjoy the place of "darker, stranger, perhaps sadder realities."[3] In their reflections, meetings to witness Vaughn Plaza, and sharing notes afterward, the coauthors found that the plaza hit this higher bar of "deep placemaking."

In addition to placemaking ethnography, qualitative interviews were conducted in the fall of 2021 to explore student perceptions of Vaughn Plaza. As part of an upper-level qualitative methods seminar (Sociology 470, under the direction of Dr. Claire Whitlinger, Sociology), students enrolled in the course conducted twenty-four peer interviews, following a semistructured interview guide. Each interview lasted between thirty and sixty minutes. Respondents were recruited using purposeful sampling, ensuring variation on gender, race, and region. An equal number of upperclassman and underclassman respondents were interviewed. After their information was transcribed and uploaded, coauthor Whitni Simpson coded it using the qualitative data analysis software, Dedoose. Analysis was inductive, utilizing line-by-line open coding to identify emergent themes and, later, selective coding to refine theoretical insights in line with grounded theory.[4] This information helps us understand different perceptions of a primary target audience, especially across race, on a space so clearly created to bridge the racial divide between Blacks and whites—at Furman and the Upstate of South Carolina. Students tell us what is *effectively* true for them to guide their experience through the space.[5]

The three other authors use critical-cultural theory and public memory studies to analyze the space as a site of campus power relations and consider the site's resistive potential on the campus landscape. Informed by *Plantation Politics and Campus Rebellions: Power, Diversity, and the Emancipatory Struggle in Higher Education*, the authors view the campus space as a site of ideological struggle in which public memory and space are tools of contestation and cooptation.[6] Informed by the Universities Studying Slavery movement and a broad racial reckoning in institutions across the United States and globally, Vaughn Plaza is an example of institutional response to a long tradition of Black-led student activism, especially on university campuses or the cities adjacent to their campus. Wendy Leo Moore's concept of "white institutional space" reminds us that systems of inequality structure the material and social development of institutions like those in higher education. This produces "racialized social institutions" that "reproduce the racial social structure—which in the United States is White supremacy."[7] The analysis of Vaughn Plaza must be informed not only by our own experience and the experience of students but also within the critical and historical context of a multigenerational racial struggle in which even moments of inclusive placemaking can easily be co-opted into temporary appeasement.

The paper blends these methodologies and disciplinary lenses rather than feature them separately. Its contribution is to be the first study of inclusive placemaking (or, what Spayde calls "deep placemaking" in his call for such work), and its mixed methodological approach serves as a potential model for further studies.[8] Not only does such a study further academic critique, it also helps us imagine future placemaking art and design for social justice, offers practical suggestions and insights to those looking to do similar, and even concludes with practical recommendations for our own local experience.

Neely and Samura, in writing about social geographies of race, blend traditions of critical spatial theory and racial studies.[9] The authors posit four key characteristics for analysis of racialized space. Specifically, they guide our reading of race and space to see both as (1) contested, (2) fluid and historical, (3) interactional and relational, and (4) defined by inequality and difference. As the authors put it, "thinking about race through the lens of space not only helps us locate and understand racial processes, it also allows us to recognize possibilities for changing existing power structures and see how people are already engaged in these resistance activities."[10]

Throughout our conversations across disciplines, racialized experiences, and institutional roles (as students, staff, and faculty), we kept returning to three paired tensions that demonstrate these racialized processes of placemaking and resistance. They are centrality versus exposure, engagement versus solitude, and celebration versus subversion. In each of the six terms, structured as headings below, we explore how the university's shared goals—at least its initial and explicit goals—come with an undercurrent of something more unresolved and ambiguous. In the end, though, these difficult undercurrents create an opportunity for even further inclusivity at the university—if understood as natural outcomes of grappling with inclusivity as a meaningful community goal.

Centrality

In 2017, Furman University centered reckoning with its roots in slavery, joining a consortium of eighty-six schools currently aligned with Universities Studying Slavery.[11] On October 16, 2016, when this movement was fairly new, Furman student Marian Baker raised questions about the university's founders in an opinion piece in the student newspaper *The Paladin*.[12] In response to student pressure and faculty leadership, the university provost commissioned the Task Force on Slavery and Justice. Its purpose was to find the answers to the unanswered questions of Furman's racist past and bring the information to upper administration and the board of trustees, with a vision of how to reconcile with this history. The task force consisted of seventeen members, including students, staff, young Furman alumni, and professors from departments ranging from sociology and political science to communication studies.

Between the spring of 2017 and July 2018, the task force gathered evidence and compiled a report that outlined their process and findings. This report is titled "Seeking Abraham," named after Abraham Sims, who is the subject of the only photo that depicts life among the enslaved persons held by the university's founders.[13] "Seeking Abraham" included recommendations for decision-making by the administration and trustees. The first section of recommendations dealt with the campus landscape and the first of these recommendations was for the Vaughn statue. It reads:

> WE RECOMMEND that a statue of Joseph Vaughn be installed at the spot of the iconic photograph in which he approaches the James B. Duke Library, capturing Vaughn's enthusiastic commitment to education. The statue should be life-size and incorporate a material that allows onlookers to see themselves in Vaughn. January 29th, the day of his enrollment (in 1965), should be the date of the sculpture dedication and thereafter should be commemorated as Joseph Vaughn Day to celebrate and encourage active student engagement and challenging the status quo. The sculpture will mark the dedication of the first permanent representation of a person of color on Furman's campus, marking a commitment toward more.[14]

The Vaughn statue was, thus, central to the recommendations of this very public, very publicized process of the university wrestling with its past.

Within the space of the university, too, the original request for a Vaughn statue is central. The iconic photo places Vaughn in front of the campus library. Architects for the 1950s campus placed the library atop a hill in the very center of campus, with all academic buildings centered around central fountains. Thus, the spot represents the literal geographic and symbolic center of activity for the entire "world" of Furman University.

Figure 8. Joseph Vaughn entering Furman University, January 29, 1965. Furman University Libraries.

This central part of campus is closed to vehicular traffic, so nearly every-body who visits Joseph Vaughn Plaza approaches on foot, walking toward the front steps of the James B. Duke Library. Coming from a parked car or other campus building, the most striking initial impressions are the materi-als and colors. Large white horizontal plinths frame the space and are etched with rich black letters. The striking contrast of black letters swallowed among majority white stones provides immediate clues about the stories of racial discrimination and integration. As one moves closer toward the plaza, the "slightly larger than life-sized" statue of Vaughn takes your eyes from these large white plinths. Made of bronze, the darkened exterior of the figure again accentuates the significance of race while also casting a slightly dark and somber tone compared with the gleaming white stones under and around him. The statue is placed within a large and open space, on a pedestal, and oriented toward incoming visitors.

When asked to recall the recommendations of the "Seeking Abraham" report, students most frequently cited the Joseph Vaughn statue. Nearly every respondent to a randomized student interview process admitted that they thought of the statue because of the centrality of its location on campus. The students interviewed were asked to think about the emotions evoked when passing the statue. One respondent reflected, "When I do walk past it, it's just a reminder that, like, there were people before me who risked every-thing and worked so hard so that people like me could come to this school." Many white respondents identified the statue as a symbol of moving forward and an indication of how far we have come. One even referenced how this is depicted by the physical appearance of the statue: "The statue has one foot in front of another as if it's walking, and his eyes are pointed upwards. So, it seems very hopeful and future-oriented." Black respondents' analysis of the structure did not drastically differ. One student stated, "I feel like it's really just kind of a movement to show the appreciation and show the growth of Black students on campus. The statue and the picture of him walking, I just feel like, is really powerful."

Together, the spatial arrangement of the objects forces the visitor to see Vaughn, to engage and interact with him, to acknowledge his presence. Rituals of experience in space create public memories; these, in turn, create group identity that informs individual identity.[15] The statue, fashioned after the iconic photo of Vaughn during his first semester at Furman in 1965, can-not be ignored or overlooked. The lack of clutter in the space, the elevation of the statue within it, and the engaging posture of the statue command visual attention. This assemblage of materials in a specific spatial configuration sends a convincing orienting message that this individual will not be hidden or tucked away. Joseph Vaughn and the act of desegregation will be central to the university's identity going forward.

Exposure

The unfortunate consequence of centrality, when making a space for inclusion, is exposure. It is as if the space asks visitors to examine, watch, perhaps even scrutinize Vaughn himself. There is, indeed, nowhere for him to hide—although fully seen, he is also fully exposed. Vaughn was exposed to white supremacist environments in his lifetime, and the plaza in some ways reenacts this exposure. Even as the majority-white campus and trustees might feel they are "lifting up" Vaughn onto a white plinth at the heart of campus, literally and metaphorically, it may be harder to see how much Furman needed and needs Vaughn, then and now. As sociologists have shown, the motivation to center difficult pasts may come from a sense of responsibility and desire to make amends with those impacted, or from a desire to prevent reputational damage from not acknowledging that such things happened.[16]

Furman University had engaged in centuries of omissions and cover-ups for its racist past. The Slavery and Justice Task Force revealed, for example, that the plantation home on campus was called a "Southern mansion" and repurposed as an "alumni house" but had never been referred to as a plantation in university communications. Records from slavery, segregation, and desegregation had been carefully eliminated and overlooked in campus archives until the 2010s. Campus racist incidents have been regular occurrences, especially when one includes microaggressions that were meant to make nonwhite persons feel lesser, even when not consciously or aggressively harmful. Yet, as a school with ambitions in the top-50 liberal arts colleges, recruiting and retaining diverse students and employees remains vitally important.

Reputational management is especially relevant when studying universities, as they pay close attention to their sociopolitical context and audiences. As a private university in the twenty-first century, Furman has a significant interest in both reputational repair with minority applicants, as well as its educational mission. Yet in doing so, it would need to approach the task conservatively knowing that the racial majority often have negative emotional reactions to learning about their privileges.[17] As a tuition-dependent institution, Furman could not risk students being made to feel guilty for past university wrongs. Thus, Vaughn offers a unifying positive image for Furman reckoning with its historical harms—he is a historical example of obvious progress that could be socially contested and discussed as well as a model for a future of multiracial inclusivity and excellence. Vaughn becomes a token figure to move past historical harms and recenter Furman's success. Work on the plaza began in October 2020 and was completed six months later in April 2021, only a year after the committee had been formed (2019–20). Trustees moved quickly, even during the pandemic, to commission architects for the plaza and a sculptor. Vaughn's statue was an expedient way to repair Furman's reputational harms with a positive endorsement of inclusivity.

The way that students learned about the plaza further reflects Furman's need to "expose" Vaughn as a symbol of racial progress. The interviews of student opinions demonstrated that nearly all students first learned about institutional repair from emails sent from the President's email account. Students described the messages as vague and speaking of diversity and inclusion in service of the university's image, which obfuscated rather than clarified the specifics of the university's past wrongs or steps of repair. Further, findings revealed that most students have not read the report, despite that it was linked to the emails. Campus leaders failed to engage most students to think deeply or constructively about repairing past harm, instead relying on institutional leaders and their public communication for exposure.

Raised at the center of campus, the sculpture's exposure can be liberating, but it can also represent the institutional powers he serves. Vaughn and other students who slowly desegregated Furman over the coming decades frequently commented they felt like the "fly in the buttermilk," and Vaughn made jokes about his uncomfortable obviousness on campus, in a sea of white faces—even as he described being made to feel welcome.[18] The statue and plaza, like Vaughn himself, are watched. Any protest or agitation here is not just viewed by students or peers but is subservient to the tower of knowledge behind it and the supervising campus staff around it.

Student activity, although appearing natural and centered around the plaza, is regulated in a way incongruent with Vaughn's subversive spirit of humor and activism. The James B. Duke Library instructs, on a frequently used web portal, that students may not undertake any "activities involving paint, liquid chalk, dyes, or any other materials that may stain or damage the Plaza." In addition, "marking the steps or porch with chalk is NOT allowed."[19] Activities, the site goes on to say, may not block or interfere with the accessibility ramp to the Duke Library porch; chairs and tables may not be moved from the porch. The Plaza is for the exclusive use of Furman-

Figure 9. Joseph Vaughn Plaza, Furman University, 2022. Photograph by Mary Sturgill, Furman University.

affiliated groups and organizations, with no solicitation by outside entities. Scheduling a special event in the outdoor space must proceed along the same rules and registration system used for events inside the building. To request tables and chairs, a person (usually a student) needs to request the materials from the campus facilities department and then also use a library-sponsored form to reserve the plaza.

The open invitation to create exposure on Vaughn's stones comes with the gaze of a sanitized, surveilled location. Students who engage Vaughn Plaza expose themselves to Furman's careful reputational management. Some tolerance is likely. Max Clarke and Gary Alan Fine write that universities are usually open to cultivating their collective persona in ways that addresses their historical injustices.[20] This is the case, given the identity of universities as places of conscious deliberation, as well as the home of reputation entrepreneurs primed to fight injustice. As Neely and Samura attest in their first characteristic, racialized spaces are key sites of contestation and thus campus politics.[21] The university has a strong interest in limiting speech that would draw further attention to racial divides existing within campus or the broader community surrounding the university.

Engagement

Although the central area of the plaza is an open landscape of brick built for person-to-person interaction, the pathways in and out of the plaza direct visitors to engage even more directly with Vaughn's off-center statue. A narrow and lengthy pathway that connects to sidewalks in both directions is engineered to force traffic directly in front of Vaughn's statue. Between these routes are landscaping beds of trees and shrubs, benches, or plaza pillars, limiting the passages through which visitors travel. A second parallel pathway guides visitors behind Vaughn's statue, whereby one encounters the statue from the back, although even still the size and significance of the heavy, dark object within the otherwise red or white backdrop invites attention. Perpendicular to those two guided routes are two sets of steps to the James B. Duke Library. Whether moving toward or away from the library using these pathways, visitors must engage in a space shared by Vaughn. Whether consciously or subconsciously, all visitors are linked to his likeness, to mix and intermingle with his legacy.

Beyond passing engagement, the large white plinths that mark the front of the plaza are positioned well for visitors to sit on them, as two parallel benches. Closer to the library, at the back of the plaza, nearly a dozen six-seat permanent grated metal tables with metal chairs can be moved to find sun or shade, depending on the weather. These elements are perpetual objects of the place, which connote meaning aligned with community and social interaction. They invite visitors and students to use the place as more than just a central pathway toward somewhere else. Cohering with Fleming's art of placemaking, the commissioned art intersects with the lived experience of the community on a deep and personal level.

Beyond initial clues designed to orient the visitor to the plaza, visitors are invited to connect with the history and meaning of the place. The scale of the statue (slightly larger than life) in such an open space appears to be merely "life-sized." As such, the statue suggests to the visitor that the three-hundred-twenty-pound mass of bronze is more like them than not. Vaughn's outstretched hand connotes a lively openness, inviting the visitor to take hold and say hello. Looking directly ahead, Vaughn's eyes "speak" with a humble kindness. The visitor can interpret the art, taken together, as not simply an object of the past but a subject of the present; as not just a historical monument but a fluid enactment of that history in the present day, Neely and Samura's second characteristic of racialized space.[22] They are material signals that the plaza participates in Spayde's "deep placemaking" using interaction, engagement, and connection to inspire while also potentially disturbing the otherwise white landscape.[23]

Although the picture on which the statue was modeled depicts Vaughn walking into the library building, the statue itself is positioned as if Vaughn is walking out of, and away from, the library. The position and outward spatial orientation send a subtle message that connects the past significance of Vaughn's presence at Furman to the present opportunity for further engagement on the rest of campus and the world beyond. Vaughn is facing out, toward a vast open mall with organic elements of water, grass, trees, and wildlife—a fluid, unbridled landscape of opportunity. Vaughn's statue becomes an "active archive," one with multiple layers of meaning that change across time.[24] He is both a remnant of the students' grandparents' generation and an active agent changing direction for the present generation.

One final spatial signal that connects Vaughn's history with the meaning and purpose of the plaza involves the vastness of the plaza itself. The "unboxed" and uncontained nature of the plaza suggests that it is meant to encourage embodied assertions and declarations of diverse identities, ideas, and causes. Around its borders, the plinths along with a few park benches and tables on the library portico also suggest that momentary meet-ups can lead to longer conversations. This open, elevated, and central campus place is designed for members of the community to be engaged and be seen, much like Vaughn as a student all-star and civil rights activist.

In the daytime, the sheer volume of traffic that moves through Vaughn Plaza indicates to visitors both the centrality and energy of the place. The diversity of routes in and out of the space ensures that humans and non-human animals (e.g., squirrels, Canada geese, American crows) engage in a constant jigsaw of movement, crisscrossing each other throughout the space. A dizzying, if sometimes chaotic, array of movement unfolds. This multifaceted, multidimensional, somewhat unorganized movement throughout the space cultivates a buzz of action that is often palpable.

The site is a prominent space of encounter—between student and faculty/staff, staff and faculty, faculty and faculty, and student and student. The plaza is frequently used by representatives of campus organizations to "table." Student groups set up various marketing, advertising, or promotional materials or activities on portable tables to recruit, educate, and engage. Aside from the two permanently anchored metal benches in the open plaza space, there are no additional permanent structures. Canvas tents, folding chairs and tables, music, and food items come and go. Whether you are a student traveling from a residence hall, a staff member completing a shift in the dining hall, a faculty member who just finished teaching a class, or an administrator gathering for a meeting in the library, the level terrain of the plaza invites all visitors to engage on equal footing in a shared and dynamic space. Connection with other members of the community is commonplace and inevitable. Individual subjects intermingle to signify an overall object—a vibrant, inclusive, and equitable community. In relationships and interactions, racialized space is co-created and tied with the icon of Vaughn, meeting Neely and Samura's third characteristic of relational and interactional development.

Yet, as these authors noted, "meanings of race and space are always created and recreated in relationship to the 'other.'"[25] Although Vaughn Plaza often displays a melting pot on campus, in practice, the space also allows various campus groups to reify their own unique identities and social boundaries, "recruiting" those with similar interests and identities, and, in effect, positioning as "other" those who are not included. Similarly, campus guests and community members, without the internal relationships as a foundation, may be positioned as "other" to the invitational space. The plaque that describes the overall purpose of the space is small and hidden in landscaping. No welcome signs or clear explanation of the space awaits the guest, who would need to piece together meaning from a one-sentence biography, a donor plaque, and dedication year on the other side of the plaza. Finally, as explored in the next section, at certain times of day and within the academic calendar, Vaughn himself stands alone—enacting himself again as "other" to campus connection.

Solitude

Vaughn's statue stands on the left side of the stairs, following the iconic photograph in its placement and accentuating the almost natural gesture of leaving the library to go elsewhere (a movement also suggested by Vaughn's stance, depicted in the act of walking). This helps mitigate the overall impression of exposure, making him engaging and "one of us," but it also introduces asymmetry. The statue's prominence is reduced. The statue is placed on a white plinth with the inscription "Joseph Vaughn '68." He towers slightly above those walking by, giving back some place of honor in one's first encounter with the plaza. Over time, however, the slight four-inch plinth serves to separate him from the crowds around. Unlike a heroic military statue that might put Vaughn soaring overhead and centered on the stairs, he becomes both commonplace at visitors' height and "a world away" from a passerby because of his slight elevation. In bestowing honor, the asymmetrical placement and slightly raised sculpture ends up making Vaughn a significantly lonely figure—recognized as part of the community, equal with the rest, but not. The slight pedestal and separation from the university as "other" creates a strong visual metaphor for the continuing tokenistic treatment and visibility of difference of nonwhite members of the Furman community.

This idea that one can be thoroughly engaged at Furman yet all the while alone, or lonely, is mimicked by the large inscriptions—reflections made by Vaughn himself on his Furman experience—on the white plinths. One reads, "I felt like a majority of one," and the other reads, "Make sure you are a part of Furman's greatness." Vaughn, biographically, was an extremely engaged extrovert. He joined the Baptist Student Union and the Reserve Officers' Training Corps (ROTC), and he was a member of the cheerlead-ing squad.[26] He succeeded as an English major with a French minor, and he played a role in campus theater productions. He was an activist for civil rights, participating in demonstrations after the Orangeburg Massacre; published in the student newspaper his leaving the Baptist faith to become Bahá'í; and founded the National Association for the Advancement of Col-ored People (NAACP) student chapter on campus. Classmates continue to share positive and humorous exchanges about Vaughn. He left Furman to become a valued teacher and president of the Greenville County Associa-tion of Teachers, and, in 1981, he was elected president of the South Carolina Education Association. Vaughn's quotes attest to his own ability to tran-scend obstacles, find a sense of belonging in Furman's engaged community, and feel powerful as a representative of one's upbringing and identity.

Yet the loneliness of these quotations seems to be obvious among the student body, perhaps a reflection of the statue's solitude. In the qualitative student interviews, students of color typically explained how the quota-tions resonated with them, whereas white students read them as symbolic of university history. For example, when discussing the quotation "I felt like a majority of one," one Black respondent explained, "I definitely relate to [the quotation] because, in a lot of my classes, I'm the only Black student in class and so I really do feel like, damn, I'm looking around and it really is only me." For Black students, Furman is attesting to their experience of social other-ness and alienation—something they felt the university tended to previously overlook in the institution's brand to be represented as minority-welcoming. Meanwhile, a white student reflected, "So the 'majority of one' really makes me feel like, I think he first joined Furman in the 60's, so you know, that was really not that long ago, and it's kind of sad that in such a short period, there was a time that there was so little diversity at Furman that it was all on that one person." The quotation made white students realize how late in Furman's history the lack of diversity on campus was even fathomed as a reputational issue, as well as the burden of solitude placed on Vaughn.

The second inscription, "Make sure you are a part of Furman's greatness," lacks the "I" that identifies the other quotation as clearly Vaughn's own words (as an alumnus reflecting on his time as a student) and so can even be read as an instruction from Furman itself. Thus, for example, a white respondent recognized, "It just, it seems more Furman celebratory than celebrating the individual. And I don't know, it makes it seem like the statue is celebrating Furman for being so accepting and welcoming versus applauding Joseph Vaughn for his accomplishment, and courage." The plinth's inscription suggests that Furman considers itself an inclusive community already and that it accomplished something in "accepting" Vaughn—a sentiment very much reflected in the study of the process of desegregation in 2015.[27] The university had professed to be granting an opportunity to Vaughn with a warm embrace, rather than as a reluctant actor who benefited from Vaughn's presence, at a minimum to avoid lawsuits and protest.

Meanwhile, a Black respondent found a way to identify with the quotation more authentically and less critically: "The one of being part of Furman's greatness is, I think, speaks a lot to me. I was a part of an athletic race campaign. And we mentioned just kind of like how important it is to give voices to the [B]lack athletes and be allies. And I feel like, kind of anything that anyone can do white, [B]lack, Hispanic, Asian, is so important and you could do so much to kind of elevate Furman racially . . . being more inclusive, so I feel like kind of playing into that greatness. I feel like everyone has a role in that." This student interprets the inscription as a celebration for the opportunity to be part of Furman's future growth toward inclusivity. Students across interviews agreed that the statue seemed like a major statement or step accomplished by the university. Nevertheless, they shared concern that Furman was not committing to further institutional action—at least not visibly. Lone individuals, like Vaughn, can inspire, but it is unclear whether they can count on institutional action to facilitate this inclusion.

Vaughn stands alone, solitary, especially at night. When one gazes at him over this tremendous landscape of fountains and buildings, feelings of loneliness necessarily emerge for students of color. Feelings of tokenization

Figure 10. Vaughn Plaza Bricks. Photograph by Mary Sturgill, Furman University.

and vulnerability come in these tranquil moments to disrupt the celebratory and iconic scene. In the immense red brick area, with huge white plinths, Vaughn's nearly life-size, nearly eyesight-level figure becomes a small Black dot on the huge predominantly white liberal arts landscape.

Perhaps aware of this effect of solitude and isolation, the architect built in a small visual "trick" in the plaza's stones that no visitors would notice without prompting. Red brick buildings rise from the red brick plaza in all directions, with the red bricks of the library merging seamlessly with the red brick pavers below the visitor's feet. The architect planted darker pigmented red (almost brown) bricks surrounding Vaughn's statue and infused the pavers in a somewhat chaotic and somewhat purposeful tapestry. Barely noticeable, lines in the bricks representing the library's columns are "pierced" by these darker pigmented red bricks. This interjection of brick diversity into the plaza replicates the impact of Vaughn and students of color, unsettling the whites-only and European-centered liberal arts paradigm. Vaughn metaphorically becomes a beacon of light or the epicenter of a ripple effect in the sea of homogenous institutions, norms, and systems.

Yet, this message is so subtle and unannounced in the current configuration as to not significantly disrupt the obvious solitude and short plinth occupied by Vaughn alone. Neely and Samura's fourth characteristic of geographies of race—that they are spaces produced and reproduced via differential and inequitable access to and use of space—is clearly represented in the tension between engagement and solitude.[28] Within the "mechanisms of white space," as theorized by Wendy Leo Moore, any first attempt at inclusive placemaking at a predominantly white campus would reinscribe the everyday racialized practices of the institution. Despite the overwhelming positive engagement by the broad community and the personal inspirations taken by many students of color, the privilege of inherently and unquestionably belonging does structure white supremacy on the landscape.[29] A broad, actively antiracist stance that challenges institutional policies and demographics could undo the isolating social power working over Vaughn and his heirs.

Celebration

After the plaza and statue are encountered, perhaps long after, the visitor might happen to read a small and understated waist-high plaque tucked away behind and beside the statue amid the landscaping. After a brief description of Vaughn, his status as the first African-American undergraduate student at Furman, and his role as a state educational leader and dedicated alumnus, the text concludes with explicit language about the purpose of the plaza itself. *"This plaza honors Vaughn and those whose contributions have cultivated a campus community that strives towards greater equity and inclusion."* Reading this, a visitor might imagine future opportunities for the plaza in disrupting Vaughn's solitude and providing space to celebrate and remember not only Vaughn but also other figures connected to the university, guided by equity and inclusion.

In its current use, the one time that Vaughn's contributions are especially noticed is January 29th each year, Joseph Vaughn Day. The date coincides with the day Vaughn enrolled at Furman and the iconic photograph was taken. Started by Adare Smith (Class of 2020) on January 29, 2019, the event has garnered broad community support and press releases. Smith formulated a walk of remembrance, simulating Vaughn's walk beside the fountains to enroll at the library and ending with a set of speeches and commemorative activities. After that first year, instigated by Smith, trustees endorsed the tradition as a true university-wide event and the City of Greenville marked it as an officially recognized day. With leadership from Furman's Community Development office, news cameras and DJs surround the plaza, honorary degrees are awarded, and performances by music groups (e.g., the Furman University Gospel Ensemble and the Baha'i Drum Circle) and speeches mark the occasion. Although only a small subsection of the campus attends such an event—perhaps a couple hundred people—the press releases and regional news coverage help build the honorific intent of the plaza. If curious visitors to the plaza conduct a web search of Joseph Vaughn to learn about him, they will likely be met with Vaughn Day news stories, press releases, and honorary degree awards.

The trustees and library use the plaza to celebrate "Furman's greatness" in ways less tied to inclusivity or equity. For example, because of the COVID-19 pandemic and the need to keep large gatherings outdoors, the plaza has been used to celebrate faculty publications in an annual event that allows faculty to showcase their research to trustees. Vaughn's statue, because it is off-centered, becomes another "guest" at such a formal occasion rather than a towering imposition. These festive, official uses of the central space allow Vaughn to intermingle with core university activities, centering inclusion and equity in events not necessarily tied to that purpose. Annual Vaughn Days require significant management and may not enjoy the same perpetuity as the statue and plaza themselves. Convocation and commencement happen at other campus arenas. Such opportunities to honor and celebrate—words used by the Task Force on Slavery and Justice and the trustees in recommending and implementing the space—are somewhat infrequent for the general campus and community.

Figure 11. Joseph Vaughn Day, Furman University, January 29, 2020. Photograph by Jeremy Fleming, Furman University.

Subversion

Despite the tight regulations, from time to time, posters, signs, flags, and megaphones have filled the space. Rather than *honoring* individuals who create a more equitable and inclusive community, the plaza participates in their *becoming*. Even as protests themselves have been small so far, they lead to signage for months, with flags and yarn wraps representing diversity in gender and sexuality, nonwhite student groups, and others. These subversions of the space of celebration and honor even go so far as to animate significant dissent against university inequities and complacency.

Given spatial centrality for campus, the plaza's area had been used for protest before its Vaughn Plaza makeover. For example, a "lie-in" and similar protests happened in the 2010s as police brutality attracted national attention and led into the existence of Black Lives Matter. Donald Trump's ascendency and the attempted repeal of DACA (Deferred Action for Childhood Arrivals) led to protests. Looking back further, in 2001, a candlelight vigil was held on the steps in the days after September 11th. Still, the remake of the plaza with Vaughn has seemed to only legitimate its resistive possibilities. Furthermore, the use of Vaughn's statue serves as a powerful visual metaphor of social justice that has been intentionally incorporated into the messaging and behavior of those subverting the celebratory space.

Racialized counter-memories are public memories that explicitly center meanings of race and racism.[30] Racialized counter-memories not only have the power to make race known in pervasively white landscapes but also offer antiracist narratives that oppose systems of white supremacy. For example, to conclude Black History Month in February 2022, representatives from Black Greek Letter Fraternities came to campus for a "Yard Show" that demonstrates steps and strolls.[31] This meeting, around Joseph Vaughn, made the not-subtle argument that Furman needs to expand its Black student population and expand Greek life centered on minority solidarity. The inanimate statue of Vaughn is incorporated into the present animation of the space, offering a particularly powerful material–semiotic interaction.

Another specific example of the plaza's value to student activists stands out from the Fall 2021 semester. During that time, a series of incidents illustrated deep-rooted cultures of white supremacy present within the student body. Anti-LGBTQI+ incidents occurred in October, and, in November, white nationalist stickers were found on campus to support "Patriot Front," a hate group formed from the "Unite the Right" rally in Charlottesville, Virginia, in

2017.[32] On November 12 and 14, students found Black Lives Matter flags that were defaced to read "All Lives Matter."[33]

In response to these racist and homophobic acts, dozens of students came together on Vaughn Plaza on November 19, 2021, both to voice their disappointment about the incidents and to criticize the university leadership's response for lacking transparency. Emily Balogh, president of the Furman Pride Alliance, argued that the university needed to offer more timely information.[34] Miles Baker, president of the Furman chapter of the NAACP, urged the administration to "listen closely, as student participation in the protest indicates the ideas and values of students."[35]

One might argue that such acts are not subversive, given that they were attended by Furman University faculty and leadership. Yet such acts visually implicate Joseph Vaughn as an ally to their cause or as one of the protesters himself. Vaughn stands, quite literally, in solidarity, as protestors surround the statue and even use his hand to hold one end of the protest banner. And given Vaughn's own history with student advocacy as an undergraduate student at Furman, his physical presence among student protestors in 2021 produced a racialized counter-memory. Vaughn and his memory were not institutionally curated as a nonthreatening symbol of diversity accomplished. Rather, he co-creates students' enduring concern about issues of white supremacy at Furman and beyond. In this moment, Vaughn was not a tool of university communications but an activator for alternative student voices.

After the racialized counter-memory placemaking by student protesters (Fall 2021), on Vaughn Day 2022, Asha Marie spoke as Furman University's 2021–2022 Student Government Association president. She expressed her desire to see the plaza utilized for student organizing. In her speech, Marie pleaded that the Furman community not let Vaughn's statue be left as "a racial symbol."[36] She continued, "his story cannot be reduced to a symbol of our institution's racial progress—a shiny gold star for our university's positionality in history." Her fear of Joseph Vaughn's memory being co-opted by the institution and only remembered in the memory site as a symbol of complacency is clear. She defined her desired use of the space as one where visitors were "challenged[ed] to invest in community, stand up for what's right and insist that we participate in making our communities a better place."[37] As she concluded her speech, she took the time to recognize the ways in which the plaza and statue were activated during the event as specifically in support for the Black community. And, in doing so, she again narrated her vision for engaged antiracist placemaking at the site: "Thank you all for coming to celebrate and honor the legacy of Joseph Vaughn. By

Figure 12. Campus Protest, Furman University, November 22, 2021. Katelyn Powell, *The Paladin*.

being here, you are showing up for our Black community, who continue to be the lifeblood of this institution, yet often do not receive the recognition they deserve. Your presence and participation today says that you see us, you stand with us, and my hope is that you will continue to walk in Vaughn's legacy, advocating always for community and to be doing what it takes to be better—committed to justice, equity, and true inclusion."[38] Marie asks the community to work toward antiracist justice in lockstep with Joseph Vaughn and his statue in midstride. Although this sort of explicit antiracist activism is not built into the site of Joseph Vaughn Plaza, Marie's vision illustrated how students, faculty/staff, and community members may choose to subvert a spirit of honor and celebration. Inclusivity is so often co-opted as a mellow and unifying sense of belonging, yet it always brings with it a radical potential for subversion of those aims.

Conclusion

One of the primary reasons Vaughn Plaza exists is the story of a six-year-old African-American child. Part of a day care class tour of Furman's campus, she returned home that afternoon to her mother who serves on Furman's faculty. When her mom asked, "How was your day?" the daughter replied that it was great, that they got to be outside and play, but that she "wanted to be white." The mother, who had never before spoken to her daughter about race, asked what she meant. The daughter replied, "White people are important and get statues made for them. I want to be important one day." This testimony, presented to the Furman Board of Trustees, was pivotal in their vote and their rush to execute Joseph Vaughn Plaza.

We hope that this essay bolsters this spirit of fostering equity and inclusion, even as it necessarily delves into the critical aspects of the space. As with any commemorative task within a free, democratic society, multiple interpretations and multiple uses will surely emerge. As a multivocal commemorative space, it carries "diverse meanings and thus can be peopled by groups with different interpretations of the same past."[39] Vaughn Plaza succeeds at creating a space of centrality, engagement, and celebration for all. This essay suggests that it might go even further, to become a space of not only multivocal commemoration but also "integrative commemoration," which allows for "the direct expression (and even celebration) of multiple conflicting values and interpretations of an event."[40] Spayde's invitation to "deep placemaking" is already happening at Vaughn Plaza, and this analysis has highlighted how racialized space in a predominantly white institution can purposefully and surprisingly unsettle passive notions of inclusivity.

In terms of Furman University's Vaughn Plaza itself, we do have specific practical recommendations to take this work further, from the insights of a social geography of race. These would include the following:

- Give future consideration of Vaughn quotations for a plinth that challenge Furman, least of which would be his challenge in the same speech already quoted on the plinths, that "Furman must continue on the path of social justice. . . ."
- On Joseph Vaughn's plinth, add a bronze set of "footprints" that symbolically invite contemporary visitors to join Vaughn—whether for photographs, for fun, or for activism, to have visitors rethink his solitude.
- Use a further plaque to draw attention to the darker bricks that already make up and will continue to even more significantly make up the literal ground beneath. Consider even using these darker bricks around campus with inscriptions for various honorees who bring equity and inclusion, whether to Furman specifically or the state and region more broadly.
- Generate classroom and digital integrations on the plaza that allow the place to do more storytelling—more about the path to desegregation at

Furman, about Vaughn's life, or about activism and minority experiences at the university. Presidential emails by their nature give the feeling of institutional brand-making, rather than authentic engagement.

- Connect the plaza strongly, through digital counter-memory tourism, to campus sites that deal with racism in the university past, as well as other examples of Black excellence. Never allow Vaughn Plaza to exist self-congratulatory, but as one "step" in a broader narrative.
- Signal somewhere in the campus landscape an official apology for specific historical wrongdoing and a commitment to further action.

Integrative commemoration, embodied in this list, makes a place for empathy for historically marginalized identities and racialized countermemory activism alongside celebration for those who need to return to campus to feel proud of alma mater. It legitimates truth-telling and inclusive disagreement, discussion, and dialogue while not sacrificing the beauty and inspiration of a space of central public memory for the university.

The conclusions of the qualitative study from student interviews clearly show that students generally recognize that there are positive contributions from the Task Force on Slavery and Justice, the "Seeking Abraham" Report, the board of trustees, and the various pronouncements from President Elizabeth Davis's email and university press releases since. Specifically, students generally praise the commemoration of an influential person of color, erasure of names of people who held racist ideologies, increased mobilization of Black students, and the facilitation of meaningful academic discussions about race. Yet, students also recognize that these positive results do not occur without negative consequences such as increased tokenism, segregation, fear, conflict, generalizations, and an unsatiated hunger for social equity on campus. Inclusion work, including placemaking in the community, follows along this difficult double-edged sword.

The three paired terms we have offered could be a guide for future analysis of inclusive placemaking. We can continue to listen and empathize with those who feel exposed for special scrutiny by their identity, as Vaughn did and now does on his plinth above central campus. We can continue to resist the urge to tokenize and thus alienate "special individuals" as representatives for their race or other identity. If Joseph Vaughn, or perhaps worse, just his act of desegregation, is viewed as part of "Furman's greatness" for letting him join existing greatness, then he will remain a solitary figure. Rather, if we see predominantly white institutions as in deep need of significant change—as the indebted in this relationship with historically marginalized

groups and individuals—then engagement can supersede othering and solitude. Vaughn, at Furman, will be surrounded by a beloved community. And
last, by realizing that celebration and subversion are two sides of the same
coin of individual- and institutional-becoming, we validate inclusive placemaking as itself a subversive act ready to undermine its own visionaries and
creators.

Rather than unique flaws or "bad" features of Vaughn Plaza, we highlight these binaries to show the necessary lessons of inclusive placemaking. It should be impossible to imagine a space already marked by perfect
inclusivity, in which centrality came without exposure, engagement came
without solitude, and celebration came without the possibility of subversion.
The ethical lapse marked by the critique would be to pretend that inclusion
is possible from a first attempt at changing white space; or that centrality,
engagement, and celebration are possible without exposure, solitude, and
subversion—the former a "buzzword" version of inclusivity that lacks for
recognizing the real, historically given and material constraints.

Sarah Adeyinka-Skold is assistant professor of Sociology at Furman University.
Her research analyzes how inequalities are (re)produced in romantic relationships and institutional histories.

James Engelhardt is lecturer in English at Furman University whose work
focuses on place-based writing, ecopoetics, and writing pedagogy.

Alyson Farzad-Phillips is assistant professor of communication studies at Furman University. As a scholar-teacher, she explores the nuances of public
memory rhetoric, racial justice, and student protests with her students, both
in the classroom and around campus.

Benjamin K. Haywood is the associate director of the Faculty Development
Center at Furman University. Trained as an environmental geographer,
his scholarship focuses on educational development and pedagogy, public
engagement in science, and sense of place.

Brandon Inabinet is professor of communication studies at Furman University.
He co-chaired the university's Task Force on Slavery and Justice. His scholarship critiques power within texts from the history of rhetoric.

John A. McArthur is professor and chair of communication studies at Furman
University. His research explores proxemics and the role of technology in
our lived experiences of space and place.

Chiara Palladino is assistant professor of classics at Furman University. Her work maps spatial narratives of the premodern world, with an interest in digital humanities scholarship that bridges these insights with modern mapping and modeling strategies.

Whitni Simpson is a 2022 graduate of Furman University with a bachelor of science degree in sustainability and sociology. She is a J.D. candidate at Tulane Law School.

Claire Whitlinger is associate professor of sociology at Furman University. Her research examines the intersection between collective memory, racial identity, and social change.

NOTES

1. Emma Berger, "Joseph Vaughn Plaza Construction Underway," *The Paladin*, October 12, 2020, https://thepaladin.news.
2. Ronald Lee Fleming, *The Art of Placemaking* (New York: Merrill Publishers, 2007).
3. Jon Spayde, "Public Art and Placemaking," *Public Art Review* 24, no. 1 (Fall/Winter 2012): 23. https://issuu.com/forecastpublicart/docs/par_47.
4. Kathy Charmaz, "The Grounded Theory Method: An Explication and Interpretation," in *Contemporary Field Research: A Collection of Readings*, ed. R. M. Emerson (Boston, MA: Little, Brown and Company, 1983), 109–26; Anselm Strauss and Juliet Corbin, *Basics of Qualitative Research: Techniques and Procedures for Developing Grounded Theory*, 2nd ed. (Thousand Oaks, CA: Sage, 1998).
5. Barbara Bender, "Time and Landscape," *Current Anthropology* 43, no. 4 (2002): 105. https://doi.org/10.1086/339561.
6. Bianca C. Williams, Dian Squire, and Frank Tuitt, eds., *Plantation Politics and Campus Rebellions: Power, Diversity, and the Emancipatory Struggle in Higher Education* (New York: SUNY Press, 2021).
7. Wendy Leo Moore, "The Mechanisms of White Space(s)," *American Behavioral Scientist* 64, no. 14 (December 2020): 1947. https://doi.org/10.1177/0002764220975080.
8. Spayde, "Public Art and Placemaking," 25.
9. Brooke Neely and Michele Samura, "Social Geographies of Race: Connecting Race and Space," *Ethnic and Racial Studies* 34, no. 11 (2011): 1933–52. 10.1080/01419870.2011.559262.
10. Neely and Samura, "Social Geographies of Race," 1946.
11. "Universities Studying Slavery," University of Virginia: President's Commission on Slavery and the University, https://slavery.virginia.edu.
12. Marian Baker, "Slavery, Memory and Reconciliation: What Is the Furman Legacy?" *The Paladin*, October 26, 2016, https://thepaladin.news/.
13. Deborah Allen, Laura Baker, T. Lloyd Benson, Teresa Nesbitt Cosby, Brandon Inabinet, Michael Jennings, Jonathan Kubakundimana, Shekinah Lightner, Jeffrey Makala, Chelsea McKelvey, Quincy Mix, Stephen O'Neill, Forrest M. Stu-

art, Andrew Teye, Courtney Thomas, Courtney Tollison, and Claire Whitlinger, *Seeking Abraham: A Report of Furman University's Task Force on Slavery and Justice* (Greenville, SC: Furman University, 2018). https://scholarexchange.furman .edu/records-taskforce-slavery/1.

14. Allen et al., *Seeking Abraham*, 39.

15. Paul Connerton, *How Societies Remember* (Cambridge, England: Cambridge University Press, 1989), 4.

16. Max Clarke and Gary A. Fine, "'A' For APOLOGY: Slavery and the Collegiate Discourses of Remembrance—the Cases of Brown University and the University of Alabama," *History and Memory* 22, no. 1 (2010): 81–112; Gary A. Fine, "Apology and Redress: Escaping the Dustbin of History in the Postsegregationist South," *Social Forces* 91, no. 4 (2013): 1319–42. https://www.muse.jhu.edu/article /509338.

17. Su L. Boatright-Horowitz, Marisa E. Marraccini, and Yvette Harps-Logan, "Teaching Antiracism: College Students' Emotional and Cognitive Reactions to Learning about White Privilege." *Journal of Black Studies* 43, no. 8 (2012): 893–911. https://doi.org/10.1177/0021934712463235.

18. Joseph Vaughn, "Racial Integration at Furman: 21 Years Later," recorded April 1986 on audio cassette. Religion in Life event of the Cultural Life Program. Furman Special Collections. Digital Recording (MP3).

19. "Joseph Vaughn Plaza." Furman University Libraries. November 29, 2021. https:// libguides.furman.edu/library/policies/joseph-vaughn-plaza.

20. Clark and Fine, "A for APOLOGY," 106.

21. Neely and Samura, "Social Geographies of Race," 1938.

22. *Ibid.*, 1939.

23. Spayde, "Public Art and Placemaking," 25.

24. Caroline Knowles, *Race and Social Analysis* (London: Sage, 2013), 80.

25. Neely and Samura, "Social Geographies of Race," 1939.

26. Brian Neumann, "Progress, Pragmatism, and Power: Furman's Struggle over Desegregation," Commemorating Desegregation, Furman University. Online PDF, https://www.furman.edu/wp-content/uploads/sites/169/2020/01/Brian Neumann.pdf (accessed June 1, 2022).

27. Neumann, "Progress, Pragmatism, and Power."

28. Neely and Samura, "Social Geographies of Race," 1945.

29. Wendy Leo Moore, "The Mechanisms of White Space(s)," 1954.

30. Alyson Farzad-Phillips, "Combatting White Supremacy on Campus: Racialized Counter-Memory and Student Protests in the 21st Century" (PhD dissertation, University of Maryland, 2022), 97.

31. Sarita Chourey, "Gallery: Black History 2022 Month Yard Show Celebration," *Furman University News*, March 2, 2022. https://news.furman.edu.

32. Helena Aarts, "Racial Reckoning Revisits Campus with Bias Incidents," *The Paladin*, November 19, 2021. https://thepaladin.news.

33. *Ibid.*, 1.

34. Reilly Murtaugh, "Protest on Campus: Student Response to Racial Bias Incidents." *The Paladin*, November 22, 2021. https://thepaladin.news/.

35. Murtaugh, "Racial Reckoning," 1.

36. Asha Marie, "Asha Marie's Short Remarks & Call to Action for Students 1/28/22," Speech at Furman University, January 28, 2022.

37. Marie, "Short Remarks," 1.

38. Marie, "Short Remarks," 1.

39. Vered Vinitzky-Seroussi, "Commemorating a Difficult Past: Yitzhak Rabin's Memorials," *American Sociological Review* 67, no. 1 (2002): 31; also see Vered Vinitzky-Seroussi and Chana Teeger, "Unpacking the Unspoken: Silence in Collective Memory and Forgetting," *Social Forces* 88, no. 3 (2010): 1103–22.

40. Christina R. Steidl, "Integrating the Commemorative Field at Kent State," *American Sociological Review* 78, no. 5 (2013): 768.

WORKS CITED

Allen, Deborah, Laura Baker, T. Lloyd Benson, Teresa Nesbitt Cosby, Brandon Inabinet, Michael Jennings, Jonathan Kubakundimana, Shekinah Lightner, Jeffrey Makala, Chelsea McKelvey, Quincy Mix, Stephen O'Neill, Forrest M. Stuart, Andrew Teye, Courtney Thomas, Courtney Tollison, and Claire Whitlinger. *Seeking Abraham: A Report of Furman University's Task Force on Slavery and Justice.* Greenville, SC: Furman University, 2018.

Bender, Barbara. "Time and Landscape." *Current Anthropology* 43, no. 4 (2002): 103–12. https://doi.org/10.1086/339561.

Boatright-Horowitz, Su L., Marisa E. Marraccini, and Yvette Harps-Logan. "Teaching Antiracism: College Students' Emotional and Cognitive Reactions to Learning about White Privilege." *Journal of Black Studies* 43, no. 8 (2012): 893–911. https://doi.org/10.1177/0021934712463235.

Charmaz, Kathy. "The Grounded Theory Method: An Explication and Interpretation." In *Contemporary Field Research: A Collection of Readings*, edited by R. M. Emerson, 109–26. Boston, MA: Little, Brown and Company, 1983.

Clarke, Max, and Gary A. Fine. "'A' For APOLOGY: Slavery and the Collegiate Discourses of Remembrance—the Cases of Brown University and the University of Alabama." *History and Memory* 22, no. 1 (2010): 81–112.

Connerton, Paul. *How Societies Remember.* Cambridge, England: Cambridge University Press, 1989.

Farzad-Phillips, Alyson. "Combatting White Supremacy on Campus: Racialized Counter-Memory and Student Protests in the 21st Century." PhD dissertation, University of Maryland, 2022.

Fine, Gary A. "Apology and Redress: Escaping the Dustbin of History in the Postsegregationist South." *Social Forces* 91, no. 4 (2013): 1319–42. https://www.muse.jhu.edu/article/509338.

Fleming, Ronald Lee. *The Art of Placemaking.* New York: Merrill Publishers, 2007.

Furman University Libraries. "Joseph Vaughn Plaza." Last modified November 29, 2021. https://libguides.furman.edu/library/policies/joseph-vaughn-plaza.

Knowles, Caroline. *Race and Social Analysis.* London: Sage, 2013.

Marie, Asha. "Asha Marie's Short Remarks & Call to Action for Students 1/28/22." Speech. Furman University, January 28, 2021.

Moore, Wendy Leo. "The Mechanisms of White Space(s)." *American Behavioral Scientist* 64, no. 14 (December 2020): 1946–60. https://doi.org/10.1177/0002764220975080.

Neely, Brooke, and Michele Samura. "Social Geographies of Race: Connecting Race and Space." *Ethnic and Racial Studies* 34, no. 11 (2011): 1933–52. 10.1080/01419870.2011.559262.

Neumann, Brian. "Progress, Pragmatism, and Power: Furman's Struggle over Desegregation." Commemorating Desegregation. https://www.furman.edu/wp-content/uploads/sites/169/2020/01/BrianNeumann.pdf.

Spayde, Jon. "Public Art and Placemaking." *Public Art Review* 24, no. 1 (Fall/Winter 2012): 23–25.

Steidl, Christina R. "Integrating the Commemorative Field at Kent State." *American Sociological Review* 78, no. 5 (2013): 749–72.

Strauss, Anselm, and Juliet Corbin. *Basics of Qualitative Research: Techniques and Procedures for Developing Grounded Theory*, 2nd ed. Thousand Oaks, CA: Sage, 1998.

University of Virginia: President's Commission on Slavery and the University. "Universities Studying Slavery." https://slavery.virginia.edu.

Vaughn, Joseph. "Racial Integration at Furman: 21 Years Later." Interview recorded April 1986 on audio cassette. Religion in Life event of the Cultural Life Program. Furman Special Collections. Digital Recording (MP3).

Vinitzky-Seroussi,Vered. "Commemorating a Difficult Past: Yitzhak Rabin's Memorials." *American Sociological Review* 67, no. 1 (2002): 30–51.

Vinitzky-Seroussi, Vered, and Chana Teeger. "Unpacking the Unspoken: Silence in Collective Memory and Forgetting." *Social Forces* 88, no. 3 (2010): 1103–1122.

Williams, Bianca C., Dian Squire, and Frank Tuitt, eds. *Plantation Politics and Campus Rebellions: Power, Diversity, and the Emancipatory Struggle in Higher Education*. New York: SUNY Press, 2021.

South Carolina and Geopolitics

Connections to the Russia-Ukraine War

Lauren K. Perez and Jennifer L. Titanski-Hooper

On Thursday, February 24, 2022, Russia began a full-scale invasion of Ukraine.[1] The resulting conflict has produced significant economic, social, and political anxieties and material repercussions that have exacerbated the uncertainty and vulnerability of our global systems. It is clear that the greatest effects of this conflict are being felt by Ukrainians, who have seen massive threats to their lives, homes, and resources. Less clear, however, are the repercussions for communities far from the battlefields. This essay considers the geopolitics of the Russia-Ukraine war as it relates to the state of South Carolina. Using a feminist lens, we argue that globalization has allowed for more interaction and mixing between places, such that events in Ukraine affect South Carolinians and, perhaps less obviously, South Carolina's economy and residents can also affect what is happening in Ukraine. In this way, globalization and world events like the Russia-Ukraine war are not just top-down but also bottom-up. We demonstrate these reciprocal dynamics through an analysis of the multilevel impacts of militarization, economics, and the members of the Ukrainian diaspora living in South Carolina.

Global Geopolitics of the Russia-Ukraine War

Geopolitics is a way of thinking about international relations and analyzing the relationships between political processes and geography. The invasion of Ukraine is a continuation of more than a century of East–West geopolitical tension over territory, political ideology, and economic dominance. Ukraine and other Eastern European states have long been a borderland between East and West, and Russia's invasion is, in part, an attempt to stop the eastward expansion of Western political organizations, such as the North Atlantic Treaty Organization (NATO) and the European Union. It also seems to be Vladimir Putin's attempt to correct what he sees as Russian weakness after the fall of the Soviet Union, to restore a balanced East–West geopolitical relationship, and to reassert control over an Eastern sphere of influence.

However, Russia has faced more pushback from the Ukrainian military than it anticipated, as well as a united West that has made it clear that it will not tolerate Russian expansion beyond Ukraine. If one of Putin's goals was to limit NATO expansion, that plan has backfired, with Finland and Sweden having applied in May 2022 to join the organization to bolster their own security against Russian aggression, bringing NATO more firmly to Russia's doorstep. The invasion of Ukraine also seems to have renewed NATO's sense of purpose, leading to increased military spending from many of its members, including the United States, which we discuss later. At the time of this writing in the summer of 2022, there is no end in sight for the Russia-Ukraine war, with Russia making gains in eastern Ukraine, but the Ukrainian government and military having regained the areas surrounding Kyiv and continuing to put up a fight in the south and east of the country. Ukrainian cities are in tatters, with more than ten thousand killed and millions of people being displaced. Russia's losses are harder to calculate, but estimates suggest that it has twice as many deaths as Ukraine.[2]

Russia's invasion of Ukraine is not just a threat to Ukrainians or East–West balance. It is also a threat to the geopolitical norm of territorial integrity, or the idea that military force should not be used to claim another country's land. This norm has been dominant since 1945 and is part of the United Nations (UN) charter.[3] Without it, states like Ukraine that are "buffers" between great powers or alliances (e.g., Russia and NATO) are particularly at risk of conquest.[4] This geopolitical norm is arguably one of the reasons why interstate wars have been decreasing, especially since the end of the Cold War.[5] One explanation for why the Western response has been so strong is that NATO and its allies are trying to reinforce territorial integrity and punish Russia for violating it. If Russia is successful in this war, it may encourage Russia and other states (e.g. China in Taiwan) to continue violating the norm; if Russia is unsuccessful, and especially if Western sanctions and support for Ukraine seem to have contributed to Russia's failure, then the geopolitical norm of territorial integrity may continue to hold and, hopefully, limit interstate wars in the future.

Toward Local Geopolitics of the Russia-Ukraine War in South Carolina

Geopolitical strife, whenever and wherever it occurs, produces ripple effects across space and scale. In the field of geography, scale essentially refers to a level of analysis. Scale is often conceptualized as local, national, or global, but it can also represent spaces in between, such as regions, or even the individual body. Globalization has increased connections between people and places and has complicated our notions of scale, making it harder to distinguish between scales and demonstrating that processes at the global, local, and every scale in between are mutually constituted.[6] As a result, it has become harder to see events like the Russia-Ukraine war as simply a conflict between the Russian state and the Ukrainian state, or even between East and West. Instead, the economic, social, and political connections facilitated by globalization mean that this conflict has implications in the everyday experiences of individuals and communities far beyond Ukraine's borders.

Like most Americans, most South Carolinians will only experience the tragedy of the Russia-Ukraine war from afar. Still, many South Carolinians have expressed solidarity with Ukrainians by displaying Ukrainian flags and attending rallies in support of Ukrainian sovereignty.[7] The Russia-Ukraine war and the tensions between Russia and NATO have also produced a significant amount of anxiety that has left many South Carolinians wondering about the impact of these global geopolitics on their daily lives. Fewer, though, have probably thought much about the processes that give South Carolina an active role in this and other geopolitical disputes. As scholars of European politics and geography, we have fielded many questions from colleagues and students seeking reassurance that the Russia-Ukraine war will not lead to a greater, perhaps nuclear, conflict. Although nuclear war thankfully remains improbable, there are still significant global consequences of the Russia-Ukraine war. This essay explores the geopolitical relationships between South Carolina and Ukraine and demonstrates that, although seemingly a world apart, these places are intimately linked to one another.

In what follows, we examine the links between South Carolina and Ukraine during this geopolitical moment while also drawing attention to the multiscalar relationships between South Carolina and global geopolitics more broadly. First, we discuss the impacts of globalization in shaping social, political, and economic relationships between places. Second, we review how theories of geopolitics—and, in particular, feminist geopolitics—illuminate the ways in which local processes and places shape and are shaped by geopolitics across scale. Third, we explore the geopolitical relationships between South Carolina and Ukraine, with a particular focus on militarization, economic relations, and the role of the Ukrainian diaspora. We demonstrate that South Carolina not only is affected by the Russia-Ukraine war and global geopolitics but also actively shapes these geopolitics in important ways.

Globalization and Geopolitics: The Uneven Forces of Globalization

The Russia-Ukraine war is significant, not just as a human tragedy or because of the tensions between Russian and Western interests but also because globalization means that most people and places are connected and, therefore, affected to some degree by the events in Ukraine. Globalization commonly refers to the economic, political, and cultural interconnectivity that has accompanied advancements in global trade, communications, travel, and technology. Jan Nederveen Pieterse, a sociologist and global studies scholar, argues that there are three main perspectives of the processes and effects of globalization on societies: (1) Differences in culture and identity will lead to conflict; (2) cultures and societies will become more related and/or similar over time; or (3) a continuous mixing or hybridization between cultures and societies will occur.[8] The first two perspectives see globalization as a monolithic process, acting top-down on local places, whereas the third allows for a more reciprocal view of how globalization works across scale. As we demonstrate in this essay and elsewhere, local people and places have varying degrees of power to shape geopolitics, which leads to the kind of mixing or hybridization discussed by Pieterse.[9]

Globalization not only affects culture, society, and politics but geography itself. People and places are increasingly and continuously connected, such that time, distance, and space seem to matter less. David Harvey referred to this phenomenon as time-space compression and argued that global capitalism increasingly annihilates space and time.[10] Harvey, a Marxist geographer, sees capitalism as the overriding structure that dictates spatial relationships. The forces of globalization are rooted in the expansion of capital. The expansion of capital increases time-space compression, and as a result, local difference gives way to global homogeneity. The consummate example of this side of globalization is the spread of corporations, such as McDonald's, which have transcended space and place while typically replacing mom-and-pop establishments. A more recent example is the prevalence and controversy surrounding social media. On one hand, social media has become a powerful force in how people transcend space and time and communicate and network with one another. For example, we discuss in the upcoming text how the Ukrainian diaspora uses social media to mobilize support for Ukraine. On the other hand, questions abound regarding the political impact of these sites, particularly after the 2016 election in the United States. Concerns include the spread of misinformation, privacy of social media users, impacts on democracy and political protests, and the lack of accountability for the creators and corporate owners of these sites. Russia has been the catalyst for much of this critique, as it effectively uses social media to spread disinformation, most recently regarding the Russia-Ukraine war.[11]

Harvey's conceptualization of time-space compression and globalization captures the role that technology and global capitalism play in shaping social, political, and economic activity. As we discuss later in this essay, South Carolina and Ukraine are connected through the defense industry, particularly through companies such as Boeing that, for better or worse, shape geopolitical activity by supplying jobs to South Carolinians and military equipment to Ukraine. This kind of global military industrial complex is made possible through globalization and time-space compression and ultimately reinforces processes of uneven development where the interests of capital control the flow of wealth. In Harvey's view, corporations such as Boeing are the agents of globalization, shaping policy, economics, and geography from the top-down, which, in turn, perpetuates the imperialist dynamics and global inequality of developed versus developing or Global North versus Global South countries. Although useful, Harvey's approach does not fully consider structures other than capitalism that facilitate globalization and time-space compression.

Doreen Massey, a Marxist feminist geographer, argues for a consideration of the role that other structures and identities (e.g., gender and ethnicity) play in these processes.[12] Perhaps most important, Massey elaborates on the different ways in which people experience mobility in a globalized world, drawing on what she calls a "power geometry," where some people and places have more access to mobility, networks, and the opportunities afforded through globalization and time-space compression. For example, we discuss later that South Carolinians of Ukrainian descent are likely to react emotionally to the conflict and be motivated to try to make a difference through actions such as donating and raising awareness. The activities of Ukrainians in South Carolina can influence the processes of globalization, even if they may be less significant than those of major defense industries or governments.

Massey reveals an inherent unevenness in the experiences of globalization and time-space compression that affects how people and places experience geopolitics or other global phenomena. NATO, Russia, Ukraine, and even South Carolina all have some capacity to influence and participate in the Russia-Ukraine war, but their ability to act is determined by the power and influence that they wield. The Russia-Ukraine war will have economic, political, and social repercussions that extend well beyond Ukrainian borders, and

South Carolina, by virtue of its diverse economics and status as a part of the United States, also has a role to play in these global geopolitics. Although not always obvious, the connections between these distant places reveal a multi-scalar geopolitics that is the product of the seemingly endless, yet uneven, connections created by globalization.

Rescaling Geopolitics

As with globalization, there are many ways of thinking about the processes and impacts of geopolitics. The field of geopolitics emerged at the beginning of the twentieth century, concurrent with the rise of the national movements and territorial contestations that would lead to World War I and World War II. Geopolitics originally concerned itself with statecraft and territorial expansion in an attempt to understand how states might grow, change, and conflict with one another to address issues surrounding resources, population growth, or identity.[13] Through the lens of these traditional geopolitics perspectives, the aforementioned reasons for Russia's invasion of Ukraine are a clear attempt to project state power and restore a territorial and political sphere of influence in Eastern Europe. For example, John Mearsheimer, a realist international relations scholar, argues that the war is principally the result of US efforts to "make Ukraine a Western bulwark on Russia's borders," which Russia views as an existential threat, leading it to invade Ukraine.[14]

Overall, traditional geopolitics views geographic and political contestation and cooperation through a very narrow lens. The state is the primary scale of analysis, with very little attention given to other scales (e.g., the scale of the body or local community). The often unintended consequence underlying this focus on the state is that social, political, and economic activity that occurs outside or within the boundaries of the state is overlooked. This leads to a "territorial trap," where states are the assumed containers for society.[15] However, in a connected and globalized world, we need a geopolitical approach that pays attention to a variety of geographic scales.

A more multiscalar view would suggest that NATO expansion is far from the only factor that led to the Russia-Ukraine war. Robert Person, an international relations scholar, and Michael McFaul, a political scientist and former US ambassador to Russia, provide a regional explanation: The war is Putin's attempt to bring Ukraine back into the Eastern/Russian sphere of influence. At the national and subnational levels, the invasion is a response to the spread of democracy in a culturally and historically close neighbor, which could lead to calls for democracy domestically in Russia, especially through protest and civil society.[16]

Feminist geopolitics has argued extensively for a deeper and wider conception of scale in the study of geopolitics, with particular attention to everyday and embodied experiences. Drawing on the feminist proclamation that the "personal is political," feminist political geography and feminist geopolitics have argued for an expansion of our understandings of what is political,[17] complicated our notions of politics in the public and private spheres,[18] and considered the roles of gender and the body in the experience of violence, politics, and security.[19] These contributions have not only broadened the field of geopolitics but also helped to illuminate how geopolitical relationships are multiscalar and are shaped by both top-down and bottom-up forces in communities, states, and global processes.

In this essay, we consider the geopolitical relationships between South Carolina and Ukraine through this feminist geopolitical lens. The connections between these seemingly distant places are not immediately clear unless we complicate our notions of scale to not only look at geopolitics at the scale of the state but also trace the connections between local, national, regional, and global communities. Although South Carolina is not a direct participant in the Russia-Ukraine war, it inevitably affects and is affected by these events. We consider these multiscalar geopolitics and the potential consequences for South Carolina through an examination of militarization, economic relations, and the Ukrainian diaspora.

Geopolitics and Militarization

One of the simplest ways to think about the geopolitical relationships between South Carolina and Ukraine is through the lens of militarization. Militarization is the ongoing process by which societies become influenced by or dependent on military values, activities, and attitudes. Militarization is, like geopolitics, a multiscalar process whereby individuals, communities, and nations are increasingly connected to global military activities and defense industries. In feminist geopolitics, Cynthia Enloe is the leading scholar demonstrating how globalization and militarization have come to feed each other, normalizing militarism at all geographic scales, including in our daily lives and in global economic processes.[20] South Carolina is heavily embedded in the processes of militarization, which creates significant economic and social patterns, as well as both directly and indirectly linking the Palmetto State to the geopolitics of the Russia-Ukraine war.

US Military Troops and Installations

In 2020, South Carolina had 39,573 active-duty service members, the ninth highest among US states. An additional 17,715 reservists resided in the state.[21] There are eight major military bases and installations in the state, including hospitals, such as the Naval Hospital Beaufort, training installations, such as Parris Island and Fort Jackson, and the Joint Base Charleston that on its own supports ninety thousand service members, civilians, and veterans.[22] Statewide, there are more than sixty-eight thousand Department of Defense personnel and nearly four hundred thousand veterans living in the state.[23] The presence of these facilities in South Carolina provides a significant source of income. Defense contracts, which we discuss in more detail later, totaling over thirteen billion US dollars (USD) were committed in South Carolina between 2013 and 2017.[24] The total economic impact of the military is over thirty-four billion dollars, and one in every nine jobs in South Carolina can be traced to the military.[25] This is a marked increase from 2017, when the total economic impact was approximately twenty-four billion dollars, creating one in every twelve jobs in the state.[26] These military installations also support migration into the state, with increasing numbers of service members and contract workers coming to live, work, and spend in the state in recent years.

In addition to these economic benefits, the presence of these military installations makes South Carolina a strategic geopolitical location for the deployment of US troops. In the past, military troops from South Carolina have been deployed to serve American interests in the Middle East (specifically Afghanistan, Iraq, and recently Egypt).[27] Although the Biden administration has insisted that no American troops will be sent to Ukraine, there has been a significant increase in American troops in Europe more broadly, and South Carolina has a part to play in that effort.

In February 2022, in anticipation of Russia's potential invasion of Ukraine, President Biden mobilized three thousand troops to Eastern Europe.[28] Notably, part of this group came from the Eighty-Second Airborne Unit in Fort Bragg, North Carolina. They were deployed on C-17 aircraft out of the Joint Charleston Base in South Carolina, highlighting the geopolitical significance of South Carolina's military installations. In June 2022, to both strengthen NATO's borders and send Putin a message that the West is unified and prepared to defend its borders, President Biden committed an additional twenty thousand American troops to Europe, bringing the total American troop presence to over one-hundred thousand.[29] It is likely that South Carolina military installations will play a strategic role in these deployment efforts.

There are also social factors that reflect the multiscalar impacts of war. The deployment of troops from any location produces significant effects on the mental and physical health of the soldiers being deployed, as well as on children and spouses, who must cope with the absence of a family member.[30] Furthermore, negative effects can be seen on small businesses, as military deployments (particularly of reservists) can hurt employment and reduce the consumer base for a time.[31] As sites of military training, logistics, and transport, South Carolina's military installations and the troops, civilians, and contractors that serve there have a role to play in the Russia-Ukraine war and global geopolitics more broadly and will have to contend with these issues.

Military Assistance to Ukraine and the Defense Industry in South Carolina

The defense industry, another product of militarization, also stands to influence the Russia-Ukraine war and affect both the South Carolina and US economies. As of the summer of 2022, over six billion USD in military and security assistance has been sent to Ukraine since the Russian invasion began. This security assistance includes weapons, ammunition, aircraft and other military vehicles, surveillance, communications and defense systems, and funding for training.[32] This is a drop in the bucket compared with the other economic aid that the United States has committed in Ukraine, totaling over fifty billion USD.[33] This larger aid package has the potential to act as a "positive economic weapon"[34] by giving money directly to the Ukrainian government to help maintain its infrastructure and to address humanitarian needs.[35] However, the utility of this aid could be limited if the funds are not used appropriately or efficiently, and as such, there has been some criticism over the lack of US government oversight in how this money will be spent.[36] Either way, for states like South Carolina, there is the potential for a lot of money to be made in the defense industry.

Throughout the Palmetto State, defense contractors and defense industries contribute significantly to employment and state gross domestic product (GDP; approximately 2.5% of the state's GDP per year).[37] In Charleston County alone, there are over eighty defense contractors that contribute to the aerospace, automotive, and tech industries, on and off existing military installations.[38] The aerospace industry, in particular, creates clear links between South Carolina and the Russia-Ukraine war. More than four hundred aerospace companies have a presence in South Carolina, including Boeing, GE Aviation, Honeywell, Lockheed Martin, and Michelin Aircraft Tire Company. The aerospace industry employs more than one hundred thirty thousand people in the state and has created more than five thousand new jobs for South Carolinians, totaling over two billion USD in investment since 2011. The industry has an overall economic impact of twenty-eight billion USD, with over four billion USD in exports in 2020 alone.[39]

The development of aerospace technology and the manufacturing of aerospace parts and aircraft in South Carolina will likely play a part in fulfilling the US commitment to security assistance in Ukraine, and, ultimately, the state could see more growth in defense industries, creating more job opportunities for South Carolinians. South Carolina's strategic geopolitical location on the eastern seaboard creates a site advantage for defense corporations looking for easy access to labor, transportation, and military facilities. This multiscalar view of militarization in South Carolina complicates our notions of wars as disruptive economically, politically, and socially. In fact, militarization and the Russia-Ukraine war may actually benefit the people of South Carolina. That being said, all of these processes are also affected by the broader economic vulnerabilities created by the Ukraine war at the international scale.

Geopolitics and Economic Relations

Although militarization reveals some of the direct geopolitical impacts that South Carolina has on the Russia-Ukraine war, the impacts of the war on South Carolinians are most directly and broadly economic. The wide-ranging impacts of the Russia-Ukraine war and the lingering effects of the COVID-19 pandemic have combined to produce record inflation, supply chain issues, and changes in global demand. Some of the big exporters in South Carolina, such as Boeing in Charleston and BMW in Spartanburg, have had to shift their production and exports in response to the war. These economic relations also have the potential to affect the Russia-Ukraine war, as economic sanctions by the West are designed to hurt the Russian economy and war effort. As with the impacts of militarization, these economic relations have multiscalar impacts—from people's pocketbooks and household incomes to the balance sheets of global corporations—and ultimately highlight the reciprocal effects of sanctions as economic tools.

Inflation and Supply Chain Vulnerabilities

Most Carolinians have already felt the effects of inflation, especially increased gas prices. The Federal Reserve Bank sets an annual inflation target of two percent, which it has met for most of the past twenty years, but by June 2022, the inflation rate was at 9.1%,[40] the highest rate since December 1981.[41] The rate for the American South was even higher, at 9.8%.[42] Inflation had already been rapidly increasing as the economy reopened amid the COVID-19 pandemic, but the war has increased supply chain concerns and, in particular, affected the price of gas and oil.

For South Carolinians, prices at the gas pump are one of the most visible impacts. Nationwide, gasoline was $1.05 more per gallon in May 2022 than it was on the day Russia invaded Ukraine.[43] By June 2022, the nationwide average went above five dollars per gallon for the first time.[44] In South Carolina, the average price per gallon was $4.31 on May 19, 2022, compared with $2.85 the year before.[45] Some of this increase may be directly related to US sanctions, which ban Russian oil imports. However, the United States only imported about eight percent of its petroleum from Russia in 2021.[46] Gas prices are driven primarily by world oil prices, which were ninety-six dollars per barrel the day before Russia invaded and shot up to almost one hundred twenty-eight dollars by March 8.[47] Russia is the world's second-ranked exporter of oil and gas, after Saudi Arabia, and many countries have decided to stop purchasing from Russia, tightening demand for the rest of the world's supply.

Food prices have also been driving inflation, both before the invasion and continuing since then.[48] Inflation for food is higher than for the all-item average, and this is worse in the South than for the nation as a whole.[49] Food prices have spiked, in part, because Ukraine is a major agricultural producer. On the basis of the 2021 harvest, Ukraine was the seventh worldwide producer of wheat and the fifth exporter, accounting for nine percent of global exports. Ukraine's exports primarily go to Egypt, Indonesia, Turkey, Pakistan, and Bangladesh, rather than the United States, but a drop in these exports affects the world wheat supply and world prices. At the time of the invasion, about ninety-five percent of Ukraine's exports from the 2021 harvest had already been shipped, so the greatest impacts on the global food market may come with the 2022 harvest (July to September) and beyond.

Ukraine also produces and/or exports large shares of the world's sunflowers, corn, barley, and rapeseed.[50] Exports of most of these crops have fallen by half since the war started. The general difficulties of war, port blockades, difficulties in transitioning to other modes of transport, and even accusations that the Russians are stealing grain have all limited global supply and increased world prices.[51] At the local scale, South Carolinians have already seen grocery prices increase, which is an added burden, especially on middle- and lower income households. However, it is important to note that the greatest impact will be in the Global South and in countries that are particularly dependent on Ukrainian crops, where threats of famine abound.

Russia produces and exports a large share of the world's fertilizer, which has dealt another blow to global agricultural production. Because rising costs of natural gas, producing fertilizer elsewhere will also be more expensive. Meanwhile, several countries have placed export restrictions on fertilizer to ensure that they will have enough supply domestically. As a result, fertilizer prices have been spiking and are likely to remain high, including in South Carolina.[52] This drives further increases in food prices, as farmers need to recoup the money spent on fertilizer and could also lead to less food if farmers choose to decrease planting. Planting decisions today affect future harvests, so there are long-term implications to these price changes: Even if the war ended today, increased prices for fertilizer could affect the food supply over the next few years. Agribusiness is South Carolina's largest economic sector.[53] As there is currently no end to the war in sight, South Carolina's farmers and the economy more broadly are increasingly vulnerable.

South Carolina's Manufacturing and Exports

In addition to these broader inflationary concerns, South Carolina holds a geopolitical position as a significant exporter of goods to Russia, which can affect both Russia's war effort and South Carolina's economy. Of all the US states, South Carolina was ranked fourth in 2021 in terms of the value of goods exported to Russia, and of all other countries that import South Carolina's exports, Russia ranked fourteenth.[54] Exports to Russia grew over the course of 2021 and were a leading driver of the growth in South Carolina's exports that year, with a one hundred sixty-two percent or $17.9 million increase.[55] This relatively high (and growing) level of trade with Russia means that US sanctions, such as government bans on certain exports or voluntary decisions by businesses to cut off trade, may affect South Carolina more than other states. Accordingly, these disruptions to Russia's trade with South Carolina may have more impact on Russia and, if sanctions work as designed, on its political decisions and war effort.

The potential impacts of South Carolina's export economy on the Russia-Ukraine war can be seen in South Carolina's largest export category: transportation equipment, including aircraft and automobiles. As discussed earlier, defense industries in South Carolina play a role in the security assistance that the United States is providing to Ukraine. However, transportation equipment exports, especially from the Charleston Boeing plant and the Spartanburg BMW plant, may face challenges in adapting to this geopolitical moment, as the war and sanctions make it difficult for these industries to get the materials necessary for production.

For example, the aerospace industry, which includes Boeing, faces challenges because it needs titanium from both Russia and Ukraine. However, Boeing has been stockpiling titanium and diversifying its supply since the 2014 invasion of Crimea and is, therefore, less reliant on current imports from Russia and Ukraine, putting the company in a better position than its main competitor, Airbus.[56] Still, Boeing has stopped importing titanium from Russia and has stopped all support to Russian customers, including supplying repair parts and engineering and maintenance support.[57] The company also marked orders for some jets as questionable, especially those to airlines in Russia and Ukraine. As a result, in April 2022, Boeing estimated losing orders for about ninety aircraft because of the conflict.[58] Boeing and Airbus have both seen their stock prices drop since the invasion, and they were in line with one another for the first few months of the war, although Boeing's did drop more after a quarterly report at the end of April 2022, and its dropoff remains greater at the time of writing.[59]

The automobile industry is similarly affected by limitations on the supply of necessary resources and parts, as well as by a loss of sales. Ukraine supplies about half of the world's neon gas, which is used for semiconductor production.[60] Ukraine also produced important automobile components, especially automotive wiring harnesses. Russia has been a key supplier of both palladium for catalytic converters and nickel for alloys and lithium-ion batteries.[61] These types of supply chain issues did interrupt production at several BMW plants.[62] Much like Boeing, BMW also halted manufacturing in and exports to Russia in response to the war.[63] The latter matters for the South Carolina plant because, in 2020, about five percent of its exports went to Russia, making it the fifth-ranked destination.[64] In response to these decisions and constraints, BMW did slightly scale down its earnings targets.[65] These types of business decisions and sanctions by Western governments also seem to be having an impact on Russian car production: Recent numbers announced by the Russian government agency Rosstat suggest that car production in Russia was ninety-seven percent less in May 2022, than a year earlier.[66] This combination of decreased domestic production in Russia and decreased imports of cars from abroad is likely to be felt by the Russian population, ideally leading them to put pressure on the government to change its behavior or, if that does not work, then arguably as an economic weapon against Russia.[67]

The Russia-Ukraine war has produced significant economic impacts for Russia and, to a lesser extent, for South Carolina. Globalization helps explain why the prices of goods such as oil, crops, and fertilizer depend on the world market and why the war affects businesses, farmers, and consumers in South Carolina. The globalization of trade and economics is also what makes sanctions against Russia useful as a possible economic tool or weapon. Globalization also opens the door for individual companies to make voluntary business decisions that can affect geopolitics from the bottom up, such as BMW and Boeing's decision to halt business with Russia. Those corporate decisions are also driven, at least in part, from the bottom-up, from the scale of individual consumers and activists who leverage the power of civil society to push these corporations to act and thereby potentially impact the course of the war.

Geopolitics and the Ukrainian Diaspora

Individuals of Ukrainian descent are particularly likely to be motivated to try to affect the course of the war. Even before the war, Ukraine had the largest European diaspora (about 5.9 million people),[68] and US Census Bureau data from 2020 suggest that there are about twelve thousand people with Ukrainian ancestry living in South Carolina.[69] These people are likely to respond to the war and news coverage of it more strongly than others. Research by Rostam and Haverkamp into how Iraqi expatriates responded to coverage of the Iraq War found that they had a heightened focus on the news, especially out of concern for relatives and their homeland.[70] More specifically, expatriates felt frustrated and angry when coverage did not focus enough attention on humanitarian concerns and cultural context. Ukrainians living in South Carolina have similarly expressed concern about relatives and others in Ukraine, anger at the destruction of their cities, and feelings of powerlessness at not being able to do more.[71]

Whereas some people may feel a sense of powerlessness, others will likely feel the need to educate others about their people and homeland.[72] Still others have turned to activism to help the war effort and people affected by the war. These efforts are not new, and previous action by the

Ukrainian diaspora has already made a difference in democratization and politics in Ukraine.[73] For example, in response to the Euromaidan protests in 2013, Ukrainian-Americans founded the activist group Razom (meaning "together" in Ukrainian), which gathered humanitarian aid, published legal reports, monitored and countered propaganda, disseminated information, supported independent media and civil society in Ukraine, and mobilized Ukrainian-Americans to vote in Ukrainian elections. In the United States, Razom also raised awareness and pushed other Americans and the US government to act in support of Ukraine.[74] Razom has responded similarly to the current war, seeking to raise awareness and action at the national scale.[75]

In South Carolina, groups like "World for Ukraine," "South Carolina Stands with Ukraine," and Charleston-based "CHS4Ukraine" have been gathering supplies to send to Ukraine, holding rallies and awareness events, and lobbying local officials.[76] Another way that Ukrainians abroad can engage is through the power of social media, which has been used for identity building, networking, and community engagement. Social media has been helpful in countering propaganda and encouraging direct participation through volunteering and donating. A Facebook group called "Ukrainians in the Carolinas" seems to be particularly active in providing information on those seeking to assist refugees to the United States.[77] Other groups, such as Lutheran Services Carolinas, are also working in refugee resettlement and anticipate settling about three hundred fifty Ukrainian refugees into South Carolina.[78] These types of activism and engagement are some clear ways that South Carolinians are influencing the conflict in Ukraine, from the bottom-up. The processes of globalization and time-space compression make it possible for Ukrainian communities living abroad to raise awareness, influence their new governments, and provide targeted assistance to those most affected by the war, thereby shaping geopolitics.

Conclusion

When most South Carolinians think about the Russia-Ukraine war, they may sympathize with the Ukrainian people and be broadly concerned that the United States will become directly involved in the conflict, either through a Russian attack or through a decision to send troops into Ukrainian battlefields. However, they are likely less aware of the numerous, often less obvious ways that South Carolina's people and economy are already an active part of the geopolitics of the Russia-Ukraine war. In this essay, we have highlighted some of the ways that South Carolina affects and is affected by the Russia-Ukraine war through militarization, economic globalization, and Ukrainian communities living within the state.

This reciprocal relationship between South Carolina and the geopolitics of the Russia-Ukraine war is made possible through globalization and time-space compression. Much of the popular discussion of globalization tends to focus on the top-down, economic elements, such as the dominance of global corporations or the spread of McDonald's around the globe. This is certainly one important aspect, as we have shown through the importance of the military industrial complex, interconnected supply chains, and world-wide changes to oil and food prices. However, it is important to also consider the bottom-up processes, where individuals and those on a local scale can affect global outcomes. The role of South Carolinians who serve in the military or who are connected to the defense industry and broader processes of militarization will both be affected by and affect the Russia-Ukraine war. The Ukrainian diaspora, even the small segment of it located in South Carolina, can make a difference through donations, raising awareness, lobbying governments, helping resettle refugees, and battling misinformation. The decisions of companies to stop sales and support to Russia can go where sanctions have not and strengthen the Western economic response to the invasion. In short, meaningful geopolitical action happens at every geographic scale.

The Ukrainian cause has found support in South Carolina and the United States for numerous reasons, including the legacy of Cold War tensions between Russia and the United States as well as a broad sense of shared identity (e.g., Christianity, Europeanness). However, the interconnectedness that we demonstrate between South Carolina and Ukraine is not due to some special relationship between these two locations—it is truly global. Similar arguments could be made about other locations and conflicts, even if there is less cultural affinity between the peoples involved. In exploring these relationships, we not only hope to demonstrate how people in the Carolinas have potential roles in the Russia-Ukraine war but also hope that this discussion serves as a reminder that we cannot consider geopolitical conflict in all its forms as ever just "over there," as somehow disconnected from our own homes and communities. This is especially important, because the longer a conflict lasts, the less likely it is to hold the attention of people and places that are far from the epicenter of a conflict. Currently, there is no end in sight to the Ukraine war and, as such, no end to the potential economic, social, and political impacts that will ripple across the globe, or our ability to influence them.

Lauren K. Perez is assistant professor of political science at Francis Marion University. Her research focuses on politics in multilevel settings, especially on the interactions between domestic and European-level legislative politics in the European Union.

Jennifer L. Titanski-Hooper is assistant professor of geography and the director of the Governor Robert E. McNair Institute for Research and Service at Francis Marion University. She specializes in European geopolitics and has written on issues of national identity and the processes of Europeanization in the former Yugoslavia.

NOTES

1. Note that the authors of this article have equal authorship and are listed alphabetically.
2. Sarah Habershon, Rob England, Becky Dale, and Olga Ivshina, "War in Ukraine: Can we say how many people have died?" *BBC News*, July 1, 2022, www.bbc.com. When writing about an ongoing conflict, we recognize that some specifics will become out of date, but we believe that the argument of this essay holds, and we hope that the data and examples provided offer valuable historical evidence of the early days of the Russia-Ukraine war.
3. Mark W. Zacher, "The Territorial Integrity Norm: International Boundaries and the Use of Force," *International Organization* 55, no. 2 (2001): 215–50.
4. See Tanisha Fazal, *State Death: The Politics and Geography of Conquest, Occupation, and Annexation* (Princeton, NJ: Princeton University Press, 2007).
5. See Kristian Skrede Gleditsch and Steve Pickering, "Wars Are Becoming Less Frequent: A Response to Harrison and Wolf," *Economic History Review* 67, no. 1 (2014): 214–30.
6. For a useful discussion to the concept of scale, see Andrew Herod and Melissa W. Wright, "Placing Scale: An Introduction," in *Geographies of Power: Placing Scale*, ed. Herod and Wright (Oxford: Blackwell, 2002), 1–14.
7. Emily Williams, "Understand SC: South Carolinians Stand with Ukraine," *Post and Courier*, March 3, 2022, www.postandcourier.com.
8. Jan Nederveen Pieterse, *Globalization and Culture: Global Mélange*, 4th edition (Lanham, MD: Rowman & Littlefield Publishers, 2019), passim.
9. See Lauren K. Perez, "Building a Bridge to Europe? National Legislators' Views on Their Role in the EU," in *The European Union and Beyond: Multi-Level Governance, Institutions, and Policy-Making*, ed. Jae-Jae Spoon and Nils Ringe (New York: ECPR Press, Rowman & Littlefield, 2020), 117–38; Jennifer Titanski-Hooper, "'The Belly of Zagreb': Identity, Development, and Europeanization in Croatia's Open-Air Markets," (PhD dissertation, Pennsylvania State University, 2017).
10. See David Harvey, *The Condition of Postmodernity: An Enquiry into the Origins of Cultural Change* (Cambridge, MA: Wiley-Blackwell, 1991).

11. See Timothy Graham and Jay Daniel Thompson, "Russian Government Accounts are Using a Twitter Loophole to Spread Disinformation," *The Conversation*, March 15, 2022, https://theconversation.com.

12. Doreen Massey, "Power-Geometry and a Progressive Sense of Place," in *Mapping the Futures: Local Cultures, Global Change*, ed. John Bird, et al. (London: Routledge, 1993), 75–85.

13. These perspectives on geopolitics were infamously deployed by Nazi Germany to justify its territorial ambitions, which ultimately worked to widely discredit the field, particularly within geography. As a discipline, geopolitics has since revived in various forms (critical, popular environmental, and feminist) as both an attempt to rehabilitate the discipline and also recognize the continued importance of the interrelationships between politics and geography. For examples of traditional geopolitics, see Halford J. MacKinder, "The Geographical Pivot of History (1904)," *The Geographical Journal* 170, no. 4 (2004): 298–321; and Friedrich Ratzel, "The Territorial Growth of States," *Scottish Geographical Magazine* 12, no. 7 (1896): 351–61.

14. John J. Mearsheimer, "The Causes and Consequences of the Ukraine War," YouTube video, 2:36, June 16, 2022, https://www.youtube.com/watch?v=qciVozNtCDM.

15. See John Agnew, "The Territorial Trap: The Geographical Assumptions of International Relations Theory," *Review of International Political Economy* 1, no. 1 (1994): 53–80.

16. Robert Person and Michael McFaul, "What Putin Fears Most," *The Journal of Democracy*, February 22, 2022, www.journalofdemocracy.org/.

17. See Lorraine Dowler and Joanne Sharp, "A Feminist Geopolitics?" *Space and Polity* 5, no. 3 (2001): 165–76.

18. See Jennifer Hyndman, "Towards a Feminist Geopolitics," *The Canadian Geographer* 45, no. 2 (2001): 210–22.

19. See Jennifer Fluri, "Geopolitics of Gender and Violence 'from Below,'" *Political Geography* 28, no. 4 (2009): 259–65.

20. Cynthia Enloe, *Globalization and Militarization: Feminists Make the Link* (Plymouth, UK: Rowman and Littlefield 2007).

21. US Department of Defense, "2020 Demographics: Profile of the Military Community," 32, 78., https://download.militaryonesource.mil/12038/MOS/Reports/.

22. South Carolina Department of Veterans Affairs, "SC Military Base Task Force," *SC.gov*, http://scdva.sc.gov.

23. Joseph C. Von Nessen, "The Economic Impact of South Carolina's Military Community," SC Department of Veterans Affairs, June 2022, https://scdva.sc.gov/sites/scdva/files/Documents/.

24. Thomas Novelly and Bryan Brussee, "From Making Fighter Jets to Food Rations, War is Big Business in South Carolina," *The Post and Courier*, June 14, 2019, updated June 3, 2021, https://www.postandcourier.com/news/.

25. Von Nessen, "The Economic Impact of South Carolina's Military Community."

26. *Ibid*.

27. See Thomas Novelly, "Where SC National Guard troops are deployed in the Middle East as tensions rise with Iran," *Post and Courier*, January 3, 2020, www.postandcourier.com; Rachel Ripp, "South Carolina National Guard deploying

50 soldiers to Egypt," *WLTX-TV*, April 20, 2022, www.wltx.com; Jeff Wilkinson, "SC has a big role to play in Afghanistan," *The State*, February 10, 2017, www.thestate.com.

28. Chase Laudenslager, "Joint Base Charleston Assisting with Deployment of Troops to Europe amid Russia, Ukraine Tension," *WCBD News* 2, February 4, 2022, www.counton2.com.

29. Jim Garamone, "Biden Announces Changes in U.S. Force Posture in Europe," *DOD News*, June 29, 2022, www.defense.gov.

30. See Stéphanie Vincent Lyk-Jensen et al., "The Effect of Military Deployment on Mental Health," *Economics and Human Biology* 23 (2016): 193–208; Alan J. Lincoln and Kathie Sweeten, "Considerations for the Effects of Military Deployment on Children and Families," *Social Work in Healthcare* 50, no. 1 (2011): 73–84; Sean C. Sheppard et al., "The Impact of Deployment on U.S. Military Families," *American Psychologist* 65, no. 6 (2010): 599–609.

31. See Martin Bressler and Linda Bressler, "A study of veteran-owned small businesses and the impact of military reserve call-ups since 9/11," *Academy of Entrepreneurship Journal* 19, no. 2 (2012): 1–22.

32. US Department of Defense, "Factsheet on U.S. Security Assistance to Ukraine," July 5, 2022, www.defense.gov/News/Releases/Release/Article/3083102/.

33. Bianca Pallaro and Alicia Parlapiano, "The Upshot: Four Ways to Understand the $54 Billion in U.S. Spending on Ukraine," *New York Times*, May 20, 2022, www.nytimes.com.

34. Nicholas Mulder, *The Economic Weapon: The Rise of Sanctions as a Tool of Modern War* (New Haven, CT: Yale University Press, 2022), 12.

35. USAID, "The United States Contributes $1.3 Billion to Support the Government of Ukraine," *Press Releases*, June 30, 2022, www.usaid.gov; USAID, "The United States Announces Additional Humanitarian Assistance to Ukraine," *Press Releases*, July 9, 2022, www.usaid.gov.

36. See Kelsey Snell, "Biden Signs a $40 Billion Aid Package to Help Ukraine Fight off the Russian Invasion," NPR, May 21, 2022, www.npr.org.

37. See Novelly and Brussee, "From Making Fighter Jets to Food Rations"; and "Military's Impact on State Economies," *National Conference of State Legislators*, April 9, 2018, https://www.ncsl.org/research/military-and-veterans-affairs/.

38. "Key Industries," Charleston County Economic Development, https://www.charlestoncountydevelopment.org/key-industries/.

39. South Carolina Department of Commerce, "Aerospace Industry Snapshot, 2021," https://www.sccommerce.com/industries/aerospace-industry.

40. US Bureau of Labor Statistics, "Consumer Price Index Summary," Economic News Release, July 13, 2022, https://www.bls.gov/news.release/cpi.nr0.htm.

41. US Bureau of Labor Statistics, "Consumer Price Index for All Urban Consumers: All Items in U.S. City Average [CPIAUCSL]," FRED, Federal Reserve Bank of St. Louis, https://fred.stlouisfed.org/graph/?g=ANNk.

42. Southeast Information Office, US Bureau of Labor Statistics, "Consumer Price Index, South Region—June 2022," www.bls.gov.

43. AAA, "Nowhere to Go but Up?" AAA, May 23, 2022, Gas Prices, https://gasprices.aaa.com.

44. AAA, "National Average Hits New All-Time High at $5 per Gallon," Gas Prices, https://gasprices.aaa.com.

45. AAA, "South Carolina Average Gas Prices," Gas Prices, https://gasprices.aaa.com.

46. US Energy Information Administration, "The United States Imports More Petroleum Products than Crude Oil from Russia," *Today in Energy*, March 22, 2022, https://www.eia.gov/todayinenergy/detail.php?id=51738.

47. "CO1 Commodity Quote - Generic 1st 'CO' Future," Bloomberg.com, https://www.bloomberg.com/quote/CO1:COM.

48. Food and Agriculture Organization of the United Nations, "FAO Food Price Index," https://www.fao.org/worldfoodsituation/foodpricesindex/en/.

49. US Bureau of Labor Statistics, "Consumer Price Index Summary," July 13, 2022, www.bls.gov; Southeast Information Office, US Bureau of Labor Statistics, "Consumer Price Index, South Region—June 2022," www.bls.gov.

50. Foreign Agricultural Service, US Department of Agriculture, "Ukraine Agricultural Production and Trade," April 2022, https://www.fas.usda.gov/sites/default/files/2022-04/Ukraine-Factsheet-April2022.pdf.

51. Wailin Wong and Darian Woods, "Russia Has Blocked 20 Million Tons of Grain from Being Exported from Ukraine," South Carolina Public Radio, June 3, 2022, www.southcarolinapublicradio.org.

52. Charlotte Hebebrand and David Laborde, "High Fertilizer Prices Contribute to Rising Global Food Security Concerns," IFPRI: International Food Policy Research Institute, April 25, 2022, www.ifpri.org; US Department of Agriculture, "South Carolina Crop Production Report | ID: 5712m658s," Economics, Statistics and Market Information System, https://usda.library.cornell.edu/concern/publications/.

53. "SC Farm Facts," South Carolina Farm Bureau, https://www.scfb.org/ag-education/.

54. US Census Bureau: Economic Indicators Division USA Trade Online, "State Exports by NAICS Commodities," https://usatrade.census.gov/data/Perspective60/View/dispview.aspx.

55. "South Carolina," OEC - The Observatory of Economic Complexity, https://oec.world/en/profile/subnational_usa_state/sc.

56. Joseph Mellors, "Boeing: Why the Ukraine Crisis Could Help It Become the World's Number One Aircraft Maker Again," *The Conversation*, March 15, 2022, http://theconversation.com.

57. Dave Calhoun, "Boeing CEO Updates Employees on First-Quarter Results," Boeing Media Room, April 27, 2022, https://boeing.mediaroom.com/news-releases-statements?item=131041.

58. Chris Isidore, "Boeing Loses More than 90 Jet Orders Due to War in Ukraine," CNN, April 12, 2022, www.cnn.com.

59. "BA: Boeing Co/The Stock Price Quote," Bloomberg.com, July 1, 2022, https://www.bloomberg.com/quote/BA:US; Bloomberg, "EADSY: Airbus SE/The Stock Price Quote," Bloomberg.com, July 1, 2022, https://www.bloomberg.com/quote/EADSY:US.

60. Samantha DeCarlo and Samuel Goodman, "Ukraine, Neon, and Semiconductors," Executive Briefings on Trade, US International Trade Commission, April 2022, https://www.usitc.gov/publications/332/executive_briefings/.

61. Klaus Ulrich, "Ukraine War: German Auto Industry Alarmed over Lack of Raw Materials," Deutsche Welle, April 1, 2022, https://www.dw.com/en/.

62. Nicolas Peter, "Statement Dr. Nicolas Peter, Member of the Board of Management of BMW AG, Finance, Annual Conference 2022," BMW Group Press Club, March 16, 2022, https://www.press.bmwgroup.com/global/article/detail /T0374315EN/.

63. Oliver Zipse, "Statement and Presentation Oliver Zipse, Chairman of the Board of Management of BMW AG, 102nd Annual General Meeting of BMW AG in Munich on 11th May 2022," BMW Group Press Club, May 11, 2022, https://www .press.bmwgroup.com/global/article/detail/T0388653EN/.

64. "BMW Manufacturing Remains Largest U.S. Automotive Exporter by Value," BMW Group, February 11, 2021, https://www.bmwgroup-werke.com/spartanburg /en/news/2021/

65. Zipse, "Statement and Presentation."

66. "Russia's Car Manufacturing Collapses by 97% in May," *The Moscow Times*, June 30, 2022, sec. news, https://www.themoscowtimes.com/2022/06/30/.

67. Mulder, *The Economic Weapon*.

68. Olga Oleinikova and Jumana Bayeh, *Democracy, Diaspora, Territory: Europe and Cross-Border Politics* (Milton, UK: Taylor & Francis Group, 2019).

69. US Census Bureau, "DP02: Selected Social Characteristics in the United States - Census Bureau Table," https://data.census.gov/cedsci/.

70. Hajera Rostam and Beth E. Haverkamp, "Iraqi Expatriates' Experience of North American Media Coverage of the Iraq War," *International Journal for the Advancement of Counselling* 31, no. 2 (June 1, 2009): 100–17, https://doi.org/10.1007/s10447 -009-9071-7.

71. Sarah Sheridan, "Ukrainians Living in South Carolina Feel 'Powerless' as Their Families Turn into Refugees," *The Greenville News*, March 7, 2022, www.greenville online.com.

72. Rostam and Haverkamp, "Iraqi Expatriates' Experience."

73. Oleinikova and Bayeh, *Democracy, Diaspora, Territory*.

74. Serhiy Kovalchuk and Alla Korzh, "The Transnational Activism of Young Ukrainian Immigrants," in *Democracy, Diaspora, Territory: Europe and Cross-Border Politics*, ed. Olga Oleinikova and Jumana Bayeh (Milton, UK: Taylor & Francis Group, 2019), 127–44.

75. "Newsletter #18: Want to Know What Kind of Impact Your Donations Are Having?" *Razom* (blog), June 7, 2022, https://www.razomforukraine.org/newsletter -18/.

76. The World for Ukraine, "About 'World for Ukraine' Nonprofit," https://www .theworldforukraine.org/, "Home," South Carolina Stands With Ukraine, https:// www.scstandswithukraine.com; CHS4Ukraine, "Home," CHS4Ukraine, https:// www.chs4ukraine.org/.

77. "Ukrainians in the Carolinas Українці Кароліни" Facebook, https://www .facebook.com/groups/937155979649761/.

78. Erin Kidd, "Lutheran Services Carolinas Anticipates Serving Ukrainian Refugees," *Lutheran Services Carolinas* (blog), May 27, 2022, https://lscarolinas .net.

WORKS CITED

Agnew, John. "The Territorial Trap: The Geographical Assumptions of International Relations Theory." *Review of International Political Economy* 1, no. 1 (1994): 53–80.

Bressler, Martin, and Linda Bressler. "A Study of Veteran-Owned Small Businesses and the Impact of Military Reserve Call-ups Since 9/11." *Academy of Entrepreneurship Journal* 19, no. 2 (2012): 1–22.

BMW Group. "BMW Manufacturing Remains Largest U.S. Automotive Exporter by Value." Last modified February 11, 2021. https://www.bmwgroup-werke.com /spartanburg/en/news/2021/.

Calhoun, Dave. "Boeing CEO Updates Employees on First-Quarter Results." Boeing Media Room. Last modified April 27, 2022. https://boeing.mediaroom.com /news-releases-statements?item=131041.

Charleston County Economic Development. "Key Industries." https://www .charlestoncountydevelopment.org/key-industries/.

CHS4Ukraine, "Home." https://www.chs4ukraine.org/.

DeCarlo, Samantha, and Samuel Goodman. "Ukraine, Neon, and Semiconductors." Executive Briefings on Trade. U.S. International Trade Commission, April 2022. https://www.usitc.gov/publications/332/executive_briefings/.

Dowler, Lorraine, and Joanne Sharp. "A Feminist Geopolitics?" *Space and Polity* 5, no. 3 (2001): 165–76.

Enloe, Cynthia. *Globalization and Militarization: Feminists Make the Link.* Plymouth, UK: Rowman and Littlefield, 2007.

Fazal, Tanisha. *State Death: The Politics and Geography of Conquest, Occupation, and Annexation.* Princeton, NJ: Princeton University Press, 2007.

Fluri, Jennifer. "Geopolitics of Gender and Violence 'from Below.'" *Political Geography* 28, no. 4 (2009): 259–65.

Food and Agriculture Organization of the United Nations, "FAO Food Price Index." https://www.fao.org/worldfoodsituation/foodpricesindex/en/.

FRED, Federal Reserve Bank of St. Louis. "Consumer Price Index for All Urban Consumers: All Items in U.S. City Average [CPIAUCSL]." Accessed June 1, 2022. https://fred.stlouisfed.org/graph/?g=ANNk.

Gleditsch, Kristian Skrede, and Steve Pickering. "Wars Are Becoming Less Frequent: A Response to Harrison and Wolf." *The Economic History Review* 67, no. 1 (2014): 214–30.

Graham, Timothy, and Jay Daniel Thompson. "Russian Government Accounts are Using a Twitter Loophole to Spread Disinformation." *The Conversation,* March 15, 2022. https://theconversation.com.

Harvey, David. *The Condition of Postmodernity: An Enquiry into the Origins of Cultural Change.* Cambridge, MA: Wiley-Blackwell, 1991.

Hebebrand, Charlotte, and David Laborde. "High Fertilizer Prices Contribute to Rising Global Food Security Concerns," IFPRI: International Food Policy Research Institute, April 25, 2022. www.ifpri.org.

Herod, Andrew, and Melissa W. Wright. "Placing Scale: An Introduction." In *Geographies of Power: Placing Scale,* edited by Andrew Herod and Melissa W. Wright, 1–14. Oxford: Blackwell, 2002.

Hyndman, Jennifer. "Towards a Feminist Geopolitics." *The Canadian Geographer* 45, no. 2 (2001): 210–22.

Kidd, Erin. "Lutheran Services Carolinas Anticipates Serving Ukrainian Refugees." *Lutheran Services Carolinas* (blog). May 27, 2022. https://lscarolinas.net.

Kovalchuk, Serhiy, and Alla Korzh. "The Transnational Activism of Young Ukrainian Immigrants." In *Democracy, Diaspora, Territory: Europe and Cross-Border Politics*, edited by Olga Oleinikova and Jumana Bayeh, 127–44. Milton, UK: Taylor & Francis Group, 2019.

Lincoln, Alan J., and Kathie Sweeten. "Considerations for the Effects of Military Deployment on Children and Families." *Social Work in Healthcare* 50, no. 1 (2011): 73–84.

Lyk-Jensen, Stéphanie Vincent, et al. "The Effect of Military Deployment on Mental Health." *Economics and Human Biology* 23 (2016): 193–208.

MacKinder, Halford J. "The Geographical Pivot of History (1904)." *The Geographical Journal* 170, no. 4 (2004): 298–321.

Massey, Doreen. "Power-Geometry and a Progressive Sense of Place." In *Mapping the Futures: Local Cultures, Global Change*, edited by John Bird, et al., 75–85. London: Routledge, 1993.

Mearsheimer, John J. "The Causes and Consequences of the Ukraine War." YouTube. 2:36. June 16, 2022. https://www.youtube.com/watch?v=qciVozNtCDM.

Mellors, Joseph. "Boeing: Why the Ukraine Crisis Could Help It Become the World's Number One Aircraft Maker Again." *The Conversation*, March 15, 2022.

Mulder, Nicholas. *The Economic Weapon: The Rise of Sanctions as a Tool of Modern War*. New Haven, CT: Yale University Press, 2022.

National Conference of State Legislators. "Military's Impact on State Economies." April 9, 2018. https://www.ncsl.org/research/military-and-veterans-affairs/military-s-impact-on-state-economies.aspx.

"Newsletter #18: Want to Know What Kind of Impact Your Donations Are Having?" *Razom* (blog). June 7, 2022. https://www.razomforukraine.org/newsletter-18/.

OEC-The Observatory of Economic Complexity. "South Carolina." https://oec.world/en/profile/subnational_usa_state/sc.

Oleinikova, Olga, and Jumana Bayeh. *Democracy, Diaspora, Territory: Europe and Cross-Border Politics*. Milton, UK: Taylor & Francis Group, 2019.

Perez, Lauren K. "Building a Bridge to Europe? National Legislators' Views on Their Role in the EU." In *The European Union and Beyond: Multi-Level Governance, Institutions, and Policy-Making*, edited by Jae-Jae Spoon and Nils Ringe, 117–38. New York: ECPR Press, 2020.

Person, Robert, and Michael McFaul. "What Putin Fears Most." *Journal of Democracy*, February 22, 2022. https://www.journalofdemocracy.org/.

Peter, Nicolas. "Statement Dr Nicolas Peter, Member of the Board of Management of BMW AG, Finance, Annual Conference 2022." BMW Group PressClub. March 16, 2022. https://www.press.bmwgroup.com/global/article/detail/T0374315EN/.

Pieterse, Jan Nederveen. *Globalization and Culture: Global Mélange*. 4th edition. Lanham, MD: Rowman & Littlefield Publishers, 2019.

Ratzel, Friedrich. "The Territorial Growth of States." *Scottish Geographical Magazine* 12, no. 7 (1896): 351–61.

Rostam, Hajera, and Beth E. Haverkamp. "Iraqi Expatriates' Experience of North American Media Coverage of the Iraq War." *International Journal for the Advancement of Counselling* 31, no. 2 (June 1, 2009): 100–17. https://doi.org/10.1007/s10447-009-9071-7.

Sheppard, Sean C., Jennifer Weil Malatras, and Allen C. Israel. "The Impact of Deployment on U.S. Military Families." *American Psychologist* 65, no. 6 (2010): 599–609.

South Carolina Department of Commerce. "Aerospace Industry Snapshot, 2021." https://www.sccommerce.com/industries/aerospace-industry.

South Carolina Department of Veterans Affairs. "SC Military Base Task Force." SC.gov. http://scdva.sc.gov.

South Carolina Farm Bureau. "SC Farm Facts." https://www.scfb.org/ag-education/food-farm-facts.

South Carolina Stands With Ukraine. "Home." https://www.scstandswithukraine.com.

Southeast Information Office, US Bureau of Labor Statistics. "Consumer Price Index, South Region—June 2022." www.bls.gov.

Titanski-Hooper, Jennifer. "'The Belly of Zagreb': Identity, Development, and Europeanization in Croatia's Open-Air Markets." PhD dissertation, Pennsylvania State University, 2017.

US Bureau of Labor Statistics. "Consumer Price Index Summary, July 13, 2022." www.bls.gov.

US Census Bureau: 2020: ACS 5-Year Estimates Data Profiles. "DP02: Selected Social Characteristics in the United States-Census Bureau Table." https://data.census.gov/cedsci/.

US Census Bureau: Economic Indicators Division USA Trade Online. "State Exports by NAICS Commodities." https://usatrade.census.gov/data/Perspective60/View/dispview.aspx.

US Department of Agriculture: Economics, Statistics and Market Information System. "South Carolina Crop Production Report | ID: 5712m658s." https://usda.library.cornell.edu/concern/publications/5712m658s?locale=en#release-items.

US Department of Agriculture: Foreign Agricultural Service. "Ukraine Agricultural Production and Trade, April 2022." https://www.fas.usda.gov/sites/default/files/2022-04/Ukraine-Factsheet-April2022.pdf.

US Department of Defense. *2020 Demographics: Profile of the Military Community.* https://download.militaryonesource.mil/12038/MOS/Reports/2020-demographics-report.pdf.

US Department of Defense. "Factsheet on U.S. Security Assistance to Ukraine, July 5, 2022." https://www.defense.gov/News/Releases/Release/Article/3083102/.

United States Energy Information Administration. Today in Energy, March 22, 2022. "The United States Imports More Petroleum Products than Crude Oil from Russia." https://www.eia.gov/todayinenergy/detail.php?id=51738.

Von Nessen, Joseph C. "The Economic Impact of South Carolina's Military Community." South Carolina Military Base Task Force. April 2017. https://scdva.sc.gov/sc-military-base-task-force.

Wong, Wailin, and Darian Woods. "Russia Has Blocked 20 Million Tons of Grain from Being Exported from Ukraine." South Carolina Public Radio. June 3, 2022. www.southcarolinapublicradio.org.

The World for Ukraine. "About 'World for Ukraine' Nonprofit." https://www .theworldforukraine.org/about.

Zacher, Mark W. "The Territorial Integrity Norm: International Boundaries and the Use of Force." *International Organization* 55, no. 2 (2001): 215–50.

Zipse, Oliver. "Statement and Presentation Oliver Zipse, Chairman of the Board of Management of BMW AG, 102nd Annual General Meeting of BMW AG in Munich on 11th May 2022." BMW Group Press Club, May 11, 2022. https:// www.press.bmwgroup.com/global/article/detail/T0388653EN/.

Reviews

Roger C. Hartley, *Monumental Harm: Reckoning with Jim Crow Era Confederate Monuments* (Columbia: University of South Carolina Press, 2021), 280 pp., cloth $89.99, paperback $29.99, ebook $29.99.

Roger C. Hartley provides an accessible, informed, and important discussion of a timely question: What should municipalities do with Confederate monuments? In our post-Charlottesville era, there are many voices calling for their removal. But as South Carolinians discovered when officials finally removed the Confederate battle flag in 2015, there are also powerful forces demanding their preservation. Hartley establishes himself as a fair broker between these competing groups. He recognizes that there are "good faith claims to leave Confederate monuments undisturbed in order to preserve Southern heritage." More important, he demonstrates that the monuments not only perpetuate "anti-Black racial stereotyping and systemic racism," but also inflict "material harm on contemporary American life." In the end, Hartley argues that officials should remove monuments from public areas, such as courthouse grounds, and place them in museums, memorial parks, or private property. His compromise will likely find little support among those who want to either destroy or celebrate the monuments. Within the context of his richly detailed historical analysis, however, it appears both reasonable and—perhaps—achievable.

The first five chapters explore whether state governments and their subdivisions should do anything about the monuments, which as Hartley notes, "virtually never mention race or slavery." Using what he terms "a *racial-reckoning* approach," Hartley challenges those who would leave the monuments in place. Specifically, he calls attention to communities' "moral obligation" to remove structures that exalt "the twin goals of the Confederacy–destruction of the Union and perpetuation of slavery." To support his claim, he traces the history of the monuments, the commissioning of which coincided with the horrific epidemic of lynchings at the turn of the twentieth century; the unsettling popularity of the film *Birth of a Nation*; Woodrow Wilson's election to the presidency; and, later, the Supreme Court's landmark decision in *Brown v. Board of Education*. The monuments, Hartley contends, embody the same creeds of segregation and white supremacy that fueled the rise of Jim Crow.

They were designed to subjugate African Americans and create an exclusionary white identity.

Moreover, the monuments present a false narrative. Calling attention to the differences between history ("what actually happened") and memory ("how we think about what occurred"), Hartley connects the monuments and the associated Lost Cause mythology to Eric Hobsbawm and Terence Ranger's idea of "invented tradition," a sort of propaganda that uses an imagined past to promote an otherwise insupportable ideology. Hartley then dismantles the pillars of the Lost Cause mythology, particularly the noxious ideas that the Civil War was fought for states' rights; that enslaved people were somehow better off in bondage; the idea that the South was overwhelmed, but never defeated, by the invading Northern forces; and the idea of a principled Confederacy nobly fighting against violent usurpers, like the fictional "plantation pastorale of racial harmony," ignores "the irrefutable historical record." To the degree that the monuments advance the Lost Cause mythology, their purpose is "to glorify, not elucidate."

Hartley provides in-depth discussions of Richmond's monuments to Stonewall Jackson (1875) and Robert E. Lee (1890). These imposing statues were constructed at a time when Confederate monuments were no longer being placed in cemeteries, where they served a memorial function, but rather in public places, such as statehouses, where they advanced a political message. Anyone attending the unveiling ceremonies for these monuments would have experienced an abject lesson in Lost Cause deception. The audience certainly "would not have known that the slaves had been emancipated, that the Constitution had been amended with the ratification of the Thirteenth, Fourteenth, and Fifteenth Amendments, or that Lincoln's Gettysburg Address had announced a 'new birth of freedom.'" Rather, they would have participated in a ceremony designed "to legitimate Southern White supremacy in the national consciousness." These efforts became even worse in the mid-1890s, when the United Daughters of the Confederacy took over Confederate memorialization and used mass-produced monuments to advance the unapologetic white supremacy associated with the "Cult of Anglo-Saxonism."

For Hartley, the efforts of the United Daughters of the Confederacy comprise a *"warping of history,"* a disingenuous enterprise through which bigots "commandeered soldiers' valor" to "promote racial bias" and "secure their own political power and cultural authority." In this way, the monuments completed the same corrosive work as the Second Mississippi Plan and other efforts to disenfranchise African-American voters. Hartley also connects the monuments to spectacle lynchings, prolonged public ceremonies of torture and killing that were memorialized with picture postcards. Drawing on Grace Elizabeth Hale's historical analysis, Hartley argues that these lynchings not only enforced African-American submission but also allowed *"Whites to maintain their own White identity."* To this degree, the lynchings and the monuments functioned as did the dirty, incommodious railway cars designated for African-American passengers. Those cars were not intended to discourage African-American travel (railroads needed Black ticket revenue) but rather to help white travelers imaginatively construct "the significance of their own Whiteness" and "the fact of their own superiority." Perhaps the most egregious example of the warping of history can be found in the proposed "Mammy Monument," designed by Ulric Stonewall Jackson Dunbar and almost constructed in Washington, DC, in 1923. Not only would the monument have reinforced the Lost Cause's toxic "faithful slave" narrative, it would also have erased white sexual predation against African-American women and advanced an ideology of "Black 'otherness.'"

Turning to education, Hartley traces the development of "Rutherford committees," through which the United Daughters of the Confederacy ensured "a proper Jim Crow education... centered on racial hierarchy." Hartley convincingly links these committees to the monuments, showing how each reinforced the message of the other. As harmful as these teaching materials were for white children, they were far worse for the African-American children subjected to the demoralizing, dehumanizing lessons contained in "hand-me-down racist textbooks." Throughout this discussion, one hears the shrill cries of today's populists, who find the fearful specter of critical race theory even in grade-school math books designed to do little more than acknowledge diversity. Still, Hartley's analysis does not entirely capture the extent of pro-Confederate indoctrination, at least not as it existed in South Carolina. He states that "even today, many who were educated in the South prior to 1970 continue to harbor the view that slavery was not a cause of the Civil War." It is worth noting that vestiges of the Lost Cause mythology persisted well beyond 1970. Lewis P. Jones's textbook, *South Carolina: One of Fifty States* (last edition 1985) and Archie Vernon Huff, Jr.'s *The History of South Carolina in the Building of the Nation* (last edition, 1991) present modernized, somewhat sanitized, versions of that same false history. School districts used these texts into the twenty-first century, and some private schools continue to do so.[1]

Turning from the history of Confederate monuments to their harmful impacts, Hartley notes that monuments helped obliterate "the history, values, and memories of the Southern African-American community" while projecting a false perception of "White unity." In one of the book's few hopeful moments, Hartley provides a compelling discussion of celebrations such as Richmond Evacuation Day, Emancipation Day, and Juneteenth, which preserved a "counternarrative to the White myth that the South's secession from the Union had nothing to do with slavery and its defense." He also considers the less well-known Black militias that flourished briefly during Jim Crow. However laudable, these efforts could not thwart the structural racism legitimized by the monuments and expressed in discriminatory practices related to employment, housing, loan lending, voting, and policing. Throughout this section, Hartley's argument remains convincing. At brief moments, however, he leaves himself open for attack. For example, he states "biases and stereotypes of the Black male as inherently criminally inclined ... arise directly form the libeling of Black males during the period of Jim Crow and Confederate monument mania." His cogent historical and cultural interpretations amply support his claim, but the argument would be stronger if he addressed documents such as the FBI's Uniform Crime Reports, which are often cited without context by those opposed to police reform. Making his point without counterargument, concession, or qualification, Hartley leaves an important idea vulnerable.

In the next section, Hartley offers three possible responses to Confederate monuments: destruction, contextualization, and relocation. Destroying monuments would, of course, provide visceral satisfaction for those harmed by the racist ideology they empower, but it would deepen social divides. It would be an act of cleansing, not reconciliation. Moreover, it would seem to attack "certain values" of Southern culture—such as a "mystical faith in agrarianism and an unabashed appreciation of home and family"—that have no connection to bigotry. *Contextualization*, the process of using signage or contrasting monuments to challenge Confederate mythology, becomes even more problematic. It would encourage the toxic moral relativism of "the dual heritage ideology," which assigns honor to both African-American culture and the white culture that oppressed it. Contextualization could also prove to be politically impossible. Hartley notes that competing interests in Harpers Ferry fought for years over the contextualization of the "Faithful Slave Memorial" only to end up with a confusing set of contradictory signs that "satisfies no one." Even worse, economic interests often use contextualization to elide African-American history. Fearful of showing "any racial conflict within the community," business leaders insist that African-American monuments minimize the horrors of oppression and present the experience of enslavement within a heroic "narrative of endurance and overcoming." Kehinde Wiley's powerful "Rumors of War" (2019) serves as a notable exception.

Relocation offers a practical and ethically sound response. Placing the monuments within a memorial park, in a museum, or on private land does not erase Southern heritage or rewrite history, as critics might charge. It does, however, remove governmental imprimatur from installations that harm large segments of the population. It also allows observers to study the monuments as "artifacts of racial hostility" rather than extolments of a fictional past.

In the book's last section, titled "Who Decides?" Hartley takes up the complicated legal questions concerning relocation, especially in states like South Carolina that have passed laws to protect Confederate monuments. At times, Hartley offers practical workarounds to restrictive legislation. A law, for example, that requires municipalities to "protect and preserve" monuments may provide an unintended argument for relocation if that monument is subject to vandalism. He also gives his reader a lucid, approachable discussion of applicable case law; notably, *Pleasant City v. Summum*. As instruments of expression, monuments raise First Amendment concerns, and Constitutional protections of free speech extend to what one chooses not to say. Municipalities, it would seem, have a right not to express hateful ideas. Local governments, however, are unlikely to be successful arguing for their own free speech rights, which are extremely limited. Instead, government subdivisions should challenge state statutes by arguing for "protecting the free speech rights of a municipality's residents." Individuals, Hartley contends, should not be forced "to support, and be associated with . . . pro-Confederate messages," which is what effectively happens when the law prevents them from removing monuments from the public spaces of their communities.

Monumental Harm is a significant book. Its meticulous analyses show the concrete connections among Confederate monuments, Jim Crow, and the Lost Cause mythology. Moreover, it demonstrates that those monuments continue to harm the same citizens who pay for their preservation. Hartley's proposals, informed by his experiences as a lawyer and professor of law, may not please those who long for the poetic justice of iconoclasm, but they provide a practical strategy for combatting a hateful ideology that continues to damage our nation and the African-American community. In this way, *Monumental Harm* offers a viable path forward.

Christopher D. Johnson, Francis Marion University

NOTE

1. For a useful discussion of these texts and their ideological content, see Alan Wieder, "South Carolina School History Textbooks' Portrayals of Race During Reconstruction: An Historical Analysis," *Journal of Thought* 30, no. 1 (Spring 1995): 19–33.

Claudia Smith Brinson, *Stories of Struggle: The Clash over Civil Rights in South Carolina* (Columbia: University of South Carolina Press, 2020), 376 pp., cloth $44.99, paperback $22.99 (2023), ebook $22.99.

Long-time journalist Claudia Smith Brinson brings together five noteworthy events from the civil rights movement in South Carolina in *Stories of Struggle*. She explains in her introduction that this book introduces readers "to the pioneers. . . . they are remarkable, courageous, inventive, persevering people willing to give everything for first-class citizenship, and, in that regard, the nation's savior." However, in her conclusion, she argues that "South Carolina functioned as a crucible." The stories she narrates highlight the significant role that the state's Black activists played in bringing about change nationally, although South Carolina was one of the slowest states to embrace those changes locally. Using extensive interviews and newspapers, she explores stories from the 1930s through the 1960s in five chronological chapters.

The first chapter is a contextualized biography of James Myles Hinton Sr., the president of the South Carolina Conference of Branches of the National Advancement for the Association for Colored People (NAACP) from 1941 to 1958. Under his leadership, the state's branches raised funds and filed lawsuits to ensure racially equal teachers' salaries, to end voting restrictions such as poll taxes, and to desegregate the University of South Carolina law school. This was also a time of significant racial violence in South Carolina. For example, Brinson recounts the story of the lynching of Willie Earle by a white mob, none of whom were convicted for his brutal death. Furthermore, white supremacists kidnapped and beat Hinton. Because of his leadership position, there was a great search effort, including what he joked was "a whole posse of preachers."

Brinson focuses on *Briggs v. Elliott* in her second chapter. Although most school textbooks discuss *Brown v. Board of Education*, few people learn that the first Supreme Court case to desegregate schools was from Clarendon

County, South Carolina. The state's segregated schools were far from equal, as the state spent eighty percent less per Black student than it did per white student. Furthermore, Black families struggled to get their children to school, as the state only provided buses for white children. As Black families signed onto NAACP lawsuits, they faced financial reprisals from the white community. Brinson explains, "White people hired and fired, rented or sold land, provided loans and mortgages, and sold farming supplies and equipment, fuel, groceries, and dry goods. So, punishment came quickly and easily." The Ku Klux Klan also threatened physical harm. When it seemed that the petitioners might win, the state attempted to improve Black schools through sales taxes and selling bonds. Despite winning *Briggs v. Elliott*, South Carolina did not begin desegregating schools until 1970.

Chapters three and four delve into the student sit-in movement and its leadership in South Carolina. Cecil August Ivory was a pastor in Rock Hill and president of Rock Hill's branch of the NAACP. He was also wheelchair bound for much of his adulthood because of a blood clot likely associated with a childhood injury. Nevertheless, he orchestrated a bus boycott and organized nonviolent demonstration training for students at Friendship College, a Black Baptist college in Rock Hill. Over one hundred students carried out sit-ins at Woolworth's, McCrory's, Phillip's, and Good's stores. Brinson states, "Rock Hill set the pace for other communities: students protested almost daily and remained nonviolent, in no small part because of Ivory's guidance and—unlike unnerved or disapproving adults elsewhere—his participation." Students from South Carolina State College, Morris College, Claflin University, Voorhees College, Allen University, and Benedict College also staged sit-ins, some of which were synchronized. Overall, they sought to desegregate public places, most memorably lunch counters.

Brinson's fifth chapter covers the Charleston hospital strike in 1969. This story highlights the often-overlooked importance of Black women in the civil rights movement. Black women working in hospitals in Charleston worked harder than white women who received higher pay, and Black women did not have areas to take breaks or eat their meals. Although the NAACP did not get involved, the Southern Christian Leadership Conference (SCLC) and New York City's Local 1199 union assisted Charleston's Black women in their strike, establishing a union, and fighting for their rights in the workplace. They also had the support of two local biracial organizations: the Concerned Clergy Committee, and the Community Relations Committee. The striking women faced state troopers and the National Guard. Despite national news coverage, journalists did not interview strikers or report on their injuries. In the aftermath, Charleston's Black women lost all the support they had during the strike, and they were unable to effectively run their own union. Mary Moultrie, one of the strikers, remarked that the women were "forgotten."

Although she chose some well-studied stories like the *Briggs v. Elliott* case and the Charleston hospital strike, Brinson does not provide any discussion of the existing literature.[1] However, with chapters meant to be read individually, this book will appeal to a popular audience and educators could assign one chapter or the entire book to undergraduate students. Unfortunately, the author does not provide a complete list of interviews in her bibliography, and she does not indicate where future researchers might access the interviews. She ends her book with what seems to be a call for other Black activists in South Carolina to share their stories. Scholars statewide should help with answering that call by making efforts to professionally obtain and preserve their valuable oral histories.

Erica Johnson Edwards, Francis Marion University

NOTE

1. For *Briggs v. Elliott*, see, e.g., Richard Kluger, *Simple Justice: The History of* Brown v. Board of Education *and Black America's Struggle for Equality* (New York: Vintage, rev. ed. 2004); Wade Kolb III, "*Briggs v. Elliot*: A Study in Grassroots Activism and Trial Advocacy from the Early Civil Rights Era," *Journal of Southern Legal History* 19 (2011): 123–75; and Delia B. Allen, "The Forgotten *Brown* Case: *Briggs v. Elliott* and Its Legacy in South Carolina," *Peabody Journal of Education*, 94 (2019): 442–67. For the Charleston hospital strike, see, for example, Jesse J. Harris, "Nonviolence as a Strategy for Change: The Charleston Hospital Strike," in *Advocacy in America: Case Studies in Social Change*, edited by Gladys Walton Hall, Grace C. Clark, and Michael A. Creedon (Lanham: MD: University Press of America, 1987): 63–80; Jewell C. Debnam, "Mary Moultrie, Naomi White, and the Women of the Charleston Hospital Workers' Strike of 1969," *Souls* 18, no. 1 (2016): 59–79; and William F. Danaher, "Framing the Field: The Case of the 1969 Charleston Hospital Workers' Strike," *Mobilization: An International Quarterly* 22, no. 4 (2017): 417–33.

Stephen H. Lowe, *The Slow Undoing: The Federal Courts and the Long Struggle for Civil Rights in South Carolina* (Columbia: University of South Carolina Press, 2021), 256 pp., cloth $89.99, paperback $29.99, ebook $29.99.

In 1954, the US Supreme Court declared that "separate educational facilities are inherently unequal" (*Brown v. Board of Education of Topeka*, 1954). The following year, the same Court ruled that desegregation of schools must proceed "with all deliberate speed" (*Brown v. Board of Education of Topeka*, 1955). Nevertheless, most segregated South Carolina public schools resisted more than token attempts at integration (and many resisted even that) until the 1970–71 school year. By then, as one school official observed, "We've run out of courts, and we've run out of time." Lowe's project is to pierce the veil of that decade-plus period of resistance, grandstanding, and refusal. His nuanced, careful analysis begins with the fight to end the white primary in the 1940s and peaks by laying bare the virtuoso use of the Federal court system throughout the 1950s and 1960s by a united array of state, county, and local officials—virtuosity that, in many cases, was abetted by similarly minded jurists—that prevented meaningful integration in South Carolina schools for far longer than was the case in other segregated states. Lowe's work is lucid and timely and should appeal to a wide audience.

Although the core of Lowe's project concerns resistance to integration, his story begins with the struggle for voting rights for Black South Carolinians, centered on the struggle to abolish South Carolina's whites-only Democratic primary. As the Democratic party invariably went on to win the general election, its primary served as the *de facto* general election for most South Carolina political offices at all levels of government. Voting rights are the heart of civil rights, but the relevant connections here appear to be political and strategic. On Lowe's account, the involvement of the National Association for the Advancement of Colored People (NAACP) Legal Defense and Education Fund, headed by Thurgood Marshall, led to a strategy focused on federal lawsuits filed on behalf of individuals who had been denied voting rights. Given the wording and context of the Fifteenth Amendment, and supremacy of federal law over state law, this seemed to Marshall to be the most likely avenue for success. Indeed, compared with the coming fight over integration, Marshall's strategy was both efficient and relatively effective. Marshall's advocacy resulted in Texas's white primary being struck down by the Supreme Court in 1944, and South Carolina's in 1948, although the latter state's significant Black participation in elections would not emerge until after the passage of the 1957 Civil Rights Act. This strategy was duplicated when the struggle to integrate South Carolina schools began and played a major role in shaping the years of entrenched resistance that followed.

Politically, South Carolina's response to early battles over voting rights anticipates and foreshadows the coming battle over school integration in one major way: unified, total resistance from one corner of the state to another. The tools that the South Carolina power structure used to resist changes to voting rights—widespread legal challenges, token adherence to court decisions, and the dismantling of public institutions—were deployed again and again throughout the 1950s and '60s to resist school integration. Although the state was forced to abandon the white primary relatively quickly, constitutional and political differences between the issues of voting rights and education set the stage for a much more protracted war and much more success for defenders of the status quo.

The Fifteenth Amendment to the US Constitution explicitly prohibits the denial of voting rights on the basis of "race, color, or previous condition of servitude" (US Const. amend. XV). There are no such protections regarding access to public education. Indeed, education had been and is still generally considered to be a state responsibility. Without explicit constitutional authority for the federal government to oversee public education, South Carolina was empowered to adopt a strategy of total resistance. This strategy encompassed a variety of elements, beginning early on with efforts (both token and more substantial) to bring the state's Black schools more into parity with White schools, including the establishment of a law school for Black South Carolinians on the campus of South Carolina State University in Orangeburg. This would show efforts to comply with the "separate-but-equal" standard set in *Plessy v. Ferguson*, the 1896 Supreme Court case allowing segregated public institutions. Showing compliance with the older standard would, South Carolina officials believed, forestall further intervention by federal jurists sympathetic to segregation. Although the Court's decrees in *Brown* and *Brown II* would undermine the merits of the state's actions, the strategy of focusing the minimum required response to claims made by individual petitioners set the parameters for resistance in the post-*Brown* era.

Perhaps the most significant element of the resistance strategy was an overwhelming focus on claims made by individual defendants, as opposed to treating Black students as a group suffering discrimination collectively.

Until the US Department of Justice became much more directly involved in supporting victims of segregation in the 1960s, federal jurists were generally inclined to hear cases limited to claims made by individual claimants and fashioned their remedies accordingly. For example, a particular school district might be sued by the parents of a student only after the student had been denied some opportunity, such as being allowed to transfer to an all-White school. Then, the case would make its way through the courts, eventually resulting in a decision in favor of the student. This piecemeal strategy, limiting remedies to individual students in particular decisions, had a remarkably effective, dilatory effect on the progress of desegregation.

The attack on segregated schools also allowed the state to cloak its actions rhetorically under the guises of "tradition," "protecting children," and "the desires of both races." Lowe makes clear that violent reprisals against opponents of segregation were rare, unlike in famous battlegrounds such as Selma, Alabama, but professional and economic reprisals were more common. Lowe also leaves little doubt that maintaining white supremacy was a paramount political goal for South Carolina political elites. Governor Olin Johnson spoke publicly of the need to "maintain white supremacy" in state institutions. In 1951, the state established the School Segregation Commission, a body whose mission was to "ensure the perpetuation of segregation" and assist segregated school districts in defending themselves from attack. As the opponents of segregation continued to build a track record of gradual success, the state responded by closing public parks in 1963 and making plans to eliminate public education entirely, transferring funds instead to districts and families to empower White students to attend segregated private schools.

It is difficult not to read Lowe's work in light of the present moment. The protracted, baseless fight against the results of the 2020 presidential election seems rooted in the strategy of total resistance adopted by segregationists throughout the 1940s and beyond. One of the book's main contributions is to highlight the challenges inherent in relying on the courts to effect policy change—something that they are frequently poorly equipped to handle, even when judges are willing to be policymakers. When they are not, as Lowe's project shows, the piecemeal, discrete nature of litigation can be obstacles to change, and even to justice.

The Slow Undoing is ultimately a well-executed legal history that answers many important questions about South Carolina's place in the struggle for civil rights for Black Americans. The relative lack of violent repression of civil rights activists in South Carolina perhaps thrusts the state's struggles somewhat out of the limelight, and Lowe has done something significant in turning the spotlight back onto the Palmetto State. His historiography is careful and meticulous, buttressed by careful editing to create a tightly written, highly focused, readable work of history. Indeed, the tight focus and editing have the effect of leaving the reader wanting more light shed on certain aspects of the struggle. What was it, for example, that led the state's leaders to eschew most violence and focus instead on a protracted legal battle? Whether that choice was some sort of "happy accident" or part of a well-thought-out political strategy seems relevant, both to the project and to our understanding of the civil rights struggle as a whole. Also, although South Carolina civil rights activists perhaps faced less forceful opposition than that which occurred in other states, many economic and political reprisals are mentioned, but only in passing, and the Orangeburg Massacre is briefly mentioned only once. Despite these quibbles, *The Slow Undoing: The Federal Courts and the Long Struggle for Civil Rights in South Carolina* is a timely, well-executed work of history that fills a real gap in our understanding of the role of the courts in both promoting and frustrating the drive for political change. Recommended to students of South Carolina history at all levels, as well as the general public.

Richard A. Almeida, Francis Marion University

Sean Patrick O'Rourke and Lesli K. Pace (eds.), *On Fire: Five Civil Rights Sit-Ins and the Rhetoric of Protest* (Columbia: University of South Carolina Press, 2021), 138 pp., paperback $19.99, ebook $14.99.

On Fire: Five Civil Rights Sit-Ins and the Rhetoric of Protest is a slim companion to Sean Patrick O'Rourke and Lesli K. Pace's fuller 2020 collection, *Like Wildfire: The Rhetoric of the Civil Rights Sit-Ins* (also from the University of South Carolina Press). As with the first book, but in more concentrated fashion, *On Fire* brings needed attention to the rhetorical and political significance of sit-ins as a complex, varied, and effective form of protest during the civil rights era. Across both volumes, O'Rourke and Pace argue that sit-ins, involving more than seventy protests and seventy thousand youths in 1960 alone, have been overlooked by rhetoric and social movement scholars. This collection focuses on five lesser-known sit-ins 1959–1961: Greenville, Rock Hill, Charlotte, Louisville, and New Orleans.

Together, the essays in *On Fire* make four key contributions to understanding these particular sit-ins and to approaching research on this topic. First, each chapter elucidates the highly localized issues that shaped different sit-ins. Each community's unique historical, cultural, economic, religious and legal contexts created distinct rhetorical situations that protesters leveraged in various ways. This insight is perhaps the collection's most valuable, as readers who are less familiar with sit-ins will have their assumptions challenged: These were not simply the exact same kind of protest happening in different cities. These chapters tell a very different and more interesting story. Second, the essays make clear that, despite the important local iterations, sit-ins did share similar philosophies and practices to provide a collective "accelerant" to the civil rights movement. In 1960, the South was, indeed, "on fire" with these related protests. Third, the research in each essay draws on a range of useful sources, including archives, interviews, oral histories, mainstream and Black media accounts, police reports, and photographic evidence. Considering that one primary aim of *On Fire* is to spur more research into the many sit-ins not yet analyzed, this diversity of materials charts new methodological and historiographical paths for future scholars to follow and take inspiration from. Finally, each author uses a different rhetorical framework for analysis; not only does this yield new understanding about the significance of specific sit-ins, but also, taken together, the applications of somatic, constitutive, Christian, and visual rhetorics as interpretive frames offer highly original analyses of this critical form of African-American protest.

Readers of this volume may be most interested in Chapters One and Three, as they focus on South Carolina sit-ins. In the first, "Reading Bodies, Reading Books," O'Rourke provides a rhetorical history of the many sit-ins that took place in Greenville in 1960. Unlike those in other locations, the Greenville sit-ins involved a "multigenerational effort" among different groups in the community beyond students, and protests occurred at the airport, library, churches, swimming pools, and skating rinks in addition to lunch counters. O'Rourke establishes the local context for these sit-ins by describing Greenville's distinct "culture of segregation" and the unique set of challenges activists faced there. O'Rourke's analysis focuses on the somatic rhetoric of the protesters' bodies "sitting, reading, walking, and surrendering themselves to the law." In Chapter Three, Richard W. Leeman contrasts the sit-ins in Rock Hill, SC, with those in nearby Charlotte, North Carolina. He finds that the different outcomes were largely the result of differences in media representations of the protests. Charlotte's newspapers, the white-owned *Observer* and the Black-owned *Post*, generally offered more even-handed coverage of the sit-ins and emphasized themes of "fairness and basic human dignity." Leeman demonstrates how the papers' rhetorical strategies of portraying broad support among African Americans and whites for the sit-ins created sympathetic audiences and responses. Leeman suggests this constitutive rhetoric led to the desegregation of Charlotte's lunch counters six months after the sit-ins began. Thirty miles away, Rock Hill presented a different situation. The *Rock Hill Herald*, followed by local law enforcement, politicians, and citizen groups, represented the sit-ins as extreme activism by outsider agitators and Communists, who threatened the peace of their community. Whites' opposition to desegregation, Blacks' divided reactions, and warnings of civil unrest were consistently highlighted over the democratic, humanitarian, and Christian principles motivating the protests. The media sowed animus, division, and fear, creating a politically fractured and stagnated public. Rock Hill erupted into violence in 1961, and lunch counters were closed rather than integrated.

The two other chapters will be of interest as well. In "Nothing New for Easter," Stephen Schneider examines Louisville's sit-in movement during 1959–1961. Louisville is another unique setting for these protests because the city was long considered among the most racially progressive in the South. Schneider recounts Louisville's history of desegregation to establish that the sit-ins were a recognized form of protest, which shifted from a specific civil rights strategy to an "important movement in their own right." Schneider illustrates how the Louisville sit-ins functioned as a "rhetoric of human action" to dramatize injustice, foster collective identity, and engender Black agency. In the final chapter, Pace highlights the significance of New Orleans's Woolworth's sit-in by contrasting photos of the protests from *The Times Picayune*, which emphasized calm and righteous integration of the city through Christian symbolism and appeals, with personal accounts of the protesters themselves, who told a different story of a city racially charged and resistant to integration. Ultimately, these protesters moved beyond the typical claims of injustice to embodied demonstrations of a divinely inspired ethos and purpose, which were rhetorical strategies well suited to the city's deeply religious culture.

On Fire offers general readers and specialized scholars alike a thought-provoking peek into the rich array of sit-ins as localized strategies within the larger civil rights movement. This smaller collection provides a highly readable and digestible version of their much longer and denser volume, *Like Wildfire*. As such, *On Fire* will either inform audiences about the rhetorical significance of lesser known sit-ins or inspire readers to delve into sit-ins as an area ripe for further research. Either way, the book is an important and timely spark itself.

Shevaun E. Watson, University of Wisconsin, Milwaukee

Robert Alston Jones, *Charleston's Germans: An Enduring Legacy* (Mt. Pleasant, SC: Bublish, Inc., 2022), 296 pp., cloth $24.99, paperback $16.99.

For today's visitors, the impact of Charleston's German community can be discerned in prominent structures, such as St. Matthew's Lutheran Church (405 King Street). Those paying close attention might also notice the German inscription on the cornerstone of St. Johannes Lutheran Church (48 Hasell Street) and the many German headstones in Bethany Cemetery (10 Cunnington Avenue). The truly inquisitive will discover that the beautiful two-story Gothic Revival building on the corner of Meeting and George Streets, now home to the Washington Light Infantry, was once the Deutsche Freundschaftbund Hall. For most visitors, however, the contributions of German-Americans remain hidden behind the attractions of Fort Sumter, City Market, and Rainbow Row. Robert Alston Jones's rich, detailed, peer-reviewed study seeks to correct these oversights. Charleston's Germans, he demonstrates, helped create the state's most vibrant and influential port city, and their influence remains appreciable. Jones presents the story of a people who struggled for prosperity, fought to maintain their heritage, and were both resistant to and complicit with the most tragic aspects of South Carolina's past.

Early on, Jones introduces several important individuals, including Franz Adolph Melchers, who published the German-language newspaper, *Deutsche Zeitung*, from 1853 until 1917, and Captain Heinrich Wieting, whose vessels brought approximately six hundred German immigrants to Charleston each year. Although the German community was well established by the mid-nineteenth century, it never achieved the prominence of similar communities in the North and Midwest. Rather, Germans acclimated to their new culture, blending in more than standing out. They did so, in part, because their numbers were relatively modest, accounting for less than twelve percent of the free white population in 1850, and because their Low German dialect, Plattsdeutsch, melded easily with English. Still, Jones pushes back against the assumption, expounded by Michael Everette Bell and others, that Charleston's Germans became "unconditionally loyal to" antebellum culture. The relationship between German immigrants and the host community, Jones insists, cannot be "tied into such a relatively uncomplicated package." Charleston's Germans not only preserved native traditions; they also challenged the bedrock mores of white Southern culture by cohabitating with, and sometimes marrying, African Americans.

Equally important, whereas resettled Germans in other southern cities displaced African Americans, Charleston's Germans encountered "employers who refused to give up their preference for free Black employees." As a result, newly arrived Germans had to find "niches in the social order where they could operate without displacing and antagonizing those who were already in place." One such immigrant, Johann Rosenbohm, who arrived in the early nineteenth century, became a grocer. His efforts helped establish an occupation for subsequent settlers. By 1870, eighty percent of Charleston's grocery stores were German-owned. Another family, the Fehrenbachs, was less fortunate. The patriarch, Nicholas, a watchmaker from Baden, could not find secure employment and abandoned his family, forcing his wife, Anna Maria, to petition the Charleston Orphan House to take custody of her son. Eventually, the son became a successful businessman who capitalized on the growing temperance movement by establishing his Teetotal Restaurant in 1859. Peter Weber, another German immigrant, chose a different path, opening a traditional tavern that would have infuriated both the nascent prohibitionists and the followers of the emerging Know-Nothing movement.

Race and enslavement, of course, affected all aspects of nineteenth-century Charleston life. Jones examines these issues with precision and nuance. He questions claims that German immigrants "approved slavery and were enthusiastic supporters of succession," noting that their earlier experiences in "landlord dominated societies" would have made them unsympathetic to "the planter class." Still, Charleston's German community, in contrast to those in the hill country of Texas and the Mid-Atlantic states, never became strongly abolitionist. To have done so would have invited marginalization. Instead, the German immigrants, few of whom ever became enslavers, lived in tension, recognizing "the fact of slavery" while aspiring to "the ideal of freedom." The Banishment Act of 1861 forced the German community to declare loyalty to the Confederacy, and many members became blockade runners. But even these actions, Jones argues, were guided more by necessity than ideology.

The decades after the Civil War put more pressure on the German community to acclimate to white Southern culture. Before the war, the Deutsche Schützengesellschraft, America's oldest rifle club, welcomed enslaved and free Blacks at its annual festival, which served as a "jovial, well-behaved civic picnic." After the war, the *Schützenfests* became something closer to "a white show of force." Jones narrates these developments largely through the biographies of individuals and families. Behind the personal stories of achievement and hardship, there is a continual struggle to balance the practical and idealistic as well as German and American identities.

As Charleston's economy deteriorated in the 1880s and 90s, the once tolerant community became less charitable and more closely aligned with the conservative Democrats who took power in the wake of Reconstruction. Editorials in the *Deutsche Zeitung* became hostile to Blacks, who were said to be taking jobs previously held by whites. The process of German acculturation to white Southern culture became particularly fervent in the early decades of the twentieth century as many families, now third- and fourth-generation Americans, lost the German language. Even more important, Teddy Roosevelt's admonitions against "hyphenated Americans" and America's eventual involvement in WWI forced many German-Americans to all but abandon their heritage. Opposing the views of the National German-American Alliance, the *Deutsche Zeitung* took a strongly pro-American stance, telling its readers, ". . . we know only the Stars and Stripes as our flag and resent the very idea that we could ever be disloyal to it." In 1915, the paper began publishing an English-language edition not only in response to a diminishing German readership but also in an effort to appear more firmly American.

The German-Americans of Charleston, Jones concludes, were "treading especially difficult waters amidst the rising tide of anti-German sentiment." Jones animates these dynamics through an insightful analysis of the *Liebenfels*, a German steamer that sank in Charleston's harbor in February 1917. The crewmen were criminally charged not only with scuttling the vessel but also with conspiracy against the United States. At the same time, the *Evening Post* ratcheted anti-German sentiment by accusing the *Deutsche Zeitung*'s editor, Paul Wierse, of collaborating with Charleston's former mayor, John P. Grace, to promote "the German point of view." In spite of these developments, Jones claims that Charleston's "culture was too uniquely well-mannered to carry out an overt anti-German campaign." Still, there were persistent xenophobic attacks to anything that "could be ascribed to a

German origin." Perhaps unsurprisingly, these events caused some German-Americans to embrace the host culture even more tenaciously. In a particularly telling incident, the newly formed Friends of German Democracy claimed that its paramilitary uniforms were "copies of Swiss design and, in fact, were closely akin to the uniform of the Confederacy." In making this statement, the Friends at once distanced themselves from their German origins and aligned themselves with the ideology of Jim Crow.

Jones provides an important, highly readable study of Charleston's German community. He substantiates his claims with abundant evidence from primary sources and effectively confronts many scholarly assumptions. He also shows the challenges of acculturation and how that process can strengthen a society's most toxic and dangerous tendencies.

Christopher D. Johnson, Francis Marion University

Lance Weldy (ed.), *BJU and Me: Queer Voices from the World's Most Christian University* (Athens: University of Georgia Press, 2021), 368 pp., cloth $114.95, paperback $26.95.

Lance Weldy makes a vital and unprecedented contribution to lesbian, gay, bisexual, transgender, queer/questioning, plus other (LGBTQ+) population studies with *BJU and Me: Queer Voices from the World's Most Christian University*. In this remarkable collection, former students from Bob Jones University (BJU), a fundamentalist Christian institution founded in 1927, speak their truths about the oppressive institution that shamed and traumatized them. Spanning several generations of students, the stories collected here provide a testimony to queer identity, survival, and triumph in the face of enormous oppression, surveillance, and mind control.

Although a collection representing a population as narrowly defined as this one risks myopic scope and homogenous narratives, that is not the case with Weldy's book. Recognizing this risk, Weldy points out that BJU's brand recognition has attracted mainstream media attention and makes a strong case that the queer experience at BJU merits book-length analysis. Indeed, each voice is as fresh and unique as the individual writers themselves. Their stories reveal trajectories from struggles with shame and fear to resolutions of healing and self-acceptance. Some students remained Christian in more welcoming denominations and institutions; others took up professions supporting LGBTQ+ youths and adults; others became atheist or agnostic as they learned to accept the truth about themselves; some found fulfilling relationships with queer partners, and others came out while staying in traditional marriages. Each writer conveys a story of remarkable struggle, liberation, and self-acceptance. As with the best literary memoirs, the reader shares this healing journey with them.

Weldy opens with an introduction that provides a comprehensive historical overview of Bob Jones University as an extremist, eccentric religious institution, whose policies and practices have changed minimally over nearly a century. As part of the indoctrination process, students are taught the university creed, which they are required to recite weekly as a student body. Foregrounding the institution's punitive practice of separation from sinners, he points out that queer students are in especial danger of this disciplinary action: "One kind of student susceptible to extreme discipline—expulsion—is one who secretly identifies or unintentionally presents as LGBTQ+." In particular, he details the anti-LGBTQ+ indoctrination process, which emphasizes a collection of six specific biblical verses, colloquially named the Clobber Passages, that provide fundamentalist "proof" that the Bible condemns queer identity. By showing how the Clobber Passages are implicated into the university creed, Weldy effectively establishes how ubiquitously queer students struggle in this hostile, traumatizing environment in which they are forced to exist: "For an LGBT+ BJU student from any decade, this repeated statement of believing in a text that condemns who they are is a recipe for religious and psychological crisis. All the contributors to this collection have been at least indirectly affected by these passages." By guiding the reader to understand that these narratives sit at the nexus of auto-ethnography, vulnerability narrative, and testimony of religious trauma, the audience is made aware of the potentially far-reaching and relevant impact of their publication. As Weldy puts it, these stories "explain how vulnerable we were to a controlling regime that has left an indelible mark on us psychologically, emotionally, physically, and spiritually." Instead of remaining silent, BJU students share their stories in this exemplary performance of speaking truth to power.

After the Introduction, the book is organized thematically. Part One, "Surveillance, Control, and Rumors," shares former students' anxieties of being watched, scrutinized, outed, interrogated, humiliated, and expelled, exposing the contradiction of the BJU brand image as a safe spiritual haven.

In Part Two, "Other Institutions," the contributors share comparisons of their experiences at BJU with the institutions they joined after their expulsion or decision to leave. Part Three, "Intersections," explores the experiences of students writing from trans, international, and nonwhite perspectives. In Part Four, "Family, Guilt, and Shame," two writers share their transformation from entrapment in shame to liberation and self-love, learning to live their lives as gay men on their own terms. Finally, Part Five, "Identifying as Religious and Spiritual," challenges the idea that queer students must choose between God and their own self-evident truths.

What is most striking about this collection is the degree to which these accounts of lived experiences at BCU echo the first-person narrator's account in Margaret Atwood's *The Handmaid's Tale*. Atwood's 1985 novel portrays a dystopian society in which a male ruling elite establishes a fundamentalist Christian theocracy that strips women of childbearing age of their most basic rights and forces them into sexual slavery to produce children as "handmaids" to powerful Commanders. In Atwood's Gilead, social roles are extremely rigid and violently surveilled; women's bodies and reproductive abilities are intensively regulated; atheists, gays, and abortion doctors are persecuted; and handmaids who step out of line are brutally executed by their own sisters. Barring execution, BJU is eerily similar to Gilead in its guiding principles and disciplinary procedures.

In her writing of the novel, Atwood declares that "one of my rules was that I would not put any events into the book that had not already happened in what James Joyce called the 'nightmare' of history."[1] She could have sourced her material from *BJU and Me*, because the stories very much reveal the ongoing "nightmare" of the queer experience at BJU. All modes of control portrayed in Atwood's dystopia (with the sole exception of execution) are foregrounded in Weldy's collection: surveillance, mind control, spying, shaming, interrogation, punishment, and "shipping" (expulsion from the university). But *BJU and Me* is not a dystopian novel. It is a collection of autobiographical accounts of the lived experiences of queer people in an enormously oppressive institution that continues to operate today. More disturbingly, instances of surveillance, mind control, interrogation, and expulsion are repeatedly recounted in these autoethnograpies, evidence that harassment of LGBTQ+ students is systematic. As one current student puts it, "We all live in fear of being caught, of being outed, of being expelled, of facing discipline for just existing."

Ultimately, however, this book features stories of triumph. In one notable account, Rachel Oblak and her husband go through a period of questioning before eventually leaving BJU. She recalls a moment when she shares with her husband that she is bisexual: "My marriage didn't fall apart as I (and others) had feared it would with my coming out. Honesty and self-acceptance actually enhanced my relationship rather than damaging it, bringing us closer together." Honesty with himself is powerful for David Diachenko as well. By breaking the cycle of sex acts followed by guilt and shame, he finally relaxes into his identity: "I suddenly realized, this feels right. Not just good, but absolutely and completely right." Jeff Mullinix, on the other hand, embraces his sexuality as integral to his spirituality and his role as a minister: "There is absolutely no conflict with accepting who I am and following Jesus, for I know God wants me to be happy, healthy, authentic, whole, integrated and my truest self." These are just a few examples of the many profound expressions of authenticity. Although it is natural for the reader to expect story after story of trauma and compromised mental health, each voice concludes on a note of liberation and self-love.

The jubilant tone of these essays is due, in no small part, to the pivotal role played by BJUnity, a support group of queer BJU students turned activists whose narratives make up this book. Through their communication on social media and in-person at Pride events, this support group made possible the healing, social connection, and self-determination that led to the creation of the book itself. Many of the contributors now work in LGBTQ+-affirming roles. The book's greatest achievement is in its visionary portrayal of an optimistic queer future for Christians and non-Christians alike, even those caught in the grips of fundamentalism. These stories open up space for everyone who is queer and has experienced religious trauma, each essay an incantatory refrain of the life-saving affirmation, "You belong, just as you are."

Right now in the United States, as many Christian institutions become more aligned with and energized by an extremist political base, as the divide between conservatives and progressives deepens and intensifies, and with a reigning Supreme Court that seems poised to strip hard-won rights from LGBTQ+ people, the voices of the survivors represented here are more urgent than ever. *BJU and Me* is essential reading for our historical moment.

M. Beth Keefauver, University of South Carolina Upstate

NOTE

1. Margaret Atwood, "Margaret Atwood on What 'The Handmaid's Tale' Means in the Age of Trump," *New York Times*, March 10, 2017.

Eric Crawford, *Gullah Spirituals: The Sound of Freedom and Protest in the South Carolina Sea Islands* (Columbia: University of South Carolina Press, 2021), 248 pp., cloth $89.99, paperback $29.99, ebook $29.99.

Eric Crawford's book, *Gullah Spirituals: The Sound of Freedom and Protest in the South Carolina Sea Islands*, is informative, insightful, and full of inspirational history that still resides off the coast of South Carolina. The author beautifully folds the inception of the Gullah spiritual into Western culture and shows how it transformed into an instrument for advancing civil rights. Crawford describes how these unique forms of song and praise provided entertainment for white listeners as well as cherished moments of respite for the enslaved. He inspires the reader to know more about Gullah–Geechee music and solicits solace through equality by expressing that "these songs are not exclusive to a specific nationality but are universal in their reach." Last, Crawford includes a Gullah songbook, in which he discusses melody, context, and rhythm. This book is a gift of music, culture, and history to all who have the opportunity to read it.

Fran Coleman, Francis Marion University

Daniel M. Harrison, *Live at Jackson Station: Music, Community, and Tragedy in a Southern Blues Bar* (Columbia: University of South Carolina Press, 2021), 256 pp., cloth $74.99, paperback $24.99, ebook $24.99.

Long before music and culture were disseminated worldwide at the speed of byte, through titans such as YouTube and TikTok, people would gather expectedly at bars and nightclubs excitedly awaiting the fresh new sounds to take the stage. The development of rock and roll and the culture that surrounds it has been well documented. Venues and clubs such as the Apollo, CBGB, and Whiskey a Go Go all stand as hallowed halls of musical expression and freedom. The many juke joints of Memphis and Mississippi have been canonized in numerous books and films. These geographic hubs are well established as the incubators of American music, but the reality is that this format was replicating itself all over the country. In *Live at Jackson Station*, Daniel Harrison takes a journey through the life cycle of one of these unique venues. Through numerous interviews and painstaking research, Harrison tells the story of a special bar and what it meant to a community, its patrons, the musicians who cut their teeth there, and the tragedy that brought it all to an end.

The introduction and first three chapters effectively present the time and place, as well as the primary characters. Hodges, South Carolina, in the mid-1980s, was an unlikely place for an openly gay bar owner to run a successful music venue. Gerald Jackson, a music-loving veteran, and his partner Steven Bryant purchased a decommissioned train station for one dollar and had it moved to a plot of family land. From here they launched "Jackson Station." From a parental standpoint, Jackson Station was decidedly off limits. Yet for its patrons and the musicians who frequented the stage, it was a sanctuary for expression and free from judgment. Through extensive interviews and quotations, Harrison paints the picture of a bar that stood against convention. The overall sentiment from all involved was that Jackson Station was a place where everyone was welcome, regardless of age, race, or sexual identity. Harrison also makes the point that, from the outside looking in, this was not always the case. For nonpatrons, Jackson Station was often referred to as a "gay bar," and parents always cautioned their children not to be caught there. Gerald and Steve ran the bar and booked the shows while Gerald's mother, Elizabeth, controlled the door like an all-seeing matriarch.

Harrison makes the case that perhaps the unlikely success of such a venue within the heart of the Bible Belt lies within the diversity of the clientele and the musicians who performed there. Located about eighty miles due east of Athens, Georgia, Jackson Station could draw on numerous colleges from the surrounding areas. An average night would also see a large contingent of local blue-collar workers of various racial backgrounds. Local and state politicians were also known to frequent the venue. Before the sun went down, one would often find entire families sitting down for a meal. Another draw for the bar was the fact that it stayed open long after all the others had closed. Here, again, Harrison draws on numerous accounts that overwhelmingly show Jackson Station to be an inviting and safe space for an eclectic slice of southeastern society.

Gerald Jackson was a lover of music, and this was most evident in the acts that he booked and the treatment that they received. In a business rife with bad actors, getting paid as a working musician was always a dubious prospect. Gerald Jackson was just the opposite. Through numerous interviews,

Harrison shows that artists liked playing at Jackson Station. Gerald would always feed the bands and pay them on time. The hours could, indeed, be grueling. Sometimes bands would take the stage at eleven o'clock at night and still be making sounds when the sun came up. Regardless of these challenges, musicians relished the chance to win over always diverse, and sometimes disinterested, crowds. Traditional rhythm and blues was the driving genre, but Gerald was always open to booking any act that interested him. Classic blues legends, such as Tinsley Ellis and Nappy Brown, performed there numerous times, but so did the New Wave band the Swimming Pool Q's. Most notable, perhaps, are the many performances by the now-famous jam band Widespread Panic. Harrison shows that each of these artists saw Jackson Station as a bit of an oasis that called out to musicians and patrons alike.

Where changing musical tastes and demographics often led to the demise of once popular destinations, Jackson Station was instead closed down by tragedy. As welcoming as Jackson Station was, disputes did, indeed, occur. In the early morning hours of April 7, 1990, Gerald Jackson followed a patron out to the parking lot to collect on a debt. Like all such incendiary situations, what happened next is a fog. Here, Harrison presents as much primary evidence as possible, but the reluctance of numerous parties to speak with him leaves a lot to court records and fading memories. Harrison does a good job presenting statements and recollections without interjecting too much of his opinion in this section. Once the smoke had cleared, Gerald Jackson was left with a debilitating wound from which he would never fully heal. It would be easy to infer bigotry or hate with regard to the attack on Gerald Jackson, but here again, Harrison leaves it to the known facts. The incapacitation of Gerald Jackson showed just how entwined he and the venue were, as it spelled the end for Jackson Station as well.

Daniel Harrison has presented a compelling story with excellent primary research. Although the details of Jackson's story are unique to him, the role that the venue and owner played in the surrounding community likely is not. The fact that there is a "Jackson Station" in countless rural communities across the United States makes the story all the more important, not less. The story is engaging, well researched, elegantly presented, and well worth the read.

Brandon Goff, Francis Marion University

Kevin Mitchell and David S. Shields, *Taste the State: South Carolina's Signature Foods, Recipes, and Their Stories* (Columbia: University of South Carolina Press, 2021), 248 pp. cloth $34.99, ebook $34.99.

Part encyclopedia, part cookbook, *Taste the State* is an entertaining compendium of eighty-two foods indelibly linked to the culinary history of South Carolina. Not a study of Southern foods, generally—no Moon Pies or R. C. Colas here—authors Kevin Mitchell and David S. Shields have researched and assembled the stories of foods ranging, appropriately enough, from "Asparagus: The Palmetto" to "Yaupon Tea." Mitchell, the first African-American chef instructor at the Culinary Institute of America in Charleston, who was named a South Carolina Chef Ambassador for 2020–21 by the state's Department of Agriculture, and Shields, Carolina Distinguished Professor of English Language and Literature at the University of South Carolina and chair of the Carolina Gold Rice Foundation, combine their unique perspectives of food and folkways to create a cultural study that covers the entire state and includes items such as the Porgy of the Lowcountry to Upcountry blackberries. Many of the entries tell the stories of food items, such as Palmetto asparagus, that although once popular, faded almost to the point of extinction only to see a resurgence in recent years. It recounts the tales of food companies tied to the state producing products such as Duke's Mayonnaise and Blenheim Ginger Ale. And it is the story of people—Native Americans, Africans and African Americans, and other cultures—who contributed their unique plants, spices, and tastes to the mélange of South Carolina cooking. It introduces cooks, planters, plant breeders, agronomists, and seedmen who, working in their unique positions, shaped agriculture and trade in the state over the course of four centuries.

Although this is not a traditional cookbook by any means, Mitchell and Shields add historical recipes from a variety of sources for each food. Intrepid cooks can attempt to interpret the instructions for rice bread from a recipe that appeared in the *Charleston Courier* on January 7, 1812; chicken pilau from the November 1892 issue of the *Ladies Home Journal*; or more contemporary recipes, such as the one for Colony House conch fritters in *South Carolina's Historic Restaurants and Their Recipes* of 1984. Interspersed throughout the book, the authors include nine new recipes, most produced by Mitchell himself, that represent a modern take on traditional South Carolina fare.

It is not a traditional academic study, but *Taste the State* is thoroughly researched. Each entry has a corresponding list of sources provided in a separate section after the text. The book is informational and written in a style to appeal to general readers, but it is also useful to academics. Mitchell and Shields stray beyond state lines occasionally when they discuss the arrival of new plants to South Carolina or recognize the importance of the style of fried fish developed just across the state line in Calabash, North Carolina. And they are not beyond waxing poetic or showing pride for their state's food. They describe Guinea Squash (eggplant) as "the most sensuous plant on one's kitchen counter"; reveal that "1874 was the year when a southerner theorized that sipping iced tea from a straw was morally, physiologically, and gastronomically more satisfying than drinking it from a glass"; and declare in no uncertain terms that "In 1954, breeder C. F. Andrus released the greatest American watermelon produced in the mid-twentieth century, the Charleston Gray." *Taste of the State* will provide hours of entertainment to people interested in South Carolina and Southern foodways, or who simply enjoying eating.

Christopher E. Hendricks, Georgia Southern University

Edwin Breeden, *A Guidebook to South Carolina Historical Markers* (Columbia: University of South Carolina Press, 2021), 448 pp., cloth $74.99, paperback $24.99, ebook $24.99.

This guidebook, as noted in the acknowledgments, is the product of more than twenty years of work by several different individuals working with the South Carolina Department of Archives and History, and it includes the text of over seventeen hundred different historical markers in the state.

Like many families in the 1970s and 1980s, we took road trips during the summer that were planned using folded paper maps and thick guidebooks. I loved going to the regional AAA office with my dad to pick up those guidebooks and watch the travel agents compile our TripTik, small spiral-bound booklets that held the maps of the interstates we'd travel. I was the map-keeper in the back seat of the car. My dad was the one who kept his eye out for the highway markers that provided us insight into the areas we traveled through, and that told us not only where we were but why we should care about the place. We would fly by most of them, but when we were traversing a particularly historical area, we'd pull over, get out of the car, and get our little history lesson.

Historical markers are self-contained stories. Sitting on sites of battle-fields, birthplaces, schools, churches, libraries—both extant and long gone—markers recount events, explain significance, present biographies, and mourn losses. While traveling down the road, we miss out on many of them. However, this guidebook allows those traveling through South Carolina to read *all* of the historical markers from the living room recliner or the back-seat of the car.

The very helpful Introduction provides a history of the SC Historical Marker Program, the process for localities to apply for markers, and recent efforts to include markers that educate the public about events and locations important for Native American and African-American histories. The book is organized by county, with markers listed in the order in which they were approved. Each listing includes the title of the marker, location, a transcript of the marker's text, name of the sponsor, date, and the GPS coordinates.

On a recent trip to Hunting Island, South Carolina, I decided to user-test the guide, regaling my family with stories of the world champion butter-fat-producing Jersey cow raised at Young Farm (Florence County, 21–26; 178); the Combahee River Raid of 1863, which resulted in "more than 700 enslaved men, women, and children" being "taken to freedom" (Beaufort County, 7–39; 60); and the history of Parris Island, which dates back to the 1500s (Beaufort County, 7–56; 64). I was able to sort out what counties we were traveling through, as I have lived in South Carolina for nearly twenty years, but a state map marking the counties would help anyone attempting to use the guide on the road.

It was a joy to keep up with the history as we quickly passed the historical markers on our travels, although I am not sure my children would agree—they hid the guidebook from me on our return trip.

Meredith A. Love, Francis Marion University

Lydia Mattice Brandt, *The South Carolina State House Grounds: A Guidebook* (Columbia: University of South Carolina Press, 2021), 192 pp., paperback $19.99, ebook $19.99.

The South Carolina State House Grounds: A Guidebook provides a superb chronological and topical history of one of South Carolina's most monu-mental and controversial achievements. Lydia Mattice Brandt's book is a well-researched and easily understandable guide to the State House monuments, its layout, and its building development since the post-Revolutionary War period. Her analysis exposes how power and identity played an inordinate role in its creation. Furthermore, Brandt's work details the complex interplay of past and present while the State House grounds took shape. This was especially pertinent to the monument selection timing and decisions, which reflected the state's sponsorship of white supremacy symbolism. As Brandt observed, "The monuments, building, and relationships between them reveal stories of what people wanted to remember at certain times and for certain reasons, not objective narratives."

Brandt's book discloses the state-centric motives of South Carolina's legislators when they expanded the grounds. Despite ongoing wrangling over various economic disputes and times of deprivation, the intentions of the legislators were clear. Even the statue of George Washington served to perpetuate an "attractive symbol of planter-politicians claiming sovereignty from the federal government in South Carolina," although the Washington statue's broken cane had been reportedly destroyed by malicious federal troops, disorderly Blacks, or both when Columbia received the brunt of General William T. Sherman's destructive 1865 march through the state's capital city.

Similarly, Brandt indicates the commemoration of the stars marking Sherman's bombardment of the exterior State House walls connoted southern heroism for each "honorable scar." Revealing the "Lost Cause" mythology's durability among white South Carolinians and their political leaders, Brandt indicates that observers "likened [the bombardment strikes to] the State House to a human body" while the markings "testified to the emotions still attached to the event more than sixty years after the end of the war." The Spanish-American War monument also displays nationalistic imagery that conforms to state-centric and white supremacy tendencies. It depicts an "idealized white soldier for the monument," Brandt emphasizes, while ignoring the pivotal "participation of African-American servicemen in the Spanish-American War." Rather, its creator, Theo Alice Ruggles Kitson, the only female sculptor on the State House grounds, constructed the monument to summon the spirit of reconciliation between the North and the South.

The State House grounds enable visitors to view monuments of controversial political figures. Brandt summarizes the intriguing history of these constructions, detailing their meanings once completed and afterward, and how the structures and the "understandings" about them comported with actual historical evidence. She describes the stories behind the statues honoring white South Carolina political patriarchs Wade Hampton, Benjamin Tillman, James F. Byrnes, and Strom Thurmond. Her descriptions not only notate the polemical aspects associated with each structure but also reveal that the legislators selected them to meld with the expansive, intricate pathways and ongoing office building construction.

Brandt describes how the individual political monuments provide physical portrayals of patriarchal white supremacy. Their heightened prominence symbolically counters the post-Civil War period of Black freedom struggles. For example, when it was unveiled in 1906, the essentially state-funded statue of Wade Hampton extolled him as the virtuous white elite who had redeemed the state from so-called Black Reconstruction dominance, depicting Hampton's face as it looked when he served as governor and as a US Senator about a decade after the Civil War. The body of the statue showed Hampton in Confederate uniform atop a horse. Combined, the dual heroic actions of his civic and military opposition to federal intrusion over state and white dominion came to define his legacy and, thus, his statue.

The grounds also offer an oversized statue of Hampton's archrival, Tillman. The monument to the so-called indomitable strongman of poor white South Carolina farmers and the state's "first New Dealer," as Byrnes commemorated Tillman upon its unveiling in 1940, serves as the ground's most blatant representation of white supremacy. The statue's overbearing, hovering depiction of Tillman stands as an exalted exemplification of Tillman's endorsement of the Jim Crow system, his advocacy for lynching and disenfranchisement, and his public effrontery to Black freedom rights after his sponsorship of the South Carolina State Constitution of 1895. The latter stripped away most of the rights previously granted to African Americans during Reconstruction.

The more contemporary monuments to Byrnes and Thurmond offer additional concrete examples of the tilted nature of the State House grounds. Each politician staunchly endorsed Jim Crow segregation and encouraged formidable acts of white resistance to integration. However, as Brandt affirms, a promising development emerged when Thurmond's daughter, Essie Mae Washington-Williams, whom Thurmond had fathered with a much younger African-American woman, got her name etched into the side of his statue, listed alongside Thurmond's four other children.

Recently, the State House grounds have become more inclusive, nationalistic, and public servant oriented. Sculptor Ed Dwight's 2001 African

American History Monument epitomizes the most glaring but refreshing aberration from the earlier trend. It depicts the horrors and long, uplifting progression toward racial justice since 1670. It reveals chronological graphic portrayals of key events, developments, and personalities, and it defines the collective forms of struggle through a "series of words," as Brandt put it, to describe the period of enslavement to freedom. "While it celebrates the very people that many of the people memorialized elsewhere on the grounds spent their lives oppressing," Brandt astutely notes, "it does not directly confront these other monuments in its design or narrative."

Even though the monument broke the mold, sculptor Dwight sanitized it to appease anxious state legislators. They feared a public controversy might erupt if it displayed too starkly the history of racial bigotry and violence. As Brandt revealed, "Dwight had imagined 'hooded Klansmen burning crosses and the bodies of Blacks hanging from trees'" but refrained from sculpting them. He did the same when it came to the early nineteenth-century Denmark Vesey slave revolt plot. He submitted to the state commission's desires, despite the fact that the budget for the monument comprised only private donations.

Further contemporary monuments focus on the civic sacrifices of South Carolinians and the nation and commemorate a hidden treasure for future generations. In 2005–06, the state legislature overrode Governor Mark Sanford's veto to utilize taxpayer funds to memorialize the law enforcement officers killed while on duty since 1797, and they funded a separate monument to honor armed forces personnel. Additionally, the 1986 Columbia Bicentennial Time Capsule generates intrigue because of its "Looking Back—Reaching Forward" granite marker that stores letters and other primary sources from 1936. In 2036, South Carolinians will open the secret treasure on the state's two hundred fiftieth birthday.

The South Carolina State House Grounds is a monumental achievement. Now that the grounds, according to a 2007 law restricting additional monuments, are essentially fixed, Brandt's work is the definitive book on the contested history of its progression into a beautiful landscape indicative of South Carolina's rich but tragic history. The 2015 removal of the Confederate battle flag after the horrific murder of nine African-American parishioners at Charleston's Mother Emanuel AME (African Methodist Episcopal) Church is among the many invaluable topics in Brandt's seminal work. Whether one aspires to use its contents as a guide, as a selective visitor's manual, or as a resource to understand the state's overall history, Brandt's book is an excellent analysis of the grounds and its fragmentary but colossal development. After reading this book, perhaps modern visitors will aim for a future that diverges from the themes that most State House grounds monuments propagate.

Jason R. Kirby, Francis Marion University